Off the Beaten Path®
Arkansas

OFF THE BEATEN PATH® SERIES

TENTH EDITION

Off the Beaten Path® Arkansas

A Guide to Unique Places

PATTI DeLANO

GLOBE PEQUOT
Guilford, Connecticut
Helena, Montana

An imprint of Rowman & Littlefield

Globe Pequot is an imprint of Rowman & Littlefield

Distributed by NATIONAL BOOK NETWORK

Copyright © 2014 by Patti DeLano

Maps by Equator Graphics © Rowman & Littlefield

British Library Cataloguing-in-Publication Information available

Library of Congress Cataloging-in-Publication Data available

ISBN 978-1-4930-0635-9 (paperback)

∞™ The paper used in this publication meets the minimum requirements of American National Standard for Information Sciences—Permanence of Paper for Printed Library Materials, ANSI/NISO Z39.48-1992.

All the information in this guidebook is subject to change. We recommend that you call ahead to obtain current information before traveling.

Contents

About the Author

Patti DeLano has been traveling the world and cruising the highways and back roads of America, spending time in her native Missouri and neighboring Kansas and Arkansas. She is currently working on a novel on the Civil War and book about sailing. She and her fiancee, David McKie, now travel along the Gulf Coast and East Coast aboard the sailboat *Didgeridoo,* with a home base in Venice, Florida.

Fawn Rechkemmer has joined Patti in revising this book. Fawn spent 4 years living in Central Arkansas and still makes frequent visits to the Natural State. She lives in Ozark, Missouri, with her husband and two young children. She is a freelance writer, editor, and social media consultant.

Acknowledgments

Finding offbeat places in Arkansas often means following directions like, "You know where that big ole tree used to be?" or "Hang a left there, you know, by that red barn?"

So I owe a lot to friends who offered hospitality and help from their homes in Arkansas and spent endless hours helping me find places as common as antiques shops and as remote as an elephant farm. My mom and dad, Sally and John Randazzo, also endured mountain roads and odd places, with the sense of humor I love them for, as we wandered around the state.

This edition is in memory of my husband, Bob, who had an instinct for finding unique eating places and unlikely shortcuts not shown on any map (even when he had never been there before). Serendipitous travel with him to odd places was always fun.

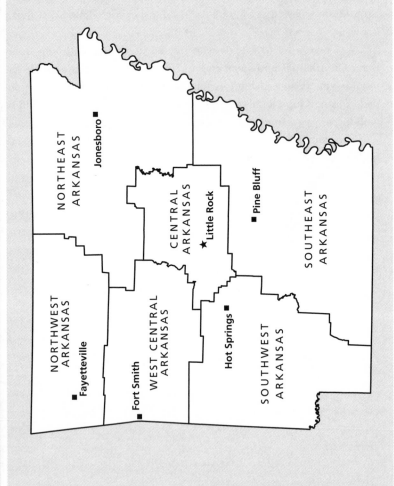

ARKANSAS

NORTHEAST
ARKANSAS

Jonesboro ■

CENTRAL
ARKANSAS

Little Rock
★

Pine Bluff ■

SOUTHEAST
ARKANSAS

NORTHWEST
ARKANSAS

Fayetteville ■

WEST CENTRAL
ARKANSAS

Fort Smith ■

Hot Springs ■

SOUTHWEST
ARKANSAS

Introduction

Arkansas is the perfect vacationland: 60-foot waterfalls and quiet sandbars seen only from a canoe or wooded hiking trail. Add trout streams and hunting lodges—nature at its best for people who want to be outdoors—plus golf courses, racetracks, and the big-city fun of fine restaurants, and you have the vacation choice of millions in the nation's heartland.

Thousands of artists and craftspeople have settled in the Ozarks. Vineyards and wineries dot the Arkansas River Valley, and an elephant breeding farm lies hidden in the foothills. Arkansans combine the friendliness of the Old South, the hardy spirit of the Southwest, and the practicality of the Midwest.

Arkansas, an undiscovered wonderland far from any ocean, may be one of the most beautiful states on the continent. It has more designated National Scenic Byways than any other state in the nation. But Arkansas is more than just the beauty of stair-step waterfalls or the thrill of Class V rapids in a canoe. It offers wine country, good Cajun food, old cotton plantations, and the only bordello on the National Register of Historic Places. If that's too much excitement for you, there's a Benedictine monastery where you can retreat, search your soul, and start over.

The climate boasts four distinct seasons—but with the Gulf Stream creating the moderate temperatures of the southern US. Spring comes early, attracting visitors from bordering states not so lucky in the weather game. Unlike its northern neighbors, Arkansas has a long spring filled with pleasant days perfect for outdoor activities.

Golfers, anglers, hikers, and canoeists flock here. So do people who have retired from the rat race and now do all their racing on whitewater rapids or at the greyhound or horse track. Arkansans are serious about outdoor activities. The 225-mile Ouachita Trail, not for wimps, allows hikers to follow the ridges and valleys from Pinnacle Mountain State Park to Queen Wilhelmina Lodge and into Oklahoma.

Yes, it's hot as the dickens in August, but as the muscadine grapes (known as scuppernongs) ripen to a reddish brown, the nights begin to cool. In late September the black gum trees change from glossy green to shining crimson—suddenly and completely—standing out from the green of the other, more hesitant trees. Then other colors begin as casual blushes of yellow and red and spread from north to south during October to finish in a blaze of color. Fall colors are dazzling, and the endless days of perfect weather and bright blue skies make this about the best time of year. Winters are characterized by brief cold snaps and a splash of clean snow. Crisp nights, bright stars, and crystal ice formations in the gleaming winter sun are followed quickly by warmer days. Mistletoe and five kinds of holly grow throughout the state, making plant hunting popular in the December woods.

Because this book is filled with listings of small crafts shops, mom-and-pop restaurants, bed-and-breakfasts in beautiful old homes, and log cabins tucked in sleepy hollers and mountain foothills, it is wise to call ahead and double-check before making a long drive to a particular place. When something disappears, something else pops up in its place, and getting off the beaten path in this state is always interesting. If a listing is gone or some other fascinating place has sprung up, let the publisher know about it so that we can include it in the next update of this book.

The tourist information centers will give you a free road map, or you can call (800) NATURAL and get a vacation guide for the area you are visiting. Bring your camera or your sketch pad and find the best Mother Nature has to offer. That's why they call it the Natural State.

Arkansas at a Glance

Arkansas: The Natural State. *Arkansas,* pronounced *AR-kan-saw,* means "South Wind," the name of the Quapaw Indian tribe whom the French Jesuits met here. The state flag is a blue-bordered white diamond on a rectangular field of red; the border contains 25 stars, the diamond has 4.

Capital: Little Rock

Motto: The People Rule

Earliest inhabitants: Pre-Columbian bluff dwellers about AD 500. They used a weapon similar to the Aztec *atlatl*—a throwing stick—to hunt buffalo and deer.

Earliest explorers: Hernando de Soto crossed the Mississippi near Sunflower Landing, June 29, 1541. The first permanent white settlement was founded by René-Robert Cavelier, sieur de La Salle, who took formal possession for Louis XIV of France in 1763. It became part of the Louisiana Purchase in 1803.

Geography: One-fourth of Arkansas is covered by standing timber. There are at least 210 species of trees, the oak group being the largest with 43 types.

Lowest elevation: 54 feet

Highest elevation: 2,723 feet

Land area: 53,187 square miles (ranked 27th in the US)

Population: 2,779,154

Statehood: June 15, 1836 (25th state; entered as a slave state)

State bird: Mockingbird

State tree: Shortleaf pine

State flower: Apple blossom

State mammal: White-tailed deer

State gemstone: Diamond

State beverage: Milk

State instrument: Fiddle

Average annual precipitation: Ranges from 45 inches in the mountains to 55 inches in the Delta.

Major newspapers: *Arkansas Democrat-Gazette, Arkansas Times, Little Rock Free Press; The Benton County Daily Record* (Bentonville); *Gurdon Times, Herald Leader* (Siloam Springs); *Morning News of Northwest Arkansas* (Springdale); *Nevada County Picayune* (Prescott); *Northwest Arkansas Times* (Fayetteville)

Travel information: Call (800) NATURAL for brochures or (800) 828-8974 for the Arkansas Department of Parks and Tourism, or visit online at arkansas.com.

Price Scale

At the end of each chapter, additional hotels and restaurants are listed using the following scale:

HOTELS

Inexpensive: Up to $100 per night
Moderate: $101 to $200 per night
Expensive: $201 and up
All prices shown are for double occupancy.

RESTAURANTS

Inexpensive: entrees in the $10 range
Moderate: entrees range from $11 to $20
Expensive: entrees more than $20

Northeast Arkansas

Things don't change much in the Ozarks—dogwoods, red-buds, and wild plum bloom in the spring; wildflowers color the meadows of summer; and thousands of acres of autumn forest splash color over the hills where the clear streams and rivers still sparkle in the sun. The colors of the Ozarks shift like a kaleidoscope, but things in the Ozarks don't change much.

The pace is slower here. The people are friendly. In a place that did not have a paved highway until after World War II, a culture emerged unique in the country. In fact, many people here insist that the Ozarks should have constituted its own state instead of meandering across two state lines.

Four beautifully different seasons bring vacationers to the Ozarks year-round. Hikers follow trails up grades to towering bluffs that cast soft shadows on the waters and offer views of pristine valleys. Gentle wildlife hides in the forest, and the scenes change with light and shadow.

These gentle, timeworn hills roll across the horizon without jagged peaks or sharp edges. A palette of colors—pale-pink anemone in the early spring, soft shades of green

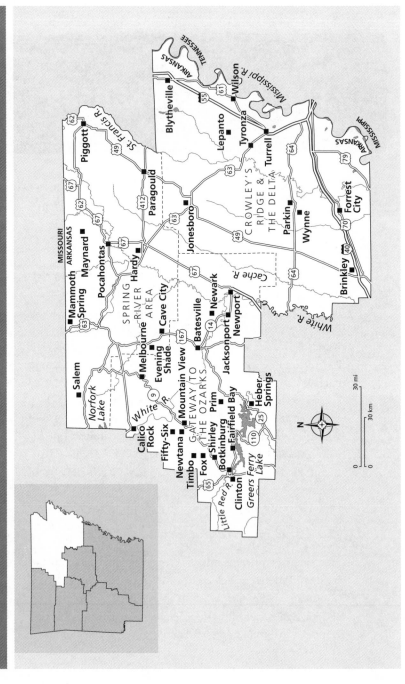

NORTHEAST ARKANSAS

in summer, blazing gold and crimson in fall, gray-green rock faces and clean white snow in winter—splash the canvas of cobalt-blue sky.

Spring slips into the state early—while snow still clings to the rest of the heartland—and woods burst with the glory of dogwoods, redbuds, jonquils, sarvis, and wild azaleas before summer's rich green canopy shades the trails of the quiet foothills.

Bed-and-breakfast inns are not too common in Arkansas, and many of them are hidden in the woods. They are all worth searching out, so many of them are included here. Arkansas and Ozarks Bed and Breakfast is a referral service for a number of the bed-and-breakfasts. Call Ken or Lynn Griffin at (800) 233-2777 or visit their website: thecedarsbnb.com.

BEST ATTRACTIONS IN NORTHEAST ARKANSAS

Blanchard Springs Caverns
Fifty-Six
(870) 757-2211 or (888) 757-2246
ozarkgetaways.com

Happy Lonesome Log Cabins
Calico Rock
(870) 297-8764
bbonline.com/ar/hlcabins

Longbow Luxury Resort
Fairfield Bay
(870) 948-2362
longbowresorts.com

McSpadden's Dulcimer Shop
Mountain View
(870) 269-4313
mcspaddendulcimers.com

NaturScent
Heber Springs
(501) 362-2449
naturscent.com

Ozark Folk Center
Mountain View
(870) 269-3851 or (800) 264-3655
ozarkfolkcenter.com

Ozark Mountain Music Makers Music Barn
Salem
(870) 895-3004

Pearls Unique
Newport
(870) 523-3638 or (800) 637-3233
pearlsunique.com

Stone County Ironworks
Mountain View
(870) 269-IRON or (800) 380-IRON
stoneiron.com

That Bookstore in Blytheville
Blytheville
(870) 763-3333
thatbookstoreinblytheville.com

Gateway to the Ozarks

Batesville calls itself the "Gateway to the Ozarks"; it is a logical place for us to start. The town was founded in 1822 where the Southwest Trail met the White River crossing. (Some folks decided not to cross and stayed.) Arkansas's oldest existing city, it is now the home of Lyon College, and there is always something interesting going on in this college town. The annual **Ozark Scottish Festival,** held in the spring, features competitions in bagpiping, drumming, dancing, and athletics at the college campus. The Batesville Air Festival, held each autumn, has 30 hot-air balloons in the air daily, along with antique and rare aircraft. The **Old Independence Regional Museum** opened in 1998 in the old National Guard Armory at 9th and Vine (380 80 S. 9th St.) in Batesville. Visitors walk into a 12,500-square-foot Works Progress Administration building made of native stone. Built in the 1930s, it is on the National Register of Historic Places. The museum represents a 12-county area and is a genealogist's dream with a climate-controlled archival vault to store rare and fragile documents, photographs, and fabrics. The large 2,680-square-foot gallery houses major exhibits, with a comfortable study area for researchers. Continuing exhibits showcase Native American and early settlement life in the area and the Civil War and Reconstruction periods. Call (870) 793-2121 or visit oirm.org for more information. Hours are 9 a.m. to 4:30 p.m. Tues through Sat and 1:30 to 4 p.m. on Sun. Admission is $3 for adults, $2 for seniors, and $1 for children.

If you have a sweet tooth, head downtown to **Arkansaw Traveller Gourmet Foods.** In this little storefront shop, you can watch Donice and Charles Woodward make molded chocolate candies—offered in white, dark, and diet chocolate—as well as jam, jelly, butters, roasted pecans, and peanut or pecan brittle, all available to taste. The Woodwards ship jelly all over the world. The shop is located at 1368 Neeley; call or fax (870) 793-7936 for information. Hours are 10 a.m. to 5 p.m. Tues through Fri and until 2 p.m. on Sat.

If you're a race fan, you'll want to plan a visit to **Batesville Motor Speedway.** Their racing schedule runs Apr through Sept and includes a wide variety of races, from comp cams to street stock to Nesmith late models. There are also races called the "Bad Boy 98" and the "Topless 100," but it's all family friendly. If you don't know what any of this really means (like me), you can visit their website for pictures and more information at batesville motorspeedway.net. For reserved seat tickets, call (870) 613-1337. There are even seating sections reserved specifically for families. The Speedway is where NASCAR racing legend Mark Martin got his start. You can visit the *Mark Martin Museum* to see several of his race cars and other racing memorabilia. You'll also learn more about his rise in the racing ranks. Call (800) 566-4461 for more information or visit mark martinmuseum.com. The museum is at 1601 Batesville Blvd., inside the Mark Martin Ford/Mercury dealership.

If you happen to be in Batesville in August, stick around for the *annual White River Water Carnival,* Arkansas's oldest annual water event. The Grand Parade, food, arts and crafts, and live music are offered every year. Call the Batesville Chamber at (870) 793-2378.

Newark is a restored 1880s community situated between Jacksonport and Batesville on Highway 69. It was an old railroad town built where the Ozark Mountains meet the flatlands of the Arkansas Delta.

The Red Rooster restaurant is at 590 Morgan St. (870-799-8700). It is right on the spot that used to house Becky's Diner, and locals give it rave

BEST ANNUAL EVENTS IN NORTHEAST ARKANSAS

Tuckerman's Hometown Days
(run by the fire department)
Tuckerman; on Mother's Day
weekend, May
(870) 349-5212

Loose Caboose Festival
Paragould; third weekend in May
(870) 240-0544
loosecaboose.net

Portfest
Newport; first Fri and Sat
in June on the banks of the White River
(870) 523-3618
portfest.org

World Championship Cardboard Boat Festival
Greers Ferry Lake, Heber Springs;
fourth weekend in July
(800) 77-HEBER
hebersprings.com

White River Water Carnival
Batesville; first weekend in Aug
(870) 793-2378
batesvillein.org

Winter Wonderland
Jonesboro; Christmas season
(870) 932-6691

reviews. Hours are 7 a.m. to 8:30 p.m. Mon through Sat. On Sun they open a little later, at 7:30 a.m.

While in Newark, check out the *Times and Traditions Fall Festival.* It is always held the second weekend in September. Times and Traditions is a gathering of local area craftspeople and entertainment, with parades, good food, and a real good old-fashioned time. For more information contact the Newark Chamber of Commerce at (870) 799-8888.

Cave City comes alive with the annual *Cave City Watermelon Festival* in August. There's not just a parade, but also live music every night at the city park, a prize watermelon auction (benefits go to Arkansas Children's Hospital), and a free watermelon feast. Call the Cave City Chamber for this year's dates at (870) 283-7333.

From Batesville the White River flows southeast to the town of *Jacksonport. Jacksonport State Park and Museum* is 3 miles north on Highway 69. Hours are 8 a.m. to 5 p.m. daily, except for Nov through Dec when Sun hours decrease to 1 to 5 p.m. Jacksonport was a riverboat town until the end. After city leaders refused right-of-way to the railroad in 1872, the population began to decline; in 1891 the county seat was moved, and the stores, saloons, and wharves disappeared. Today, exhibits in the park's 1872 courthouse and programs by park interpreters share the story of this historic river port. Admission is free. Jackson State Park also has 20 Class A campsites, a barrier-free bathhouse/restroom, a tree-shaded picnic area within a stone's throw of the river beach, a covered pavilion to rent for large gatherings, a gift shop, and the 28-acre wildlife conservation area called the Tunstall Riverwalk. There is a boat ramp for access to the White River. But a word of caution: According to the locals, in the murky waters where the White and Black Rivers join, a creature called the "White River Monster"—known as "Whitey"—has been sighted. (I'm not making this up.) Sightings of this elusive monster date back to when Native Americans lived in this county. The most recent "reliable" (chamber of commerce quotes, not mine) sightings were in 1937 and the 1970s. So positive that there is a White River Monster, the state legislature proclaimed this section of the White River to be a "White River Monster Refuge." (Hey, if the Arkansas legislature says it's true, it must be.) And now that the Loch Ness Monster has been declared a sham, this could be the only monster left in the world, so be careful not to hurt it. Call (870) 523-2143 for information. Contact *Ozark Gateway*

Tourist Council for information on this area at (800) 264-0316.

US 67 follows the White River south to *Newport,* where, since the turn of the 20th century, the White and the Black Rivers that converge nearby have yielded delicately tinted natural pearls that are highly valued, becoming heirlooms for families lucky enough to find them. In fact, the Royal Crown of England has a lustrous White River pearl in it.

trivia

A bronze plaque on the Holmes building on the corner of Front and Hazel Streets in Newport designates the location of Sam Walton's first Ben Franklin store.

Pearls Unique is the place to find these rare beauties. The freshwater natural pearls are found in mussels in the cold river waters and, because of channeling, dredging, and pollution, are becoming rare. They come in all sizes, from tiny ones to large collectors' pearls, and range in price from $5 to $50,000. The pearls are not just round; they come in shapes carrying such romantic names as *angel wings, rosebud, snail,* and *popcorn.* Customers have the option of selecting from loose pearls and having a setting custom-designed or finding a piece already made. Manager Phyllis Holmes has studied pearls most of her life and will explain how the value of the pearls is determined—by size, luster, shape, and color. Colors can be in shades of peach, apricot, rose, lavender, bronze, silver, gold, cream, white, or even blue and green. The shop has some very rare collectors' baroques, including a large white snail shape. Pearls Unique can be found at 1902–D McLain, Newport, in Pratt Square. Hours are from about 8

trivia

Arkansas is the only state to produce both pearls and diamonds. (Did you know the best way to clean pearls is to use Woolite and water, rinse, and air-dry?)

a.m. to 4:30 p.m., and tours are conducted from 9 a.m. to 4 p.m., but call ahead to make an appointment at (870) 523-3638 or (800) 637-3233. You can also send a fax to (810) 523-3639, or visit pearlsunique.com.

The *Bob E. Jackson Memorial Museum of Funeral Service* is at 1900 Malcolm Ave. in Newport. A horse-drawn, glass-sided funeral coach and a vintage 1880 family buggy are the highlights of this unusual funeral service collection. An 850-pound bronze casket, manufactured in 1927, is on display (needs *big* pallbearers!). It is one of only five made—three were used for burials; the other is on display in Texas. This unique museum has toe-clincher and glass-sealer caskets (ask about them) and home embalming tools. A "must-see" museum, if you like this kind of thing. If you are just along for the ride, the museum also includes a small chapel and an extensive collection of Mr. Jackson's World War II memorabilia. Call (870)-523-5822 to arrange a tour.

One unique museum is not enough for Newport. In the upstairs of the Newport Business Resource Center at 201 Hazel St., you'll find the **Rock & Roll Highway Museum.** Prosecuting Attorney Henry Boyce founded and maintains the museum, which is a tribute to the stretch of highway between Newport and to Pocahontas that became famous for the clubs that played host to Johnny Cash, Elvis Presley, Roy Orbison, Jerry Lee Lewis, Conway Twitty, Sonny Burgess, and Billy Lee Riley in the 1950s. Vintage photos and other memorabilia from the Silver Moon, Porky's Roof Top, and King of Clubs are on display. The museum is open whenever the Business Resource Center is, which is usually Mon through Fri 8 a.m. to 4 p.m. Call ahead to confirm your visit at (870) 523-7428.

Portfest "Rollin' on the River" in Newport is a celebration of River-boat Days. It began in 1982 and has continued to be a time for the community to gather annually for fun and fellowship. It is held the first weekend in June and always features a Nashville star as the headliner. The event takes place on the banks of the White River in Jacksonport State Park. More than 10,000 people gather to celebrate their heritage and to pay tribute to the river. Don't miss the annual Arkansas State Catfish Cooking Contest for some mighty good eating. Portfest offers lots of fun events for the kids. Contact the Newport Area Chamber of Commerce for details by phone at (870) 523-3618, or visit portfest.org.

MJ's Restaurant & Catering To Go has a unique concept: home-cooking without the cooking. Call ahead and order a casserole to go, Mon through Fri until 6 p.m. Pick it up on the way home from work for a quick fix for dinner. They have a daily lunch special of half a sandwich with potato salad and a cup of their delicious homemade soup. Lunch is served Mon through Fri from 11 a.m. to 2 p.m. Call (870) 523-5788 for more information.

The local airbase/industrial park on Highway 18 is the home of **Newport Raceway Drag Strip,** if you are thrilled by the roar of drag racing. Races are held every weekend on the 2-lane blacktop. Call (870) 698-1345 for times.

The Holmes Building, at the corner of Front and Hazel Streets, is the location of Sam Walton's first Ben Franklin store. A bronze plaque honors this spot. The **Old Iron Mountain Railroad Depot,** at 425 Front St., has been restored and is open to the public. Railroad and train memorabilia bring railroad history to life here. Call (870) 523-8078.

Travel northwest from Newport on Highway 14 as it flows along the curve of the White River; the scene changes as mountains pop up, trees line the highway, and cattle graze on the rolling hills and valleys. The drive to **Mountain View** is an event in itself. For a tour through some lovely Ozark countryside, travel north on Highway 69, then east on Highway 58. You can also stay on Highway 69, turning east on Highway 9, a twisting 2-laner from Melbourne along a ridge with a view of White River Valley. No matter how you do it, the last 30 miles scribble through hills with rocky streams and spectacular vistas. All roads lead to Mountain View, so it becomes the center point from which directions to other attractions in the area begin.

Free Saturday musicals held in the Mountain View town square have been a tradition for some 30 years, and "pickin' and grinnin'" goes on well into the night, as local strummers gather by the courthouse and folks bring lawn chairs to get comfortable on balmy evenings. Folk music lovers by the thousands come into town to hear the fiddles and dulcimers sing. Favorite son Dick Powell, crooner and leading man of the forties and fifties, was born here. Mountain View also hosts the annual **Bean Fest.** More than 30 huge iron kettles of pinto beans, along with corn bread and onions, are cooked and served free to everyone. The tall tale–telling contest (and they get taller every year) is part of the event called "The Big Blowout." But the highlight is the Great Outhouse Race—each privy is decorated and, after the musket shot, pushed along the course with the driver sitting on the seat inside. The coveted gold, silver, or bronze toilet seat trophies and cash prizes for best-decorated comfort station and best-dressed driver are awarded on the courthouse steps. This is not the only outhouse race in the state, but it is—citizens here will tell you—the only one fueled by beans.

Courthouse Square is the heart of the community, and most of the shops there have no address; in fact, there are only a few street names. Highways become streets, streets become highways, and the names are interchangeable. Ask directions, and the people who live in Mountain View will just point or say it's near some other place on the square. If you walk around the square, you will find everything sooner or later. It is illegal to buy liquor and impossible to find a good restaurant meal, but good music is easy to find. Visit ozarkgetaways.com.

Woods Pharmacy, at 301 West Martin St. in Mountain View, has an early-1900s restored antique soda fountain that serves deli sandwiches and old-fashioned ice-cream treats. Remember thick, rich milk shakes and malts, phosphates, hand-dipped ice cream, and fresh limeade and lemonade? They are still here, just 1 block west of Courthouse Square. Hours are 8 a.m. to 5 p.m. Mon through Sat. Call (870) 269-8304 for more information.

A number of bed-and-breakfasts are clustered near the square. The **Wildflower Bed and Breakfast on the Square** (100 Washington St.), on the northeast corner across from the old jailhouse, is owned by J.R. and Pam Rivera and calls itself a "vintage guest house." This bed-and-breakfast, at the convergence of Peabody and Washington Streets, has six rooms, all with private baths and queen-size beds. Named to the National Register of Historic Places, this old hotel was built for traveling salesmen in 1918. In 1998 it went through extensive renovations. Rooms range from $65 to $135, including a hearty buffet breakfast served in the sunny parlor dining area. Lots of games, puzzles, and reading materials are available for the guests. The bed-and-breakfast's location is perfect for guests who come to hear the old country tunes picked by impromptu gatherings of musicians. Call (870) 269-4383 or (800) 591-4879 for reservations, or visit wildflowerbb.com or arkansas-inn.com.

Corner Stone Gifts, at 101 North Peabody St., is owned by Debra Verilla and is housed in the building that used to be home to the busiest Chevrolet dealership in the entire state. The store carries an eclectic selection of sophisticated gifts. Call (870) 269-8826 for more information. Winter hours are 10 a.m. to 5 p.m. Mon through Sat. Summer hours are longer and include Sun.

Tommy's Famous (Pizza) specializes in handmade pizza and won second place in the state for best pizza. Call (870) 269-FAST to place your order.

Tommy is also famous for his Memphis-style barbecue and ribs. You can't miss Tommy's bright purple building, 4 blocks west of the square off Highway 66 West. He is open 7 days a week from 3 p.m. until whenever—7, 8, or 9 p.m., depending on how many people are still there. If it's too crowded inside and the weather is nice, eat on the picnic tables outside.

Peabody Street crosses Main at the south end of the square, and just past the post office is where *Ozark Country Inn Bed and Breakfast* sits in the shade of old maple trees. Many of the musicians you will hear on the square stay here. It was built in the early 1900s. Maple trees surround the second-story porch where people pick and play well into the night when the weather is warm. Because the inn is only steps away from Courthouse Square, where good music making and jiggin' can be enjoyed almost every night, it is often booked up. Bring your fiddle and join in. Don "Brickshy" and Sissy Jones invite you to enjoy their hospitality. Call (870) 269-8699 or (800) 379-8699. The inn's website is ozarkcountryinn.com. Rooms at the inn—located at 219 South Peabody St. on Highway 9 South—all have private baths. An old-fashioned breakfast is served at 8 a.m.

trivia

The word *Arkansas* comes from the word *Kansas,* "people of the south wind" or "downstream people." But spelling the state name has never been easy. Explorers used *Arkansoa, Arkancas,* and *Arkensa,* to name a few. Not everyone agreed on the pronunciation—was it *Ar-KANSAS* or *AR-kan-saw?* The legislature settled on *AR-kan-saw* in 1881.

The *Stone County Ironworks* manufactures and distributes heirloom-quality iron furniture and accessories. The historic building is on Courthouse Square. It has a complete line of hand-forged iron from the ironworks. Owner Paulette Nichols has recently opened the upstairs with more crafts, decorative accessories, and goodies of all kinds. Hours are seasonal and different almost every day. Usually opening at 9 a.m., the shop remains that way until 5 p.m. on Mon, 6 p.m. on Tues and Wed, 7 p.m. on Thurs, and 9 p.m. on Fri and Sat. Sun hours are from noon to 5 p.m. Winter hours are Mon through Sat 9 a.m. to 5 p.m.; call (870) 269-IRON or (800) 380-IRON for the exact closing time, or visit stoneiron.com. Their address is 17430 Hwy. 66.

Another favorite spot is *PJ's Rainbow Cafe* at 216 Main St. (870-269-8633), a nonsmoking restaurant owned by Pat and Chuck Mahaney. Really good home cooking is what is going on here: soups made from scratch (scratch being a pot of water), homemade pies, and hand-breaded chicken-fried steaks. Winter hours are 7 a.m. (biscuits and gravy, homemade cinnamon rolls the size of hubcaps) to 8 p.m. (dessert could be the infamous Mountain Ozark Pie—a chocolate-coconut-walnut pie served warm with a dab of ice cream). It all begins at 6 a.m. weekdays in summertime until 8 p.m., and Sun 7 a.m. to 2 p.m. Closed Mon.

The Inn at Mountain View, just off Courthouse Square at 307 Washington St. in Mountain View, dates to 1886 and features a porch that is great for sitting and rocking. A large stone fireplace in the living room warms guests on cool autumn nights. Owners Mark and JoAnn Nelson (and Tigger, who greets and loves everyone as only a yellow Lab can) keep up many of the traditions of the famous old inn while adding great new ideas. The antiques and handmade quilts are still there, and every morning, JoAnn and Mark cook up a breakfast smorgasbord. This is more than just a full country breakfast. Internet access and a big-screen TV are available for corporate meetings. The restored inn is air-conditioned, and large mini-suites range in price from $88 to $140 for two. All have private baths. Call (870) 269-4200 or (800) 535-1301, or visit innatmountainview.com.

A popular activity while enjoying music on the square is to take a buggy ride around town. Starting about 7 p.m. on Fri and Sat nights, Mar through Oct, folks from the *OK Trading Post* bring their horses and buggies to the square. You can also book trail rides and hayrides through the Trading Post by calling (870) 585-2217. Owners Terry and Denisa Malott offer trail rides in the woods. A half-hour ride is $12, a 1-hour ride is $20, or 1.5 hours for $25; a ride through the woods and along the creek and bluff for 2 hours is $30. The half-day ride ($60) includes a meal, but the overnight ($125) is the best deal. You bring your own sleeping bag and fishing gear, and the guides cook you a steak dinner that night and ham and eggs in the morning. You can also take a hayride to the creek for a hot dog roast.

Also east of the square, but on Sylamore Road (which is also Highway 9), is where Jim and Betty Woods and their team of craftspeople make dulcimers at *McSpadden's Dulcimer Shop.* The shop is filled with local artists' crafts—pottery, wood carvings—all natural items. You can watch through the glass wall as five woodworkers make mountain dulcimers (the kind that goes on your lap). If you ask, someone will play one and give you a quick lesson. They'll have you playing "Mary Had a Little Lamb" in no time. Prices here are quite reasonable—from $180 with a case, music, and instructions, to $1,000 for a custom-carved beauty. The shop is open Feb through Nov; hours are Mon through Sat 9 a.m. until 5 p.m.; call (870) 269-4313 for information. Their website is mcspaddendulcimers.com.

The **White River Furniture Company** is across the street from the courthouse. Al Cunningham has a large selection of rustic furniture for your cabin or country home. The wood selections are made by families who have been crafting furniture for more than 60 years.

Arkansas Craft Gallery, 104 East Main St., showcases the best artists from all over the state. Several guild shops dot the state. Kathy Sheskey, executive director, says that more than 300 artists are members of the guild, and they have been sending top-quality handmade crafts here for more than 20 years. The guild also has the largest selection of pottery in the state, as well as five styles of working spinning wheels, furniture, wooden bowls, and candles. Works from seven glass artists, five basket makers, two broom makers, and 30 jewelry makers are also available. Each month the gallery highlights a different artist. The shop is open 9:30 a.m. to 5:30 p.m. Mon through Sat. Call Kathy at (870) 269-3897 or (870) 269-4120. You'll find a website at arkansascraftguild.org.

Two miles north of Mountain View on Highway 5/9/14 is the **Jimmy Driftwood Barn and Folk Museum.** If you don't know who Jimmy Driftwood was, you will by the time you leave Mountain View. He built the barn for the Rackensack Folklore Society, a loose-knit group of locals who are dedicated to preserving the folk music of the hills. It is operated by the University of Central Arkansas. Driftwood has been called this country's finest folk balladeer, although he started his career quite by accident at age 50, when he wrote "The Battle of New Orleans" for his 6th-grade American history class and it became an instant success. Jimmy died in July 1988, but his style of music lives on here. The barn welcomes folk musicians and the public to free Fri and Sun musicals at 7:30 p.m. throughout the year. Other programs and activities are offered at various times during the week. Call (870) 269-8042 for information or visit jimmy driftwoodmusicbarn.com.

Don and Suzie Mellon had the Mellon Patch business in a converted chicken house in Mountain View. It was built around a wooden train whistle, musical spoons, wooden trains, and other wooden items, which they sold wholesale. Their dream was to build a new workshop and retail store on property they owned near the Jimmy Driftwood Barn. The dream has become an old country store, "the kind of place you like to pull into" when traveling across Arkansas, according to Don.

The white clapboard building, now called *Mellon's Country Store,* has tall, narrow windows. A 35-foot tower is out front with a circa 1930 aeromotor windmill. A 1924 vintage gas pump with Don's pride and joy—a 1939 Ford—parked in front of it will certainly stop traffic.

Inside there are hanging hams, barrels of hard candy, and the scent of coffee being ground. You can buy sausage grinders, cast-iron pots, horseshoes (and mule shoes), and washboards. Felt hats are displayed on an old hatbox dresser, and lots of vintage musical instruments—banjos, fiddles, and guitars—are all over the place. In fact, Don will sit a spell on the porch with you and do some pickin' if you've a mind to. Or you can have an RC Cola and a Moon Pie and listen to Don, a toy maker by trade, talk about his own handmade wooden toys—checked out by his own grandchildren—of which he is justifiably proud. "Our motto is 'If they can't break it, then we'll make it,'" he says. Aisles are crowded with reminders of a time when metal trademark signs for Coke, Hershey, Lipton, and Nehi were common. You can have homemade jellies, chow-chow, smoked hams, and stone-ground cornmeal or browse among antiques, curiosities, marbles, iron skillets, books, and handmade crafts. This is the place to see hats from the Clearwater Hat Company, too.

Mellon's Country Store is 2 miles north of Mountain View on Highway 9 at the windmill. Seasonal hours are Apr through Oct, 9 a.m. to 5 p.m. daily; in Mar, Nov, and Dec, 9 a.m. to 5 p.m. Fri, Sat, and Sun. In Jan and Feb it is open on Sat and Sun. Call (870) 269-3354 for information or visit mellons countrystore.com.

The *Stone County Museum* on School Avenue is for history buffs, especially if you are from this area. Most items have been donated by families in Stone County, so there are handwoven bed covers and curtain panels, crocheted bedspreads, wedding clothing, and homemade furniture. There's a spinning wheel and cider press and lots of military relics. The museum has copies of birth, marriage, and death certificates and rubbings of tombstones. Hours are 1 to 4 p.m. on Thurs, Fri, and Sat from Apr through Oct. *Cash's White River Hoedown,* 507 Sylamore, Mountain View, offers a rip-roaring good ol' time. Bumpy and Aunt Millie Miles showcase a musical and comical cast in a performance that reflects the homespun humor of the area. If you like mountain music, this is the place to be. Aunt Millie says, "Laughter is the best medicine, and I am the doctor." For reservations and current schedule, call (800) 759-6474 or (870) 269-4161.

If you don't want to stay in town and listen to all the music, or if you just want a good night's sleep before you hit the Ozark Folk Center, then check out *Country Oaks Bed & Breakfast,* just 1 mile from town off Highway 9 south of Mountain View (on the road to Shirley). Here you can have the feeling of yesterday and the comfort of today. Antiques, lace curtains, claw-foot bathtubs, and marble showers create ambience at this lush hideaway on 69 acres. Surrounded by majestic oaks, it has its own (catch and release) fishing lake, with a path for morning strolls and a 2-mile hiking trail. Queen- and king-size beds, fireplaces, and ceiling fans give you all the modern comforts, as do three upstairs sitting rooms with television and free snacks and beverages. A full gourmet breakfast, prepared by innkeepers Carole and Jerry Weber, is served in the dining room each morning. Three rooms are available, all with showers. This is a new house but done in Victorian style, so there is a porch with rockers (no children under 12, which makes it even quieter). A second building offers five more guest rooms and a meeting room for corporate groups. Rooms run $100 to $110. Call (870) 269-2704 or (800) 455-2704 for information and reservations. You can also visit countryoaksbb.com.

The Olive Tree Gallery is the dream, after more than 35 years in the gallery business, of Eric Whitley and his wife Penny. They have created the gallery to see. Local, regional, and national artists display here. Originals, prints, and giclées can be purchased. (Giclée is a picture that has been printed directly onto the canvas with a French process that brings more life, clarity, and vibrant color to the print). Handmade hats and purses abound. There are garden hats, toddler hats, fuzzy hats, plain hats, funky hats, and fussy fru fru hats, as well as one-of-a-kind purses. There are elegant handmade copper fountains of all sizes that can be displayed on tables, walls, or floors that came all the way from Idaho. Best of all, right in the middle of the gallery is a specialty coffee shop. According to Eric, the Amish pastries served here are guaranteed to cause hip expansion. The gallery is located at 116 A West Main in Mountain View. Call (870) 269-6580 or go to theolivetreegallery.com.

What brings people to the Mountain View area, though, is the *Ozark Folk Center,* north of town off Highway 5/9/14 on Folk Center Road. Built to maintain the unique folk traditions of the Ozarks, the center preserves almost-forgotten arts and music of the hill people who lived on the hillsides and hollers of the mountains. The center features artists like Dutch Wigman, who makes bowed psalteries; Terri Bruhin, a weaver who makes lace-weave table linens and rag rugs (more about her later); and Owen Rein, a master chair maker who creates white-oak rockers with drawknife and bending forms, or "jigs," to curve the green wood to the measurements of the person planning to use it. This showcase for hill-life traditions was founded by descendants of the river valley pioneers to preserve the lore and crafts that were quickly disappearing. Twenty-five "cabin crafts," practiced in rustic shops scattered across an Ozark hilltop, and a heritage herb garden are open daily 10 a.m. to 5 p.m. May through Oct. If you have never experienced the sweet scent of cedar from a cooper's shop or the sharp tang of coal smoke from a blacksmith's forge, this is your chance to travel back to simpler times. The park re-creates a time when plain materials like white-oak sheaves or apples became baskets and dolls and when common farm implements such as saw blades and buckets became musical instruments. Music is made here with such instruments as the bowed psaltery, dulcimer, pickin' bow, and spoons, as well as fiddles, banjos, and guitars. Concerts are presented Mon through Sat at 7:30 p.m. in the center's 1,000-seat auditorium. Sun night gospel concerts are held once or twice a month through the season. Call (870) 269-3851 or (800) 264-3655 for a schedule or visit ozarkfolkcenter.com.

The century-old Shannon Cabin at the center is open to visitors. It has a stone fireplace, homemade furniture, front and rear porches, and a sleeping loft typical of the rural log homes of the past. Scheduled for demolition, it was brought to the center from Happy Hollow in Stone County. Tina Marie Wilcox, Ozark Folk Center herbalist, did the landscaping, planting an assortment of homestead flowers, herbs, and bushes around the cabin, the way a pioneer woman might have done.

Although the *Ozark Folk Center Skillet Restaurant and Ozark Cabins at Dry Creek* is located in the middle of the state park, innkeeper

Iona Borhem takes care of you as though you were her personal guest. The octagonal cabins are built from native cedar and scattered around the grounds. Three sliding glass doors let in the breeze and a wide view of the trees outside, and the dining room serves traditional southern cooking—beans and ham, greens, and corn bread. Call (870) 269-3871 or (800) 264-FOLK for room reservations, or visit the center's website at ozarkfolk center.com.

At the far end of the Folk Center's main parking lot, you'll find *Loco Ropes.* This is an adventuresome must-do for everyone taller than 43 inches (that's the minimum requirement) and less than 290 pounds. You can choose your daring act here. Tower Adventures include rock wall climbing, the HotShot controlled free fall, or a ride on the Screamin' Pig zip line. Each of these is $7.50 per person. Otherwise, you can take to the treetops, where you can choose from three different ropes courses (or complete them all!). While harnessed in to an overhead guideline, you'll traverse rope bridges and negotiate plank wood crossings. In between each challenge you can hug a tree trunk, as you'll be 10-20 feet off the ground. It's an empowering (and completely safe) challenge for kids and grandmas alike! The cost for the Treetop Adventures is $15 to $50 depending on how many courses you do. Hours are 10 a.m. to 5 p.m. daily, Mar through Nov. It's best to call ahead for reservations if you want to do the treetop ropes courses, but you can usually just walk up for the Tower Adventures. Phone is (870) 269-6566, or you can visit their website at locoropes.net.

You can tour about 25 studios near Mountain View by coming in Sept and doing the annual *Off the Beaten Path Studio Tour.* It's a self-guided tour of the private studios within 30 miles of town. See pottery, jewelry, stained glass, paintings, folk art, woodcarving, and more. Works are on exhibit and for sale. Maps and studio guides are available at the Mountain View and Calico Rock Chambers of Commerce. For more information call (888) 679-2859 or go to offthebeatenpathstudiotour.com.

Traveling along scenic Highway 9 between Mountain View and Melbourne, you will see the beautiful Wildcat Mountain. Sitting smack-dab on the top of the mountain are 2 two-bedroom log cabins surrounded by flower gardens and scenic views. These are the *Wildcat Mountain Cabins.*

Artistic owners Ed and Pamela Alexander have a studio on the mountain. Pamela specializes in unique one-of-a-kind garden art. Wind sculpture, bottle trees, trellises, birdbaths, and whimsical flag holders are just a few of the items available. Ed is an extraordinary photographer. His wildlife and scenic views are breathtaking. You can reach Pam at (870) 219-3280 for rates and availability for the cabins.

Barbara Carlson is also part of the Off the Beaten Path Studio Tour. Barbara specializes in portrait quilts, which belong in a subgroup of art quilts. Art quilts are smaller quilts that are hung on walls as artwork. Because they are used as decoration only, many nontraditional quilt media are used. Barbara's quilts are exhibited at the Historic Arkansas Museum in Little Rock and the Arkansas Craft Gallery in Mountain View. Barbara can be reached at (870) 297-3479.

An underground stream flows into **Blanchard Springs Caverns,** which are just 14 miles north of Mountain View off Highway 5/9/14 at the town of Sylamore (where Highway 5/9/14 splits), then east on Highway 14. The water emerges as Sylamore Creek, winding its way through the Ozark National Forest to the White River. It is an important part of the cavern; 216 feet beneath the lush green of the Ozark National Forest lies the underground world of massive stalactites and towering sandstone columns, sculpted by water and time and home to blind salamanders and albino crayfish. This is a living cave because the continuous water supply keeps the formations growing. The uppermost caverns consist of two huge rooms, the Cathedral Room and the Coral Room, which are each large enough to hold several football fields. The explored part of the lower section, where the river flows, is almost 5 miles long.

The Dripstone Trail passes through the uppermost part of the caverns for 0.7 mile, with stone curbs or handrails. Every type of calcite formation can be found in the limestone caves—stalactites, stalagmites, hollow soda straws, massive flowstones, and giant columns in colors ranging from snow white to dark brown because of the varied minerals found in the deposits.

The Discovery Trail—discovered when someone fell through a hole in the floor—is 1.2 miles long and has more than 600 steps that take you deeper into the caverns, where there are water-carved passages, a cave stream, and the natural entrance. One spot looks as though billions of diamonds had spilled into the cavern, the crystals sparkling in the lights. The skeletal remains of a Native American who explored the cave more than a thousand years ago were found next to a bundle of reeds—perhaps used to make torches—but no one knew much about the cave until it was explored in 1956. It has been open to the public only since 1973. You might want to wear a long-sleeved shirt or maybe even a sweater when exploring the cave, because it's a constant 58 degrees inside, and with the humidity near 100 percent, dampness adds to the chill.

Blanchard Springs Caverns are in the town of **Fifty-Six** (870-757-2211). Hours are 10 a.m. to 4 p.m. daily Apr through Oct and Wed to Sun Nov through Mar. Admission is $10 for adults, $5 with a Golden Pass for seniors, $5 for children ages 6 to 15. There is a $3 per car day-use charge for the picnic areas with a spring-fed stream for swimming (complete with bathhouse); camping facilities are $10 per night with a 5-night minimum. From Mountain View take Highway 14 west to Fifty-Six. Granted, these caverns are a well-known tourist spot, but they are among the most beautiful caves in the world. It would be a shame to miss them. To get the most impressive feeling of the caverns, come by in December for the annual **Caroling in the Caverns** event. Guides will escort you into the acoustically perfect Cathedral Room, and the incredible voices and stringed instruments of the area folk musicians raise goose bumps in the semi-dark. It begins around Thanksgiving and is at 2:30 and 4:30 p.m. on Sat and Sun through the middle of Dec. You can do a walking tour of the caverns with the 2:30 p.m. show, if you want to. This has been going on for more than 6 years and all performances have sold out, so advance tickets are required. Call the Mountain View Chamber of Commerce, (888) 679-2859, or download tickets at ozarkgetaways.com.

The **Clearwater Hat Company** owners, Kay and Bob Burton, are believed to be the only makers of historical fur-felt hats in the country. They work in **Newtana,** west of Mountain View, at 1007 Clearwater Rd. The Burtons searched the Smithsonian archives to study hats worn in Europe and America from 1750 to 1900 and now can produce anything from the French-Indian War period to the 1920s. Reenactors are the couple's best customers. Colonial hats, worn by men like Thomas Jefferson and George Washington, had three corners turned up to show off the powdered wigs stylish then. Civil

trivia

Notice Jude Law's pecan-colored slouch hat in the movie *Cold Mountain?* Russell Crowe and Peter Fonda are also wearing hats made at Clearwater Hats in *3:10 to Yuma.*

War hats include the "hardee" hat: one side of the brim turned up with a plume. All are made with fur felt just as they were 200 years ago. Even most of the equipment used in the factory predates 1920. Crowns and brims are hand shaped after the bodies of the hats are steamed, sized, and shaped. But mercury nitrate is no longer used, as was done in the old days, so there are no "mad hatters" here. Kay tells the story of the day the beautiful Porsche pulled up to the shop (which is so far off the beaten path as to be a challenge to find), bringing everyone out of the shop. The driver stepped out of the little car with this book and a GPS in his hand. Ah, the wonders of electronics! And speaking of electronics, their website is clearwaterhats.com, or call (870) 612-7011 to order a catalog. Please call weekdays between the hours of 9 a.m. and 4 p.m. This is their cell phone, and sometimes they are hard to reach. Keep trying! You can also see the hats at Mellon's Country Store in Mountain View.

Timbo Dairy Bar, west on Highway 66 in **Timbo,** advertises itself as having the best burgers in town. Never mind that it's the only place to eat in town, the food is pretty good. Open Tues through Thurs 11 a.m. to 7 p.m., Fri and Sat 11 a.m. to 8 p.m., and Sun 11 a.m. to 3 p.m. Closed Mon. Call (870) 746-4733.

On top of Fox Mountain is the small, small town of **Fox** (two grocery stores and a post office) on Highway 263 just south of Timbo. Fox is about an hour's drive from Mountain View, with two ways to get there. One is to travel on scenic Highway 66 to Highway 263, but this route has a terror of a hairpin turn onto Highway 263 that you might find exciting if you are an Ozark Mountain Daredevil driver. Or try Highway 9 south to Highway 263. This is a more pastoral drive along a road of soft hills lined with old barns. About five artists live in the area. Some work at the Ozark Folk Center; others don't, and they are a challenge to find.

Fox Mountain Pottery is the home shop of Joe and Terri Bruhin, the weaver you met at the Ozark Folk Center. Joe is a potter whose pride and joy is a Noborigama-type, three-chambered, climbing natural-draft-wood-fired kiln ("I don't think there's another one like it in the state," remarks Terri). Here he creates one-of-a-kind stoneware and porcelain pottery, everything from traditional casseroles and mugs to large urns that stand 2 feet tall. The kiln reaches temperatures of 2,500 degrees, so the resulting high-fired pottery is good in the oven, microwave—or kitchens on Mercury or Venus. It's pottery meant to be used, as well as being original artwork. To find the shop once you're in Fox, turn onto the dirt road next to the post office and begin the trek into the hills. Call Joe for directions at (870) 363-4264 or you may never find it. Joe says that they are "in the middle of nowhere out here," and that's very accurate.

Joe can also direct you to the other craftspeople around Fox—a woodworker who makes fishing lures, a shop where glass beads are made—and Terri Bruhin can usually be found at the Ozark Folk Center in the weavers' shop, where she weaves handwoven clothing.

Calico Rock is a pretty little town of about 1,000 people on the bluffs of the White River exactly halfway between Mountain Home and Mountain View on Highway 5. The many colors of the sheer vertical cliffs along the river make it easy to see how the town got its name—steamship captains used to say, "Stop by them calico rocks," because it was the northernmost accessible port for steamboats in the spring of the year, and the name stuck. In 1901 the railroad came to town and blasted away the beautiful calico-colored cliffs. There's a view of the river from Main Street, and the old buildings, made of the colored rock and brick, reflect the 1920s and 1930s, when the railroad and sawmills that had made the town led to its destruction: A passing locomotive sparked a fire on a warehouse roof, and Main Street was destroyed. The town was rebuilt, however, and now the buildings are filled with crafts, collectibles, and antiques shops. Visit calicorock.com.

Mills can still be seen in the older part of town, and wood homes of the 1920s and 1930s perch on the river bluffs. The 1923 **River View Hotel** at 100 Rodman Ave. is 1 block from the Main Street of Calico Rock. The white cement-block hotel (not fancy but built for railroad workers who passed through the town in the 1920s, when the woodmills were active) is now a bed-and-breakfast. This old-fashioned inn is filled with antiques and collectibles of the 1920s; it has iron beds in some rooms and oak Mission furniture in others and overlooks the White River. Owner Linda Boulton serves up a hearty breakfast. There are eight rooms, five of which are two-bedroom suites—each with a private bath—some with tubs, others with showers.

Prices range $75 to $100 and include breakfast, which is served buffet-style in the small sunroom off the lobby. You can make reservations by calling (870) 297-8208 or visiting ozarksriverview.com. The hotel is closed Nov through Feb and for two weeks in Mar.

See You at the Movies!

If Calico Rock looks slightly familiar, it may be because you saw the movie *Boot-Leggers* starring Kate Smith. It was shot in Calico Rock in 1973 and continues to air regularly on cable TV. The incredible scenery of the Ozarks and the charming personalities of towns like Calico Rock make Arkansas a popular state with Hollywood. In all, about 75 movies have been shot in the state, including the opening credits of *Gone with the Wind*—that's the Old Mill in North Little Rock. Other movies that were shot, at least in part, in Arkansas, include:

White Lightning	1972	*Rosa Lee Goes Shopping*	1988
Crisis at Central High	1980	*The Tuskegee Airmen*	1995
The Blue and the Gray	1981	*Sling Blade*	1997
A Soldier's Story	1983	*Walk the Line*	2005
Biloxi Blues	1987	*Mud*	2012

Plus, much of John Grisham's *The Client* and *The Firm* were shot in West Memphis and other parts of eastern Arkansas. And all of the exteriors of the television show *Designing Women* are homes in Little Rock.

The **East Calico Historic District** is the only ghost town located inside of an existing town in the US. There's a walking tour that will guide you through the history of the area and the 22 buildings that remain here. Some of these include a pool hall/tavern, a barber shop, a theater, a cafe, a lumberyard, the telephone exchange, a cotton gin, a funeral parlor, and an electric company. Once you've seen it all, you can visit the old jail and have your photo made. The tour starts at the west edge of the district and ends at Roselawn Cemetery. Visit calicorocket.org to learn more and download the walking tour.

Probably the most romantic setting for a bed-and-breakfast is that owned by Carolyn and Christian Eck. The Ecks' two log cabins, called **Happy Lonesome Log Cabins,** are surrounded by the Ozark National Forest. These are 1.5 miles from anywhere. In fact, after you reach the property, it is still a half mile of woods to the cabins, with a fabulous view from a 200-foot bluff overlooking the White River. Talk about a perfect location for a honeymoon hideaway! There are hiking trails and mountains to climb. Each cabin has a sleeping loft and a wood-burning stove, and both are unhosted for maximum privacy but provided with coffee and homemade fruit bread (the pumpkin bread is a favorite)—all for $78.50 for two, $85 weekends and holidays; $10 for each additional person. There are now two more cabins, one with two bedrooms and a sleeping porch. You can bring the entire family, because one sleeps 11 for $160 per night (plus $10 additional for each extra person) for the first 4 nights. A smaller cabin is handicap accessible; it has one bedroom and a dog run for $78.50. The actual address is 1444 Forest Home Ln. according to the website bbonline.com/ar/hlcabins, or call (870) 297-8764 or cell (501) 626-4237. The cabins close in winter, so call ahead for sure.

Downtown Calico Rock has a number of interesting places worth checking out. Chris and Carolyn Eck's hardware store on the east side of Calico Rock's Main Street has an outdoor display of sturdy pieces of country furniture handmade by Walter and Martha Hagan. A gigantic rocking chair they built is every visitor's favorite photo op. It's the kind of place where you can go in to buy just one screw, if that's all you need. What used to be Edith Floyd's grocery is now **Don Quixote's Calico Kitchen**, at 103 Main St., owned by Gloria and Bob Gushue. The bakeshop in front, where Gloria does all the baking, is filled with rye, whole-wheat, and other interesting breads and pastries. A favorite is hummingbird cake. Ask Gloria about her bird collection, visible in the rustic, woodland decor of the restaurant. She started with placing one or two fabric birds in tree branches; now customers bring birds and nests to add to her collection from their travels all over the world. Bob is also an antiques dealer specializing in Tiffany glass (he is a registered Tiffany dealer). There are Tiffany pieces for sale in the restaurant along with other antiques, such as American brilliant cut glass. Continental cuisine is their specialty—Northern Italian and French dishes dominate the menu, but Bob also makes a great Polish stew called *capusta* with sauer-kraut and beans. The restaurant serves nothing but choice meats. Often, folks from Mountain View or other nearby towns will call ahead to order a meal, and Bob and the crew will begin work so that lunch is ready when they arrive. That says something about the food, doesn't it? The bakery opens at 10 a.m., and lunch is served from 10:30 a.m. until 4:30 p.m. Dinner begins at 4:30 and continues until 9 p.m. Sun hours are 11 a.m. to 4 p.m. Call (870) 297-8899 for reservations, or visit donquixotes.net. They do close in winter, so call ahead.

Melbourne is on Highway 9, east of Calico Rock. The *Ashley House Bed and Breakfast* is at 618 East Main, just 2 blocks east of the courthouse square. Terry and Susan Smith are the innkeepers at this seven-bedroom home that has a huge wraparound porch, complete with rockers and ceiling fans. All seven bedrooms have king- or queen-size beds, cable TV, high-speed Internet, and private baths; prices range $50 to $100. Complimentary snacks, coffee, and an ice machine and microwave are in the public area. This century-old home looks very cozy. If you need more than just a room, Jeff House, a small white cottage with three bedrooms, is adjacent to the main house. Sporting shade trees and a big front porch, the house is fully equipped with kitchen and bedroom supplies and has cable TV and one bath. A small cottage on the west side of the Ashley House, Kate's House, has two bedrooms, one bath, cable TV, and a fully supplied living/kitchen area. This cottage and the Jeff House are $50 to $100 per night. Breakfast is available at the Ashley House for $5 per person for all guests in the cottages. Meeting facilities are also available. Call (870) 368-4577 for reservations, or visit ashleyhouse.net. You can also e-mail sfs@centurytel.net.

Greers Ferry Lake Area

The Aromatique Factory, a multimillion-dollar business on the outskirts of *Heber Springs,* started on a whim in 1982. Patti Upton created a pretty arrangement of pinecones and gum balls, brightened with green bay leaves, and gave it a Christmas scent with cinnamon, cloves, and such for her friend Sandra Horne's gift shop. The result, called "The Smell of Christmas," was a sellout hit. What started as a small two-woman business has grown into a corporation employing more than 400 persons. You'll find the Aromatique Factory at 3421 Hwy. 25B North, Heber Springs.

A showroom for the factory, called *Panache,* is filled with the lovely scents created here. Described as an "A'romantic shop," it is part of the factory complex and carries the decorative room fragrances sold elsewhere only in upscale gift shops and the finest department stores. It's a treat just to walk into the little shop and be bathed in the delicate scents. Choosing among them is fun, too. Now there are 15 scented mixtures of wood chips and botanicals, more than 100 ingredients in all, with aromas romantically named "Smell of Spring"—a hyacinth-scented collection of bougainvillea;

German statice in purple, pink, and white; bright-green bay leaves; and curled poplar in mauve—or "Gentleman's Quarters," comprising "rugged, exotic botanicals" with a masculine, outdoors smell. All combine colors and textures artfully and carry a delicate but definite scent. Prices range from $8 for a small cellophane bag to $125 for elegant holiday baskets. The shop is open 9:30 a.m. to 5 p.m. Mon through Fri and Sat 10 a.m. to 5 p.m. Call (501) 362-7919 or (800) 875-3111 for information, or visit aromatique.com.

Not to be outdone, *NaturScent* has a three-room gift shop at the factory owned by Darrel and Martha Bufford at 1259 Wilburn Rd., Heber Springs, on Highway 110 near the Winckley Bridge. Thirty fragrances of potpourri, candles, and bath oils are displayed with shampoos and lotions. The most popular is the original mulberry potpourri. Hours are 8 a.m. to 4:30 p.m. Mon through Fri. Call (501) 362-2449 for information, or visit naturscent.com.

Morbid Curiosity

Okay, maybe this is not the kind of museum the kids will jump up and down about, but the **Olmstead Mortuary Museum** has a certain morbid pull to it. It is in the building that housed the Olmstead Funeral Home until the business required larger quarters. The circa 1910 stone building is on the National Register of Historic Places. Fire destroyed the original wood-frame undertaker shop built there in 1896. Thomas Dwight Olmstead is the grandson of Thomas Edward Olmstead, who arrived from Indiana in a covered wagon in 1896 and opened a funeral parlor. Over the years the paraphernalia became more and more interesting. The museum's centerpiece is a somber, black horse-drawn hearse, the finest of its kind. After that, the displays mainly appeal to a curiosity for things we never get to see. There is a home cosmetics kit used to make the deceased look less deceased and more "natural." Books on embalming and funeral directing that date back to the early 1900s line the shelves. The funeral home's first electric Porti-Boy embalming machine (1938) looks like a giant blender. An 1896 grave tamper will give you the willies if you read any Edgar Allan Poe. Also here are the first sealed metal coffins, from about 1908, and an impressive and expensive-looking (you can take it with you) oversize casket made of cypress and covered with doeskin that was built in 1926 for someone who, for whatever reason, never had to use it. All in all, it is a very interesting museum, at 108 South 4th St., Heber Springs. Call (501) 362-2422 to schedule a visit. Open Fri 10 a.m. to 4 p.m.; olmstead.cc.

The town of Sugar Loaf was founded in 1882 and became Heber Springs in 1910. Heber Springs is a tourist mecca but keeps the small-town ambience of those earlier days.

Heber Springs is at the foot of Round Mountain and still has, downtown in Spring Park, the original spring for which it was named. You'll also want to visit **Bridal Veil Falls,** a beautiful waterfall just south of town. Take highway 5/25 south and turn right onto Bridal Veil Falls Road to get there. It's a short, easy hike down to the falls. If you manage to time your visit after heavy rainfalls, you'll really get a treat.

Cafe Klaser, at 1414 Wilburn Rd., Heber Springs, is a favorite spot to eat. Billy Klaser is a five-star chef and makes a great tenderloin stuffed with rice and crawfish. Klaser and his wife, Lea, offer a fine mix of specialties— shrimp being a very good base for many—and some old favorites (they won Best Steak honors in the lake area). The special hamburgers are huge (try the Bleu Ox burger with bleu cheese crumbles, sautéed onion, and bacon); the po' boy sandwiches come in catfish, crawfish, oyster, or shrimp; and the awesome salads include a blackened shrimp salad with black olives, tomatoes, cheese, and egg. Then there is the seafood buffet Fri and Sat nights 5 to 9 p.m. or the Sun buffet 11 a.m. to 2 p.m. One last temptation is a counter of handmade chocolates at the door. After the meal you can follow the walkway down to the river and watch a fly caster hip-deep in water landing the biggest fish ever. Hours are Mon and Tues 4:30 to 8 p.m. and Wed through Sun 11 a.m. to 8 p.m. Phone (501) 206-0688.

North of Heber Springs you can visit the **William Carl Garner Visitors Center** between Memorial Day and Labor Day. Staff members will lead you through the dam and powerhouse located here. Nature trails, both easy and challenging, begin at the center. A US Fish and Wildlife Service hatchery just north of the dam stocks the Little Red River and other cold waterways below dams in the region with more than a million trout each year. The center is open daily 10 a.m. to 6 p.m. May through Sept. In Apr and Oct, hours are 10 a.m. to 6 p.m. Thurs through Mon. Call (501) 362-9067.

Overlooking Greers Ferry Lake in Heber Springs is the posh community of Eden Isle, a grand retreat built by Dick and Patti Upton, owners of Aromatique. What better theme for an inn in Eden than **The Red Apple Inn and Country Club**? Apples even appear on markers at the 18-hole golf course with panoramic views of the lake. This unspoiled landscape is just as

Traversing Big Creek

The **Big Creek Natural Area,** 12 miles east of Heber Springs, embraces 3.5 long, winding miles of Big Creek. Rocky streamside bluffs rise 200 feet above the creek, creating quiet and solitude. Within this natural area you will find a number of rare plants that prefer a cool, moist, and heavily shaded environment. Wild pink azaleas and maidenhair fern adorn the area. You are asked to leave nothing but footprints and take nothing but photographs while walking the fairly rugged 2.4-mile trail. For more information call (501) 324–9619 or visit naturalheritage.com.

lovely from the window seating in the restaurant at the inn, where you can enjoy entrees such as raspberry chicken and their specialty, cherries jubilee for two. Guests at the inn can use five tennis courts, two swimming pools, steam rooms, and massage rooms. Each guest room is filled with Spanish and Mexican antique charm; some have fireplaces. Just a short distance away is the Little Red River, famous for fly fishing. Call (501) 362-3111 or (800) 733-2775 or visit redappleinn.com.

The Bottle Tree Gallery is both an art gallery and a home and garden decor store. Located at 514 West Main St. in the historic old city hall building, the shop is open Fri and Sat 11 a.m. to 4 p.m. The gallery is filled with handmade items by both local and national artists. You'll find jewelry, art prints, pottery, and of course, the ever popular bottle trees the store is named for. Call (501) 590-8840 for more information.

Somewhere in Time Antique Mall can be found at 304 W. Main St., Heber Springs. You'll discover antiques, gifts, and jewelry amongst other treasures here. Call (501) 362-9429 for hours and more information. *The Browsing Post* is another gift shop in town, but it has something that sets it apart from the others—cupcakes! Down the road a piece from Somewhere in Time at 1101 W. Main St., you can get retail therapy and fix up your sweet tooth. They've also started serving lunch at *The Browsing Post Market Cafe.* Hours are 9 a.m. to 5 p.m. Mon through Sat. Call (501) 362-5560 to find out what's on the menu.

At *Ozark Country Market,* you can stock up on some goodies to take home with you. They sell jams, pickles, salsas, relishes, pie fillings, ciders, noodles, peaches canned the old-fashioned way, and bulk foods. You'll also find a large variety of cheeses, Amish roll butter, salami and summer sausage, jerky and beef sticks, bacon, dip mixes, Amish noodles, cookbooks, and popcorn. If that's not enough, they also have Amish art, candles, baskets and wooden toys. Outside there are plants and flowers to enjoy too. The market is at 999 Heber Springs Rd. South. Call (501) 206-0127 or visit ozarkcountrymarket.com for more info.

The **Abbé House Inn** at 3144 Riverbend Rd. in Heber Springs provides a beautiful setting for some rest and relaxation. Innkeeper Mark Herrington designed and built the Abbé House on land that his parents bought along the Little Red River. Completed in 2000, this 13,200-square-foot home has 2,700 square feet of verandas and 10 rooms, each with a private bath and whirlpool tub. Rates range $80 to $115 per night. Mark is also the resident chef and offers a dinner menu along with a southern-style breakfast. Many of the ingredients for his culinary creations are grown in the gardens right at the inn. Call (501) 250-2223 or visit abbehouse.webs.com for more information.

Head south on Highway 25 out of Heber Springs, and you'll come to the town of **Quitman.** At 6060 Heber Springs Rd. West, you'll find a unique little shop called **The Vintage Rose.** The store holds an eclectic mix of antiques, gifts, and home decor. Many locals proclaim this to be their favorite place to shop and promise that it is worth the detour. You'll have to time it just right, though. The Vintage Rose is only open Fri and Sat 10 a.m. to 5 p.m. For more information call (501) 589-3092.

Mystic Gardens and Gifts & Family Flea Market is on Highway 25 south of Quitman. Watch for the sign—if you get to the intersection of Highway 107, you've gone too far. Owner Patricia Marie Williamson proffers flowers, birdhouses, furniture, gifts, and jewelry. She has an expansive collection of hanging baskets and flowering plants in the spring and summer. She also does floral arrangements and can even make wedding cakes. Stop by and visit—she is open Thurs through Sat 11 a.m. to 5 p.m.

There are a couple of routes around **Greers Ferry Lake** by highway to the towns on the other side. **Sugar Loaf Mountain** is between Heber Springs and the town of Greers Ferry, too, but you need a boat to get to it because it rises 560 feet in the middle of the lake. The first National Nature Trail established by Congress climbs to the 1,001-foot summit. The trail is an easy and has spectacular bird's-eye views of the lake. (There is another

Sugar Loaf Mountain, a landlocked mountain that shares its name with the one in Greers Ferry Lake. It is on Highway 110 and also has a foot trail to the summit for great views.)

The drive from Heber Springs to Fairfield Bay on Highway 16 is more scenic than the one on Highway 92.

Longbow Luxury Resort is unlike anything you have ever seen. Ben Pearson, legendary archer and member of the Archery Hall of Fame, the Bowhunter's Hall of Fame, the Arkansas Outdoor Sportsman's Hall of Fame, and the Sporting Goods Hall of Fame, bought these rugged original 400 acres in *Prim* after reading an ad in the *Wall Street Journal*. His son, Ben Jr., has remodeled the cabin and named Longbow after his dad's first bow, maintaining the surrounding canyon's natural beauty while adding some modern conveniences.

The land is covered with sheer cliffs, enormous boulders, and a 30-foot waterfall. The cabin is an integral part of the landscape. Some of the interior walls are jagged cliffs, and a natural rock wall rises 20 feet from the living room floor and shows earthy colors from mineral deposits. There are skylights and a sleeping loft that lets you wake up at treetop level. The living room and full kitchen are wedged between two cave walls and overlook a waterfall cascading into a 6-foot-deep pool. Stone steps lead from the back door down to a patio at the pool's edge. A hammock is tucked under a rock overhang that shades it from direct sunlight.

The creek has bream, and you can see kingfishers, deer, and beaver. In the winter, bald eagles soar overhead. The property is now 1,400 acres, and a second cabin with a whirlpool tub has been built. Full of fossils, Native American spear points, and petroglyphs (rock carvings), this may be one of the most beautiful places in the state. This is a romantic getaway for adults, but small children need careful watching because of all the rocks and steps. Rates are from $175 per day for double occupancy. Call (870) 948-2362 for information.

Ben continued his father's tradition when he built the Bushmaster, also in honor of a famous bow. The cabin is far enough from Longbow to ensure privacy, yet close enough that a family could rent both and share this remote canyon. In the Bushmaster cabin, aged rocks form two bathroom walls. The cabin is built directly over a rushing stream. Decks on two levels overlook a 250-million-year-old rock formation, which was once part of a massive river system that carved out the bluffs. The canyon changes dramatically with the seasons, from the lush green foliage of summer to bare-tree views of the frozen waterfall in winter. *Southern Living* magazine calls this place "the most beautiful spot this side of Eden." The rate is from $175 per day for double occupancy for this cabin. The website for Longbow and Bushmaster is longbowresorts.com.

Now head for the Historic Railroad Trail, a 2-mile round-trip excursion that starts at Highway 9 near the hardware store and runs along the historic Missouri and North Arkansas Railroad. It goes by an Indian burial ground, and the end of the trail is at the old pioneer Cottrell-Wilson Cemetery.

Driving along US 65 is always interesting, as several emu farms are in the area. You might be amazed at all the things that are made from the emu. Nothing is wasted; they use everything but the beaks and toenails.

Off Highway 16 in **Shirley** you may do a double take as you pass a couple of camels standing in a pasture, chewing their cud. The camels, Clyde and Crystal, live with David and Yvonne Barron. The Barrons purchased Clyde from a zoo and rescued Crystal from a petting zoo where she injured her foot. The two camels hit it off right away. Now they are living a fine and comfortable life with all the alfalfa and carrots—and water—they want. (Clyde can drink 21 gallons of water in one slurp.)

The **Fairfield Bay Library,** on Dave Creek Boulevard across from the mall, also displays paintings by local artists; the displays rotate every 60 days. Five large wood carvings by the Fairfield Bay Woodcarvers depict various stages of reading experience from childhood to old age. There is also a 140-pound specimen of Arkansas quartz mounted on a wooden pedestal. You can enjoy the day outdoors in the Memorial Reading Garden.

Also in Fairfield Bay is a massive 100-foot-wide cave that goes back 97 feet into the hillside. It is called **Indian Rock House,** and archaeological evidence shows that it was home for someone about 1000 BC. Native American tribes of Osage, Sioux, Cherokee, and Shawnee populated this area, hence the name. Diggings have uncovered skeletal remains, jewelry, spears and knives, baskets, tools, and dried vegetables. Primitive art decorates the walls of the cave, and rock art in the shapes of circles, squares, crosses, and diamond patterns found here are unlike anything else in the state. Geologists think that the natural spring flowing through the rear of the cave formed this grotto over a period of millions of years and believe it may be the beginning of a natural bridge formation (that will take several

Mushrooming Town

The little town of **Shirley** (population 350) is 10 miles northeast of Clinton on Highway 9. There's not much there anymore except for a nice little cafe for lunch. But there's something else going on in Shirley. A number of people here grow a gourmet delicacy: shiitake mushrooms.

Growing shiitake here is the brainchild of Tom Kimmons, a professor at the University of Missouri before he retired to Shirley. Shiitake contain all eight essential amino acids in better proportion than soybeans, meat, milk, or eggs. They also contain a good blend of vitamins and minerals, including vitamins A, C, and D and niacin. As little as 5 grams of shiitake taken daily can reduce serum cholesterol and blood pressure dramatically. Shiitake produce interferon and interleukin compounds, which strengthen the body's immune response to protect against cancer and viral infections, and produce a fat-absorbing compound that aids in weight reduction. A shiitake a day really can keep the doctor away, experts say.

Shiitake originated in the woodlands of China on oak-like shii trees. They have been used with acupuncture for 2,000 years. The Japanese discovered the full-bodied flavor of the delicacy and soon became the world's leading producer. Shiitake grow on white oak, which is abundant in this part of Arkansas—as is humidity. They are organically grown in logs. In early December, the planting begins. A high-speed drill creates a series of holes in the logs, and moist shiitake fungus is injected into the holes. To keep the fungus moist, the holes are sealed with cheese wax heated to 400 degrees Fahrenheit. The logs are stacked in square crisscrossed piles—called crib stacks—covered with burlap, and left to sit in the shade for several months. The fungus requires care and must be taken inside if it is too hot or too cold and uncovered and allowed to dry after a rain. Mushrooms are harvested in the fall, when the logs are flooded with water for 24 to 72 hours to fool the fungus into believing a rainstorm has occurred. About 4 days after white pinholes appear on the logs—early stage of mushrooms—it is picking time. Tours are available on Thurs or Fri morning or by appointment. Call (501) 723-4443 for information.

For a lot more information about the health and medicinal properties of this organic treat, shiitake products and gifts, or how to grow these mushrooms, visit shiitakecenter.com.

million more years to complete). Visitors are welcome to the nearby **Old Log Cabin Museum** (circa 1850), where they can find a path to the cave as well as information on several nature trails along Lynn Creek, through scenic woodlands, and by a small cove. The museum is open Apr through

Oct, Mon through Thurs 10 a.m. to 2 p.m., Fri 1 to 4 p.m., and Sat and Sun 10 a.m. To 4 p.m. The Old Log Cabin complex is off the parking lot that serves the Indian Hills Country Club and Golf Course. To reach it, drive in the entrance on Highway 16 and follow Snead Drive. Call (501) 581-1638 for more information.

Tired of driving? Does your back ache? Stop at **Garden Oaks Therapeutic Services** in the Lynch subdivision off US 65. Here Susan Fox will turn on mellow music, anoint you with aromatic oils, and relax away all of your aches. A sauna is available, too. Call (501) 745-6110 for an appointment.

The **Van Buren County Museum** is in **Clinton** at 3rd and Poplar Streets, just west of School Hill. Historical displays show life in Van Buren County, beginning with early Native American artifacts—grinding stones, laundry stones, cooking utensils—of tribes who have lived here or passed through on their way to reservations. A glimpse into life in the 1700s is in the hallway—a heavy ball and chain used on the only prisoner ever hanged in the county when he was found guilty of killing his wife. The story is on the wall as well. Other rooms display such artifacts as old musical instruments; an early oil painting of Old Choctaw, now lying beneath Greers Ferry Lake; and a special room called the History Room, where people can look up old family records for genealogical research (there is usually a volunteer to help with this), including extensive census and cemetery records, marriage indexes, and court papers. Hours are 10 a.m. until 3 p.m. Mon through Thurs. For more information about the museum, call (501) 745-4066.

If you are in Clinton the last week in August, join the western fun at the annual **National Championship Chuckwagon Races.** There is more than just the racing chuckwagons: You can watch bronc fanning, or the Snowy River Race. Western music and barn dances, and a western trade show and food as well as a nondenominational church service on Sun morning round out the event. For more information, visit chuckwagonraces.com.

Going north from Clinton on US 65 will take you to places tucked out of sight (the backcountry keeps its secrets to itself unless you are in a canoe) or in plain view on the highway. The highway passes the **Antique Warehouse** in **Botkinburg,** the largest collection of antiques in the country (according to the owner), at US 65/Highway 110, and it's open 7 days a week. Owner Don Keathley buys and restores European furniture, all of excellent quality and ready for the finest home. The back rooms also have unrestored pieces to browse among. Along with the furniture, there are decorator items of brass and silver, mirrors, and hundreds of stained-glass windows, and everything in the seven warehouses and five showrooms—90,000 square feet—dates from the 1860s to the 1880s. Hours are 9 a.m. to 5 p.m. Mon through Sat and noon to 5 p.m. Sun. The telephone number at the warehouse is (501) 745-5842. For more information and a preview visit antiquewarehouse.com.

Spring River Area

If you've headed north from Batesville on US 167, take US 62 and US 63 to **Mammoth Spring,** so named because of its size, not because of any pre-historic elephant remains. Almost straddling the Arkansas–Missouri state line, it is the outlet of a subterranean river, and legend has it that the spring was found when an Indian chief dug a grave for his son, who had died searching for water during a drought. The Spring River is created by the flow from Mammoth Spring in the foothills. It is the largest spring in the state and one of the largest natural water flows in the nation. Because of a constant release from the huge natural spring—nine million gallons each hour—it has canoeing and trout fishing year-round. The spring also makes **Mammoth Spring State Park** one of the most picturesque parks in Arkansas. In addition to the spring, the 8-acre lake formed by the stream, and the beginning of the Spring River, you'll also find the bright red 1886 Frisco railroad depot. Kids and adults alike love exploring the depot and the caboose that is located just outside the depot. Remnants of a mill and hydroelectric plant also remain as evidence of Mammoth Spring's history. The visitor center features exhibits that depict the area's history and natural resources, and also serves as an Arkansas Welcome Center. There are picnic sites, a trail, and a playground at the park. The visitor center is open daily 8 a.m. to 5 p.m. and until 6 p.m. between Memorial Day and Labor Day. The train depot is open Tues through Sat 8 a.m. to 5 p.m.

The park marina rents paddleboats and kayaks Apr through Sept 10 a.m. to 5 p.m. daily. For more information, call (870) 625-7364 or visit arkansas stateparks.com/mammothspring.

There's plenty to do in Mammoth Spring during the spring, summer, and fall months. For example, every Thurs night square dancing takes place downtown, and every Fri night a free musical show, with a live band made up of local people, offers good country music. It's an open-mike arrangement, so if you want to get up there and show off your own banjo or fiddlin' skills, the crowd welcomes you. There's a two-step dance on Sat night, also with a live band.

The town is country music crazy because of George D. Hay, the founder of the Grand Ole Opry. He traveled to the springs in the 1920s as a reporter with the Memphis *Commercial Appeal.* Invited to a hoedown, Hay was inspired by the local band that played well into the night and by the crowd that stayed up with it. "No one in the world has ever had more fun than those Ozark mountaineers did that night," Hay said. "It stuck with me until the idea became the Grand Ole Opry. It's as fundamental as sunshine and rain, snow and wind, and the light of the moon peeping though the trees. . . [I]t'll be there long after you and I have passed out of this picture." And so it is. Every Labor Day weekend the town now has the **Solemn Old Judge Days** celebration to remember that enthusiasm—it's a regular hoedown with jig dancing and all. Then Sat night the townsfolk get very serious about the flattop guitar and fiddle contest that anyone can enter. The winner is guaranteed a spot at Fanfare in Nashville—the Grand Masters' fiddle contest.

If you are looking for a place to eat, check out **Fred's Fishhouse**—not just because it's the only place in town but because it happens to be pretty darn good, too. You can get chicken or a burger, if fish isn't your thing. Fred's is at 204 Main St., Mammoth Spring. Call (870) 625-7551. Hours are Mon through Thurs 10 a.m. to 7:30 p.m., Fri and Sat until 8:30 p.m., and Sun 11 a.m. till 2 p.m.

In the town of **Salem,** southwest of Mammoth Spring on Highway 9, music has always been a tradition. Every Sat night instruments get tuned up, and crowds gather to hear country, folk, and bluegrass music.

A tradition in the area is sponsored by the Ozark Mountain Music Makers at the **Music Barn,** 2 miles east of Salem on US 62/412. Here you can listen to more traditional country, bluegrass, and folk music and dance a little, if you like. Shows start at 7 p.m. every Sat. Call (870) 895-3004 for a schedule.

Country music star David Lynn Jones has a recording studio at his home in Bexar, less than 20 miles from town, so you may see him on the streets of Salem when he is not touring.

Salem also has a farmers' market and trade days every Fri, Sat, and Sun, beginning around 7 in the morning and ending at dusk. The best one is the Christmas Market, copied from German towns, where you'll find warm

Natural History

The **Rock Creek Natural Area** is on the Ozarks' Salem Plateau, which extends from northern Boone County east to Pocahontas. Surface rocks are dolomite and limestone formed during the Ordovician Period 510 million years ago. Bubbling Spring Run is an upland headwater run, and Rock Creek is the upland stream. The rare Riddell's goldenrod and a species of skullcap, a member of the mint family, are restricted to the glades found here. You might also see a spotted sandpiper if you are lucky.

drinks and Santa giving children rides on a hay wagon or tractor regardless of the weather.

The Spring River flows from Mammoth Spring to Hardy. On the banks of the Spring River, the historic village of **Hardy** is where professional artists have settled, and trout anglers and canoes have filled the summertime river for more than a century. The main street is filled with turn-of-the-20th-century storefronts that have been converted into a collection of antiques, crafts, and gift shops. Though the restored area is not big enough to tire you, it does hold more than 50 shops full of antiques, collectibles, and most unusual things in the 3 blocks of Main Street known as "Old Hardy Town."

The **Olde Stone House Bed and Breakfast** is right on Main and School Streets, within easy walking distance of all shops. Owned by Greg and JaNoel Bess, the 2-story, native-stone house has two large porches along the front and one side. A jumbo country rocker is on the front porch, and the side porch has white wicker furniture. Located at 108 West Main St., the establishment is just across the street from the Spring River, where you can always see rafts, canoes, or kayaks floating by. Three bedrooms and baths are on the second floor, where vaulted ceilings and ceiling fans move cool air; antiques grace both these and the three bedrooms and baths on the first floor. Guests can use the living room, and the Besses have an extensive library of books and board games. Coffee is provided on the side porch for early risers, and breakfast is served 8 to 10 a.m.—homemade granola and fresh fruit with homemade bread or muffins for the diet-conscious and something really decadent, like baked German apple pancakes, for the rest of us. Rooms begin at $69. Check the website for information on their

Murder Mystery Weekends and special packages which include canoeing and golf. Call (870) 856-2983 or (800) 514-2983 for reservations; oldestone house.com.

Cluttered Cupboard is a unique shop with beautiful new and old glass antiques and collectibles. The shop is open 7 days a week 9 a.m. to 5 p.m. You can find it at 130 East Main St. For more information call (870) 856-5641.

Jeff and Debbie Kamps's **Flat Creek Dulcimer Shop** is at 644 Main St., Hardy. Jeff's mountain dulcimers are entirely handcrafted in the glass-front workshop, as are door harps and other crafts. But the dulcimers and dulcimer tapes are what bring folks in. The instruments are made of walnut and butternut and cost around $300, a price that includes a case and instruction book. Jeff's whole family plays the dulcimer. Hours are 10 a.m. to 4 p.m. 6 days a week. Call (870) 856-2992 or go to flat-creek.com for more information.

Hardy's downtown maintains the appearance of a 1920s business district. Bronze markers hang on 24 storefronts and denote Hardy's National Historic District, established in 1995. The oldest, housing **Hardy Pottery,** was purchased by Dale and Liane Maddox in 1980. Dale and Liane create pottery at 200 East Main St., and sell it along with hand-forged fireplace sets, white oak baskets, porch swings, wooden toys, hand-tied brooms, and a host of other craft items. The pottery is both functional (mugs, serving pieces, canisters) and decorative (lamps, vases). Dale works at the potter's wheel at the back of the shop, and visitors are invited to watch him there. Liane has a workshop at their home, where she develops new designs. The shop is open 9 a.m. to 5 p.m. Mon through Sat; call (870) 856-3735 or go to hardypottery.com for information.

The town of Hardy hosts the annual **Fall Arts and Crafts Festival** in the middle of Oct. There is a huge variety of handmade artwork for sale, live musical performances, and very interesting food—including deep-fried Twinkies® and alligator-on-a-stick—as well as the traditional festival food. Contact Main Street Hardy at (870) 856-3571 or visit oldhardytown.net.

Take US 167 south to **Evening Shade,** a town with more buildings on the National Register of Historic Places than any other city of its size. But of course that is not the reason you are driving to Evening Shade, is it? No. You want to take a photo of the city limits sign. And why is that? Well, because Burt Reynolds made the town famous with his television show of the same name, popular in the late 1980s, that's why.

There is a tribute to Burt Reynolds, for putting the town on the map, in the Burt Reynolds Gymnasium/Thompson Auditorium. The $750,000 gym/auditorium was built from the profits on sales of the *Evening Shade Cookbook,* which residents of the town and Reynolds combined to produce. In fact, Charlie Dell, who played Nub on the show, came to Evening Shade to marry actress Jennifer Williams at the local Methodist church.

The town of **Maynard** lies by the Missouri border, north and east of Hardy and Cherokee Village. If you pass through Maynard in the third week of Sept, you will become part of the **Pioneer Days Festival**, with its hour-long parade, dress revues, frontier games, and free musicals. This little town—population 381—swells to beyond 6,000 for the 2-day event, which includes a crafts festival, a chicken and dumpling dinner, a gospel sing, and a bluegrass music festival in the park. About the same time the **Annual Old Folks Singing Convention** features live gospel music. Call (870) 647-2701 for more information about these events.

The **Maynard Pioneer Museum** is housed in a century-old log cabin not far from the business district of this small town. The museum is on Highway 328 and Spring Street, and a city park surrounds it. The cabin was to be demolished in 1979, but the citizens of Maynard took it apart log by log, numbered them, and reconstructed the whole thing in the park. The inside depicts a typical rural home of the late 1800s, with handmade furnishings, old photos, tools, and heirloom needlework; a muzzle-loader rifle hangs over the fireplace. The museum, said to be one of the finest pioneer museums in the region, is open May through Sept 10 a.m. to 4 p.m. Tues through Sat and 1 to 4 p.m. Sun, though you can see the museum just about anytime by calling Bea Hearn at City Hall (870-647-2701). No admission fee is charged.

Imperial Dinner Theatre, in nearby **Pocahontas** at 1401 Hwy. 304 East, features Broadway shows in a family dining atmosphere. The box office number is (870) 892-0030, or visit them at imperialdinnertheatre.com for show information and times.

Crowley's Ridge & the Delta

One of the surprises of this part of the Mississippi Delta is that it has hills. Rising abruptly above the Delta region is a narrow band of gently rolling hills known as *Crowley's Ridge;* stretching north to south, it breaks the flat plains and is one of the great oddities of the world. It extends nearly 210 miles from the northeast corner of the state to the Mississippi River at Helena and covers a half-million acres. These tree-blanketed hills were formed by wind and water over millions of years just prior to the Ice Age, when the Mississippi and Ohio Rivers cut vast trenches into the great plains of eastern Arkansas. The ridge was an island left when the two rivers retreated to the west. Crowley's Ridge Parkway, which stretches 200 miles through the Delta from St. Francis to Helena, was declared a National Scenic Byway in 1999.

The "highland" area of the ridge and the Ozark foothills, a region bounded by I-40 and US 167, contains a cluster of state parks, 11 of them to be exact, including two state museums and a memorial. Sixteen miles east of Crowley's Ridge State Park is downtown *Paragould.* But it's not called downtown anymore. The townsfolk decided that "uptown" sounded more, well, uptown than "downtown," and so downtown Paragould is now called uptown Paragould. The pride of the town is a lighted mural of an old steam engine and depot. When driving on the US 412 overpass, you can look down into uptown Paragould.

The *Hamburger Station* at 110 East Main St. is home of the famous "hum-burger" with grilled onion, a burger so good it was mentioned in *USA Today* as one of the best hamburgers in the country. Bert Daggett is the owner of this carryout-only spot housed in an old train depot. Since its beginning in 1985, Hamburger Station has served sandwiches that rate high on the charts in this fast-food world: a roast turkey sandwich on a sesame-seed bun with bacon, cheese, lettuce, and tomato—and made from real turkey, roasted right there at the station. The roast beef sandwich is also made of "real beef," roasted in the station's oven. No pressed-meat, imitation stuff here. The station also makes great shakes and malts. Hours are 10 a.m. to 8 p.m. Mon through Sat; call (870) 239-9956 for information.

trivia

Arkansas's earliest inhabitants were the pre-Columbian Bluff Dwellers about AD 500. Burial remains indicate that the Bluff Dwellers planted corn, beans, pumpkins, sunflowers, and other plants. They used bows and arrows and a weapon similar to the Aztec *atlatl*—a throwing stick—to hunt deer and buffalo.

22 Lou is a cute little boutique store at 2405 Linwood Dr., in Paragould. They carry ladies fashions and accessories for all sizes, and nothing is priced over $50. The gals who work there will help you assemble the perfect outfit, too. Hours are Mon through Fri 10 a.m. to 5:30 p.m. and Sat till 4 pm. Call (870) 215-7752 for more information.

Kiss the Cook has been the place to stop for lunch for over 12 years. Daily lunch specials include wraps, soups, and quiche, as well as the occasional comfort food like homemade spaghetti. Find them at 118 North Pruett or call (870) 335-2665 for directions. Hours are 11 a.m. to 2 p.m. Mon through Fri.

At 611 Court St., you'll find Paragould's first bed-and-breakfast. **The White House Inn** is a historic federal revival–style home that was constructed in 1892. Innkeepers Marilyn and Bob White have completely renovated and "revived" the historic home and now offer four rooms, each with a private bath. There's also a small fitness center and spa on-site. For more information, call (870) 236-4087 or visit them online at whitehouseinn.net.

Paragould is the county seat for Greene County. It's worth the time to stop by its old **1888 Courthouse,** located on the old courthouse square in Paragould. Extensive restoration work has been done on the building, including replacing the original cupola clock tower that was removed when the clock stopped working. Now that the old stucco facade has been stripped away, the courthouse also sports its original redbrick exterior.

If the kids need a place to run, visit **Reynolds Park** at 3307 Reynolds Park Rd. There's a stocked fishing lake, a nice playground for the kids to play on, and pavilions and grills available for picnic lunches. The Children's Fishing Rodeo is held here on the second Sat each June. Children age 15 and under can hook their share of the 400 pounds of fish added to the lake by the Arkansas Game and Fish Commission for the event. Lunch is provided and prizes are awarded. If you want to stay a while, there are also 11 RV pads available that rent for $15 per night. Tent camping is $5 per night. For more information, call (870) 239-7530.

Discover writer Ernest Hemingway's Arkansas connection at the restored home and barn-studio where he penned portions of *A Farewell to Arms* and other famous works. The **Hemingway-Pfeiffer Museum and Educational Center** is at 1021 West Cherry St., **Piggott.** This is where Hemingway's second wife, Pauline, lived. Call (870) 598-3487 for more information, or visit hemingway.astate.edu. Hours are 1 to 3 p.m. Sat and 9 a.m. to 3 p.m. weekdays. Price of admission is $5 ($3 for seniors and groups).

The **Rosedale Farm Bed and Breakfast** is just down the road at 1577 E. Main St. Eighteen acres of pastoral fields surround this 1917 home. Each room has a queen bed. There is also a fully stocked kitchen with complimentary snacks and drinks. For availability, call (870) 634-7100.

The **Inn at Piggott** is another historic place to lay your head. Housed in the 1925 Bank of Piggott building, the inn's rooms have queen beds and private baths. It is on the square at 193 West Main St. For more information, call (870) 598-8888 or visit theinnatpiggott.com.

Donna's Country Kitchen at 260 W. Court St. serves home-cooked comfort foods. Try one of the daily lunch specials and follow it up with some cobbler for dessert. Lunch hours are Mon through Fri 11 a.m. to 2 p.m. Dinner hours are Mon through Thurs 4:30 to 7 p.m. Call for more info (870)598-5753.

There's a handful of boutique shops in downtown Piggott that combine for a fun shopping experience. They're all within a 3 minutes' walk of one another. Start at **The Treasure Shop** at 239 West Main St., which has been a fixture in Piggott for over 40 years. Here you'll find gifts, home decor, clothing, shoes, handbags, and more. Hours are Mon through Fri 10 a.m. to 6 p.m. and Sat till 3 p.m. Phone is (870) 598-2385. Just down the block is **Feather Your Nest** at 209 West Main. Their hours are Mon through Fri 10 a.m. to 5 p.m. and Sat till 3 p.m. Phone is (870) 598-1004. From there, hang a right on 2nd Street and stop at **Sugar Creek Kids.** They have lots of fun and unique gifts, toys, and clothing for the short people in your life. Hours are the same as Feather Your Nest, and the phone is (870) 598-3923. Finally, hang a left at the end of the block onto Court Street. **Madpie's Flea Market and Tea Room** is at 118 W. Court. Once you've finished perusing here, you can visit the tearoom to replenish all that energy you just spent

trivia

Hernando de Soto crossed the Mississippi near Sunflower Landing, June 29, 1541. His search for food and gold took the Spaniard through the central part of the state, across the Arkansas River to Hot Springs, and down the Ouachita River to a site near Camden.

shopping. Madpie's is open Mon through Sat 10 a.m. to 5 p.m. Phone is (870) 324-0568.

A town that didn't have a paved road until 1937, **Lepanto** now has a four-room living model of the Delta's heritage called **Museum Lepanto USA,** at the intersection of Berney and Main Streets. Patsy McClain is the museum's director, (870) 475-2043. When the town was first founded, the only way into Lepanto was by boat on the Little River. Later the train came through, although it still took all day to get out and another day to get back. This unique city shares the history of the Delta—the agricultural days, the Civil War and Indian conflicts, the Victorian era—in a museum supported entirely by donations.

The people are proud of their history and show it in the town and the all-volunteer museum. The blacksmith shop, roofed with hand-hewn shingles, contains a huge iron anvil and all the tools and items created there, with a printed guide to identify and explain each one. A Victorian parlor, a general store full of supplies, and a doctor's office and barbershop have been rebuilt there, too. Fossilized Delta mud, old tintype photos, an early printing press, and one of the first Maytag washing machines, made in 1902, offer a perspective on the changes that swept the Delta region over the years. A collection of artifacts shows the life of the Woodland Indians, who were native to the area. The museum is right on Main Street and is open Wed and Fri afternoons 1 to 4 p.m. Apr 1 to Nov 1, or anytime by request. At other times of year, just wander into the **Victorian Rose Antiques** shop (870-475-3247) at 244 Greenwood Ave., two doors down (full of glassware, china, and furniture). Hours are 9 a.m. to 5 p.m. Another manifestation of this town's pride is the mural at the four-way stop at Highway 140/135, depicting the town's Medal of Honor winner.

If you are in Lepanto the first week in Oct, you can help the town celebrate two of its longtime events. The **Annual Terrapin Derby and Festival** is held on Greenwood Street in downtown Lepanto. Watch as the turtles race to the finish line to snap up the watermelon waiting for them there. The turtles have been racing here for over 80 years. Call (870) 930-6427 for details. Stevens Square is where the Annual Craft Fair and Flea Market is held at about the same time. It features not just booths filled with antiques but live music and homemade desserts as well. Call (870) 475-6150 for more about the fair.

Wilson was founded as a company town in 1886 by Robert E. Lee Wilson, who owned a nearby logging and sawmill operation. After the land was cleared, Wilson built a cotton empire that made the city the most important company town in the South. In 1925, Wilson's son honeymooned in England. After that, all of the town's buildings were rebuilt in Tudor revival architectural style. All residents of Wilson except the postmaster and railroad employees were company employees. They had access to company doctors for $1.25 a year, and jobs created by other services like dry cleaning and a grocery store kept the standard of living high. At one point, Wilson even had its own currency. However, the advent of mechanized farming caused a decline in the Wilson company's value, and the town's population gradually shrank to about 900. Wilson has been purchased by a businessman who has plans to revitalize the little city. In the meantime, you can still see the examples of Tudor revival architecture throughout the town. The reopening of the *Wilson Cafe* marks the beginning of the town's revival. The lunch menu features home-cooked soups, salads, and burgers, as well as specials that range from fried catfish to smoked ribs. Hours are Tues through Sun 11 a.m. to 2 p.m. The cafe is also open for dinner Thurs through Sat 5 to 9 p.m.

trivia

During the Civil War about 58,000 men joined the Confederate army and perhaps 6,000 served in the Union forces. After the Confederate surrender, the state was controlled by the US Army.

The *Hampson Museum State Park,* one of the state parks along Crowley's Ridge, features a most unusual museum, given to the state by James K. Hampson, a medical doctor with a successful practice who turned his boyhood fascination with arrowheads into the research and study of the physical remains of the early inhabitants of his family plantation, the Nodena. He and his family excavated, studied, and inventoried the mounds and subsurface remains of a complex civilization that lived on the meander bend of the Mississippi River in a 15-acre palisaded village from AD 1350 to 1700. The result is an educational facility devoted to the study of these, the state's earliest inhabitants, that exhibits artifacts from the Late Mississippian Period culture. The Nodena people were farmers who developed a civilization of art, religion, political structure, and trading networks. The park is 5 miles east of I-55 at the junction of US 61 and Lake Drive. Admission is free. Hours are 8 a.m. to 5 p.m. Tues through Sat and 1 to 5 p.m. Sun. Call (870) 655-8622 for more information or visit arkansasstateparks.com.

Traveling south along the Mississippi from the Nodena site will take you through the 5,500-acre *Wapanocca National Wildlife Refuge,* 5 miles west of the Mississippi River in *Turrell.* The heart of the refuge is the 600-acre Wapanocca Lake, a shallow old oxbow of the once-meandering Mississippi River. Surrounded by 1,200 acres of cypress and willow swamp, the other two-thirds of the refuge is equally divided between remnants of once-extensive bottomland hardwood forest and cropland of the refuge's farm unit. Take the Nature Drive to observe a variety of birds and wildlife in each habitat. More than 228 species of birds are known to pass through here. Log on to fws.gov/wapanocca for more information or call (870) 343-2595.

If you are headed north on I-55 to *Blytheville,* up in the northeast corner of the state, you will notice that it is a bit different from the rest of northeastern Arkansas. This area has Delta roots laid down by the settlers who came to this region and the slaves who worked the land. The county courthouses have land, marriage, and death records for genealogy buffs, and many of the city libraries have genealogy rooms and extensive history collections. Old cemeteries are everywhere along the Delta Byway, dozens more than 100 years old. Go online to deltabyways.com for additional sources of information.

Take a little detour off on Highway 63 to the town of *Tyronza.* Here you'll find *Tyboogie's Cafe* at 101 North Main St. in the historic old grocery store building. Owners Keith and Jill Forrester spent months renovating the space. This is a farm-to-table cafe, meaning many of the ingredients for the dishes served come straight from local farms. At lunchtime there is a serving line with cafeteria-style service, offering rotisserie chicken, pizza, as well as a featured entree of the day. If you visit on Friday, try the catfish. Dinner is an all-you-can-eat buffet. If the day is nice, sit outside on the covered patio and enjoy the breeze. The restaurant is very new, so call (870) 815-9519 for hours.

The *Southern Tenant Farmers Museum* is in the historic Mitchell-East Building at 117 S. Main St., Tyronza. The museum tells the story and history of sharecropping, tenant farming, and the farm labor movement through exhibits, photographs, and artifacts. Hours are Mon through Fri 9 a.m. to 3 p.m. and Sat noon to 3 p.m. Admission is $5 for adults and $3 for seniors and children. Call (870) 487-2909 for more information or visit the museum's website at stfm.astate.edu.

The **Delta Gateway Heritage Museum,** at 210 West Main St. in the Kress Building (a 1938 art deco commercial building listed on the National Register of Historic Places), houses Mississippi County records. Hours are Wed through Fri 1 to 4 p.m. and Sat 9 a.m. to 3 p.m. Visit deltagatewaymuseum .weebly.com for more information.

Highway 61 Arch, US 61 at State Line, was erected in 1924. The arch, spanning US 61 at the Arkansas–Missouri state line, was built to commemorate completion of the first paved highway in Mississippi County and is listed on the National Register of Historic Places. Search out **That Bookstore in Blytheville,** at 316 West Main St., to see the storefront, which they call "a folk art celebration of books." You can browse their fine book selection, many volumes of which are autographed by the best contemporary authors (John Grisham, for one, was there to sign books). You can sit in a rocker by a woodstove and sip a cup of their special coffee. Call (870) 763-3333 or visit thatbookstoreinblytheville.com. Store hours are Mon through Sat 10 a.m. to 6 p.m.

The Cupboard, at 213 West Main in downtown Blytheville, has Arkansas souvenirs and accent furniture. Hours are 8:30 a.m. until 5 p.m. Mon through Sat. Call (870) 762-2015 for more information.

Great southern barbecue, they say, is at **The Dixie Pig,** 701 North 6th St., family run since 1923. Hours are Mon through Sat 9:30 a.m. to 8 p.m. and Sun 11:30 a.m. to 1:30 p.m. But ribs are served only on Thurs and Sat nights after 5 p.m. So get in line. Call owner Buddy Halsell at (870) 763-4636.

Are you a real sportsman, not just a tourist? Then find the **Pluck-a-Duck** goose lodge in **Wynne.** This is prime duck-hunting country right in the middle of the Mississippi Flyway, with more than 15,000 acres of rice fields, flooded timber, and river blinds. Highly experienced guides take you to productive areas. Trained hunting dogs are provided, or you can bring your own dog. The comfortable lodge is famous for its outstanding meals prepared by Barbara Owens and accommodates up to 26 people. The day begins early with coffee and sweet rolls. After the morning hunt, you can return to the lodge for a country breakfast and a few hours of relaxation before heading out for the afternoon hunt. A big evening meal follows. The lodge is within minutes of the best hunting in the area. All you need to buy are shells, which must be steel shot, with nothing larger than T-shot. Licenses and duck stamps are available at the lodge. Chest waders are highly recommended for hunters. The rate is $445 per day per gun, $400 for four people or more. For goose season only, it's $100 per day per gun. For more information call Cecil (Shorty) Owens (or Barbara, who says—with a smile in her voice—that she takes care of most of the business) at (800) 545-5944 or (870) 588-5608. During hunting season only, the lodge telephone number is (870) 697-2139. You can consult their website (pluck-a-duck.com) or contact them via fax (870-238-4481) for more information.

Northwest of Marianna on US 49 and off I-40 is the city of **Brinkley.** **Marion McCollum Lake Greenlee** is a 300-acre fishing lake, stocked with bluegill, bass, and catfish. The Arkansas Game and Fish Commission conducted a $3 million renovation to the lake and surrounding banks. It now features two handicap-accessible fishing piers, two boat ramps, and 3 miles of maintained levy around the lake to provide access to land-based anglers. A cross levy built to divide the lake has a bridge for pedestrian traffic. For more information, contact the Arkansas Game and Fish Commission at (800) 364-4263 or (501) 223-6300.

The **Louisiana Purchase Historic Marker and State Park,** at the junction of three counties east of Holly Grove, preserves the 1815 benchmark used to survey the Arkansas area of the Louisiana Purchase Territory. It contains about 36 acres within a headwater swamp, a fast-disappearing ecological setting in eastern Arkansas. A 950-foot barrier-free boardwalk provides access to the monument in the swamp's interior that marks the "point of beginning" for the survey. The boardwalk has a number of exhibits along the way focused on the sights and sounds of the swamp. To find it from I-40 at Brinkley, take US 49 and travel 21 miles south to Highway 362; then drive 2 miles east on Highway 362.

The **Central Delta Depot and Museum** features photographs and other memorabilia from the Rock Island and Cotton Belt Railroads, as well as photography of area sawmills and timber-related businesses that were spawned by the arrival of the railroads. This museum also serves as a visitor center for the Louisiana Purchase State Park (see above). Located in a beautifully restored 1912 Union Railroad Depot, it is on the National Register of Historic Places. Behind the main depot building, you'll find a 100-year-old

Arkansas Midland-MoPac depot from Monroe, Arkansas, and a furnished sharecropper house. The museum is at 100 West Cypress St. Call (870) 589-2124 for hours and information.

Los Pinos is a nice little Mexican place on Main Street in Brinkley. In addition to a full menu of authentic Mexican dishes, the brightly colored booths, tables, and chairs with carvings of flowers, sun and moon, and other scenes makes for an interesting atmosphere (and fun for playing I Spy). Hours are 11 a.m. to 9 p.m. daily, and they stay open till 10 p.m. on Fri and Sat. Go see them at 2005 North Main or call (870) 734-1855 for more info.

If it is late Sept, stick around for the Lick Skillet Festival. Monroe County is a duck hunter's paradise, and there is White River fishing and lots of antiques and gift shops.

Low's Bridal Shop carries one-of-a-kind and high-end bridal gowns not found in any other part of the state. With 25,000 square feet of display area and over 60 of the world's best known wedding gown designers, this is a must-stop place for the betrothed. At 127 West Cedar St., Low's is open Tues through Fri 10 a.m. to 5 p.m. and Sat 9 a.m. to 4 p.m. Call (870) 734-3244 for more information, or visit lowsbridal.com.

Another good spot to eat in Brinkley is *Gene's Restaurant & Barbeque* at 1107 North Main St. Gene Depriest is the owner, and his place is open 7 days a week from 7 in the morning until 9 at night, so you really can count on this one. Phone (870) 734-9965.

Now hunting geese is what it's all about in this part of Arkansas, because it is in the path of a major flyway. And the best place to do it is at *Paradise Wings Lodge,* south of Brinkley Gibbs Road. You will enjoy good hunting as well as great home cooking. There is plenty of action in this agricultural area with flooded rice fields, soybean fields, and timber. You can hunt snows, blues, Canadas, and specklebellies "Texas Style" with rags and shell decoys. So if lying on the ground with geese landing all around you is your idea of paradise, then Paradise Wings Lodge is the place for you, because they have the four-wheel drive vehicles to take you where no car can go. Call (870) 734-2030 or go to paradisewings.com for rates, dates, and instructions on how to get there.

The *Brinkley Fall Round-Up* has a lot of fun activities and arts and crafts, but it also includes the *Cache River Regional Duck Calling Contest.*

Hop on I-40 east to **Forrest City** and find 603 Front St. and the **St. Francis County Museum**, where every room in the historic building has a story to tell. One contains prehistoric artifacts found in this area; another has ancient Native American pottery and stone points. There are displays about early medical doctors, an antique doll collection, and an African-American history room. Hours are Tues and Fri 10 a.m. to 4 p.m. Call (870) 261-1744 for more information.

The town of **Parkin** on US 64 is worth a side trip if you enjoy archaeology. The **Parkin Archeological State Park** is excavating a site occupied from AD 1000 to 1500.

Evidence developed since the site was opened in the 1960s supports the theory that Hernando de Soto visited here in 1541, making the Spaniards the first Europeans to cross the Mississippi River into what is now Arkansas. Tiny European-made glass beads, Spanish bells, and lead shot from a primitive 16th-century firearm have been found. The site dates from the Mississippian Period, an age when Native American villages were scattered across the Delta. The visitor center offers exhibits, a historical movie presentation, and a gift shop. A 0.5-mile trail provides a tour through the ancient village site. The park is situated just north of Parkin at the junction of US 64 and Highway 184. Hours are 8 a.m. to 5 p.m. Tues through Sat, noon to 5 p.m. Sun. Admission is free for the visitor center and exhibits. Guided tours are $3.50 for adults and $2.50 for children 6 to 12, or you can get a family pass for $12. During certain times visitors can assist at the dig. Call (870) 755-2500 for more information, or visit arkansasstateparks.com/parkinarcheological.

Highway 1 leads to Jonesboro, home to Arkansas State University.

Arkansas State University Museum, 110 Cooley Dr., Jonesboro, will not remind you of the dusty museums of your grade-school field trip days. This museum connects yesterday with today and ancient Native American cultures with early settlers, all done in colorful links that adults and children can easily follow. It shows artifacts from the world's oldest known cemetery, found near Jonesboro, burial place of the Paleo-Indian culture of the Pleistocene Age—a settled and domestic people once thought to be nomadic hunter-gatherers. Especially interesting are the bones of a Palaeolama, an ancient 1,000-pound species of llama, excavated near here. It is the farthest north that remains of the species have been found.

Visitors can compare prehistoric tools with the farm implements used by pioneers a century ago and see a reconstructed log cabin built by a family 125 years ago. The museum shows both Confederate and Union uniforms, weapons, and equipment.

The museum's newest permanent exhibit is Old Town Arkansas, which was 7 years in the making and covers the turn-of-the-20th-century period. Visitors enter the old Main Street through a replica of the courthouse tower, complete with the original bell. Everything here is original; there are no reproductions. The physician's office includes the city's first X-ray machine.

The museum is open 9 a.m. to 7 p.m. Tues and 9 a.m. to 5 p.m. Wed through Sat. Admission is free. Call (870) 972-2074 or visit museum.astate.edu.

West Washington Guest House, 534 West Washington Ave., Jonesboro, is architecture and elegance of the 1900s—classic four-square style—overlooking the West Washington Avenue Historic District. Twelve distinctively decorated guest rooms—each named after and inspired by a native Arkansan—offer private bath, cable TV, telephone, and private temperature control. Each room has a queen-size bed, with additional amenities such as sofas; whirlpool tubs are available in selected rooms. There is a spacious porch for lounging and a relaxed atmosphere. A buffet breakfast is available in the morning.

The original construction of this home was completed in 1914 for the Snyder family. Their son, John, grew up in the house and later became secretary of the treasury under President Truman. During the Depression the house was converted into eight apartments. It is estimated that families of four lived in each apartment, for a total of 32 persons in the house. Notice the pineapple on the mantel? In earlier times, the host would place a pineapple on the mantel at the beginning of a party. When the hostess decided to end the party, the pineapple would be removed from the mantel. The guests would take notice, thank their host and hostess, and leave. At West Washington Guest House, innkeeper Pat Simpson says that the pineapple will always be on display to welcome guests. Rates are $65 to $95 for the rooms; suites are $120. To contact the inn, call (870) 935-9300, fax (870) 802-3299, or visit them online at jonesborobedandbreakfast.com.

Skinny J's in downtown Jonesboro is a favorite local restaurant. Started by Jonesboro native, Chef James Best, this is the spot for great steaks, juicy burgers, and nightly live music. They are at 205 South Main St. Hours are

Mon through Sat 11 a.m. to midnight. Call (870) 275-6264 for more information or visit skinnyjsjonesboro.com to start making your selections from the menu.

More Places to Stay in Northeast Arkansas

BATESVILLE

Comfort Suites
1227 N. St. Louis St.
(870) 698-1900
Inexpensive

BLYTHEVILLE

Holiday Inn
1121 East Main
(870) 763-5800
Inexpensive

CALICO ROCK

Cedar Rock Lodge
303 Main St.
(870) 297-3474
Inexpensive

CLINTON

Best Western
1025 Hwy. 65
(501) 745-4700
Inexpensive

FORREST CITY

Holiday Inn Express
220 Eldridge Rd.
(870) 633-3700
Inexpensive

HARDY

Best Western
3587 Hwy. 412/62W
(870) 856-2176
Inexpensive

JONESBORO

Holiday Inn Express
2407 Phillips Dr.
(870) 932-5554
Inexpensive

MOUNTAIN VIEW

Days Inn
703 E. Main
(870) 269-3287
Inexpensive

NEWPORT

Newport Days Inn
Highway 67N
101 Olivia Dr.
(870) 523-6411
Inexpensive

PARAGOULD

Quality Inn Suites
2310 West Kings Hwy.
(870) 239-2121
Inexpensive

SALEM

Cottonwood Inn
360 US 62
(870) 895-4999
Inexpensive

More Places to Eat in Northeast Arkansas

HEBER SPRINGS

Janssen's Lakefront Restaurant
7209 Greers Ferry Rd.
(501) 723-4480
Inexpensive

Lindsey's Pot O' Gold Restaurant
350 Rainbow Loop
(501) 362-3139
Inexpensive

CHAMBERS OF COMMERCE IN NORTHEAST ARKANSAS GATEWAY AREA

Batesville Chamber of Commerce
409 Vine St., Batesville 72501
(870) 793-2378
mybatesville.com

Calico Rock Chamber of Commerce
102 Main St., Calico Rock 72519
(870) 297-4129
calicorock.us

Hardy Chamber of Commerce
Main and Church Streets, Hardy 72542
(870) 856-3210

Mountain View Chamber of Commerce
(870) 269-8068 or (888) 679-2859
ozarksgateways.com/chamber

Newport Area Chamber of Commerce
210 Elm St., Newport 72112
(870) 523-3618
newportarchamber.org

CROWLEY'S RIDGE

Brinkley Chamber of Commerce
1501 Weatherby Dr.
Brinkley 72021
(870) 734-2262

Jonesboro Chamber of Commerce
Box 789, Jonesboro 72401
(870) 932-6691
jonesborochamber.org

Paragould Chamber of Commerce
Box 124, Paragould 72451
(870) 236-7684
chamberparagould.org

GREERS FERRY LAKE AREA

Fairfield Bay Chamber of Commerce
Box 1159, Fairfield Bay 72088
(888) 244-4386
ffbchamber.org

Heber Springs Chamber of Commerce
1001 West Main St.
Heber Springs 72543
(501) 362-2444
heber-springs.com

SPRING RIVER AREA

Mammoth Spring Chamber of Commerce
Box 185, Mammoth Spring 72554
(870) 625-3518

PARAGOULD

Kimono Japanese Steakhouse
1600 W. Kingshighway
(870) 236-7788
Moderate

MOUNTAIN VIEW

Mi Pueblito
103 N. Peabody
269-5400
Inexpensive

NEWPORT

U.S. Pizza
1204 Hwy. 367 North
(870) 523-3623
Inexpensive

Northwest Arkansas

The Buffalo River literally gets you off the beaten path and into a beautiful wilderness. It was the first National River Park, established by Congress in 1972. Now about 12,000 canoes are rented during June and July, along with roughly the same number of private boats. Add the number of motorized fishing craft, and you have something like 50,000 folks floating down the 125-mile river. That's a lot of sunscreen. But the Buffalo cuts a path through some of the most unspoiled beauty in the country—towering limestone bluffs, whitewater rapids, and natural wilderness—drawing campers, anglers, and others bent on getting away from city stress.

Buffalo Point, at Highways 14 and 268, was once the only fully developed park on the river. In 1997 Tyler Bend, on US 65, was added. Both offer camping, hiking trails, and rustic cabins and are run by the National Park Service. Outfitters can be found at every access point, in almost every town along the way.

The Buffalo River is a tributary of the majestic White River, along which settlers built log cabins. These hardy settlers, isolated as they were from the rest of the world,

NORTHWEST ARKANSAS

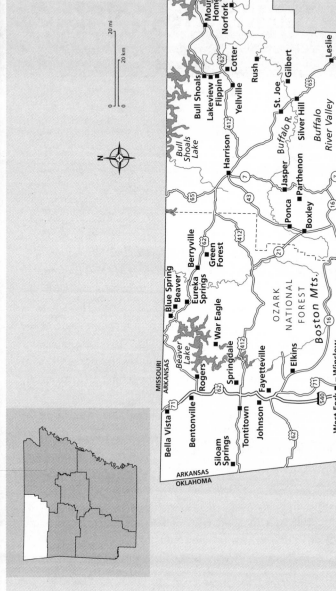

BEST ATTRACTIONS IN NORTHWEST ARKANSAS

Arkansas and Missouri Railroad
Springdale
(479) 725-4017 or (800) 687-8600
amrailroad.com

James at the Mill
Johnson
(479) 443-1400
jamesatthemill.com

Trout Fishing on the White River
Roundhouse Shoals Fishing Service
Cotter
(870) 404-7757
roundhouseshoals.com

Turpentine Creek Wildlife Refuge
south of Eureka Springs
(479) 253-5841
turpentinecreek.org

War Eagle Mill
War Eagle
(479) 789-5343
wareaglemill.com

Zip Line Canopy Tour
Ponca
(870) 861-5514
buffaloriver.com

developed a folk culture that still flourishes today in the backwoods and hollows along the creeks that feed the historic river.

It can reach 80 degrees or get plenty chilly by the middle of October, when dozens of arts and crafts fairs lure thousands of autumn tourists to the area. November and December have their own beauty; the winter has many mild days, with dramatic new scenes uncovered after foliage falls. Snow in these mountains can be from 2 inches to 2 feet, but it can also disappear quickly.

Crossing the Buffalo River

Like so many other small towns across the country, *Leslie,* 20 miles southeast of Buffalo River on US 65, fell on hard times when the railroads moved on. This was the end of the "Dinky Line," the railroad that hooked up to the Missouri and North Arkansas Railroad. The rail line was used to "log out the hollers" around here, carrying lumber to the mills. When that industry faded, the town faded, too, in spite of the proud rock homes. The seven hotels mysteriously burned, one at a time, and Leslie went from being one of the biggest towns in northwest Arkansas to a shadow of its former self. Then longtime residents of Leslie donated money to help refurbish the town.

The ***Ozark Heritage Arts Center and Museum,*** 410 Oak St., is a surprising treasure that any town would covet. This hill town of only about 500 people has a 400-seat theater, art gallery, and museum thanks to the philanthropy of Daphne Killebrew and her late husband, Rex. The museum covers the history of whiskey barrel manufacturing, which made Leslie a boomtown in the early 1900s. The Killebrew Theater was built over the high school gym and now offers the community repertory players made up of volunteers from the region. It offers a large stage, comfortable high-rise seating, and twin balconies. The theater hosts musical performances, ranging from light opera to Ozark fiddlers, and throws in some heavy metal, too. A must-see event is the annual ***Arkansas Fiddler's Contest*** in June. There is a concert or other event at least once a month, and the theater has a "resident ghost" named Leroy. What more could you want? The museum contains a nearly complete 1920s dentist's office. The Arts Center is open Apr through Dec, Tues through Sat 10 a.m. to 4 p.m. The gallery emphasizes the art of northern Arkansas, featuring primitive artists as well as abstract painters. Tours of the museum and gallery are free. For more information call (870) 447-2500 or log on to ozarkheritagearts.org.

Leslie is also home to ***Serenity Farm Bread,*** at Main Street and Highway 66 in the old Farmers Bank Building. The aroma of healthy bread baking in old-world brick ovens greets visitors to Chris and David Lower's bakery. Each morning the ovens are fired up to 1,000 degrees Fahrenheit to heat the bricks. The floor of the oven is then scrubbed and allowed to cool to about 430 degrees for baking. The loaves are placed inside using a long-handled peel. Some starter is saved every day for the next day's batch, because the Lowers won't use yeast in the sourdough-type bread. (Actually, it's Flemish *desem*—pronounced *da-sum*—bread.) Only organic grains, filtered water, and sea salt are in it. The culture that starts the bread is fed only whole-wheat flour. There are other fruit-filled loaves, like the walnut raisin bread, which contains organically grown fruits and nuts. In all, the bakery carries more than 50 types of bread and pastries.

Lower wraps the loaves in bakers' linen—a tight wrap is part of the secret—which slows the growth and makes the bacteria work harder. Each

BEST ANNUAL EVENTS IN NORTHWEST ARKANSAS

Annual Fiddlers Convention
Harrison; in the middle of Mar
(870) 741-1789; features jam sessions,
stage performances, and food.
Admission is free, but donations are
accepted.

Tontitown Grape Festival
Tontitown; second weekend in Aug
call St. Joseph's Church
(479) 361-2612

**Annual Arkansas Hot Air Balloon
State Championship and Festival**
Harrison; Sept
(870) 741-2659
arkansasbaloonfest.com

Hillbilly Chili Cook-Off
Upper Bull Shoals-White River State
Park, Lakeview; first weekend in Sept
(870) 404-2864

Fall War Eagle Fair
War Eagle; third weekend in Oct
(479) 789-5398; arts and crafts

Bella Vista Arts and Crafts Festival
Bella Vista; third weekend in Oct
(479) 855-2064
bellavistafestival.org

Lights of the Ozarks Festival
Fayetteville; Wed before Thanksgiving
to Sat after New Year's
(479) 521-5776
thelightsoftheozarks.com; 300 miles of
lights illuminate the historic downtown,
Old Main Building at
University of Arkansas

batch is different because of the effects of barometric pressure and temperature. With all this care, five kinds of gourmet bread are produced, and are they worth the effort! There is, of course, 100 percent whole-wheat bread. But try the apple and fig almond-filled loaves, garlic herb and tomato olive focaccia, or the walnut raisin or European rye. You can sit and enjoy the gourmet coffee served here, including a local brew, Rozark Hills.

You can buy a loaf in the bakery for $5 to $7, but don't cut it or eat it for several hours, because internal cooking is going on. The bread is best the third day after it is baked, allowing it to be shipped to retail stores in the Midwest. It also freezes well. Call (870) 447-2211 for information. Serenity Farm also has an informational website, serenityfarmbread.us, which includes the menu of available breads. But to order, you still have to call and talk to a real person—as it should be. Bread store hours are

Mon through Thurs 8 a.m. to 5 p.m., Fri 8 a.m. to 4 p.m., Sat and Sun 9 a.m. to 4 p.m. Take US 65 to Leslie, turn east on Highway 66, go 1 block and turn right at the yield sign, go 1 more block, and you're there! It is directly across the street from Dave's Auto Parts and kitty-corner from Lewis Grocery.

David and Chris acquired a lovely old house 0.5 mile south of Leslie on US 65 South, overlooking 2 acres on the creek. The more delicate pastries are baked here in a gas oven. It's a 100-year-old historic Sears kit house. They sell bread from the in-town bakery here, as well as fresh decadent pastries, health foods, and other fine items. They will offer soup and sandwiches made on the great bread baked at the bakery—a gourmet menu with things grown right there, as well as the usual brown beans and corn bread so popular here. The menu will suit almost anyone who wants to sit on the porch that covers two sides of the house and enjoy the view. The shop is filled with arts and crafts, fabulous desserts, health food, and gift items. Hours are 8 a.m. to 5 p.m. Wed through Sun (Fri until 6 p.m.). The gazebo will be surrounded with flowers in summertime, and the restaurant will be closed in Jan and Feb. The house is 0.25 south of Highway 66 on US 65. Call (870) 447-2210.

Old Mercantile Antiques, at 402 Main St. back in Leslie, is an interesting antiques store in a circa 1908 historic building. Open Mon through Sat 10 a.m. to 5 p.m., here you'll find a little bit of everything, ranging from Wild West–inspired furniture and decor to items from Asia. The only thing all the shops contents have in common is that they all have a story to tell. Call (870) 447-2731 for more information.

A few doors down at 407 Main St., ***Elk & Eagle Trading Post*** has its own selection of interesting wares for sale, including a nice selection of local travel resources. You'll also find a variety of Arkansas-made products, and you can even purchase a bigfoot hunting license here (it's good for a lifetime, and no, I'm not kidding). You'll also find old-fashioned games, a selection of metal signs, local wood carvings done with a chainsaw, and an eclectic mix of pottery. Hours are Fri and Sat 10 a.m. to 4 p.m. Call (501) 941-4828 to get your sasquatch hunting report.

Stop by ***Cove Creek Emporium*** for a pick-me-up. Here you can "Have a Latte in Leslie" as the town's sign proclaims or pick from their selection of other beverages while you shop their selection of organic coffees, gifts, and antiques, as well as a clothing resale shop. Their phone is (870) 448-6287.

Sentimental Journey, at 101-199 Oak St. (corner of Oak and Main) offers an eclectic blend of antique, vintage, collectible, shabby chic, handmade, and present-day merchandise. Owner Pamela Kelley is a self-taught artist of 19 years. Her accomplishments include serving as an artist in residence at Yellowstone Park. Here in Leslie, she has created a store that includes work from various artists, craftspeople, and collectors with products including handpainted artwork, handmade rustic furniture, pottery, antiques, natural bath and body products, collectibles, and a host of unique quality gifts. Hours are Mon through Sat 9:30 a.m. to 5 p.m. Call (870) 221-1527 for more information.

If all that perusing works up your appetite, head around the corner from Main Street and visit the **Skylark Cafe** at the corner of High Street and US 66. The cheerful little blue house is over 100 years old and is on the Historic Registry. Inside, you'll find a menu of fresh fare prepared using healthy cooking methods and local ingredients. Daily lunch specials include dishes such as garlic pepper chicken on cheesy black bean rice with pico de gallo, a garden salad, and French bread—say that out loud and see if your mouth doesn't water. Save room for dessert too—the selection of pies, cakes, and cookies changes each day. Hours are Mon through Thurs and Sat 11 a.m. to 3 p.m., Fri 11 a.m. to 8:30 p.m. Call (870) 447-2354 for more information.

The Buffalo National River flows under US 65 north of town, and the Tyler Bend Recreation Area follows the river. **Gilbert,** on Highway 333, is a gathering place for canoers paddling the river. With its 1901 saloon-style front, the **Gilbert General Store (Buffalo Camping and Canoeing)** is the same now as then. Well, maybe not exactly the same—in 1906 the owner added on to it a bit. But the town post office is still in a front corner, and the potbellied stove, circled by rocking chairs, still makes a warm spot for the locals to gather. The store is the heart of this quaint town on the banks of the Buffalo River, where the population can swell from 43 to 543 on any summer day. Managers Ben and Cynthia Fruehauf have been here since the 1970s and can not only provide you with anything you need in the way of canoe gear but also tell you how to find all the secret waterfalls and cliffside swimming holes. Listed on the National Register of Historic Places, the store is open 8 a.m. to 5 p.m. daily during the season, which runs from about Mar through Oct. Ben says they "shorten up the hours in the winter," which might mean it's closed entirely, but you never know unless you call (870) 439-2888. Take US 65 to Highway 333; then go east on Highway 333 to the end of the road. If you want a preview, visit gilbertstore.com.

Tyler Bend Recreation Area has handsome camping facilities and a 6.5-mile-long hiking trail at the put-in point just off US 65 at the Buffalo National River. The trail creates foot access to some of the best scenery along the river—high bluffs, long sandbars, and fast-water shoals. Most of the walk is along easy grades, but more difficult stretches occur along the ridgelines, where the vistas of Calf Creek are worth the effort. The trail is a series of loops adjoining one another and varying from just under 2 miles to nearly 4 miles. A 1,000-foot-long stone wall built during pioneer days and a 1930s log homestead are also found along the trail.

North of Tyler Bend on US 65, **Coursey's Smoked Meats** in **St. Joe** has been smoking bacon and hams for more than 50 years. The place has the original old smoker out front, but now it's all done inside in stainless steel smokers. Hours are 9 a.m. to 6 p.m.—"only 7 days a week" (closed in Jan). Jack Coursey is the owner, Mary Lu Coursey Neal is the manager, and they still make the best smoked bacon in the state. If you don't believe it, call (870) 439-2503 and order some, or fax (820) 439-2300. She says, "Like country music, we'll always be here."

Also in St. Joe is **Ferguson's Country Store and Restaurant,** on US 65 just up from the scenic Buffalo River. The road to Gilbert, where canoeists drop into the river, turns off US 65 at Ferguson's. Down the road at St. Joe are other cutoffs to the river. The restaurant caters to busloads of tourists who come to eat the home-cooked fried chicken, pork chops, beans with corn bread, and cinnamon rolls and browse in the country store filled with handmade quilts, wood products, and doodads. The owner of this one-stop-for-everything store is Wayne Thompson. Call him at (870) 439-2234 for information. They are open mid-Mar to mid-Dec 7 days a week, 8 a.m. to 3 p.m. at the restaurant and until 4 p.m. in the store. Behind the restaurant is the year-round Ferguson Furniture Manufacturing. Folks who eat at the restaurant can wander through and look at the solid red oak tables, chairs, and hutches being made by the vanishing breed of craftspeople who once populated the Ozarks.

Northeast in the Northwest

The town of *Norfork* began as a changeover point for pioneers who followed the White River, then switched from boats to oxcarts. Norfork today is equally reliant on the river. Tourists come to the area for fishing, and the many guide services and resorts are a major source of employment for locals.

P.J.'s White River Lodge is a renovated fishing lodge and B&B with full restaurant. It's at 384 Lodge Ln. in Norfork. Les Stevens and his wife, Julie, are the owners and operators of the lodge. Julie is the chef and has created many specialties such as Stevens whiskey rib eye and Tranquility Run Trout. The lodge was noted in *Sports and Field Magazine* in 1998 as one of the top 10 fishing spots. "Solitude is embraced but not enforced at the lodge, according to *Southern Living* magazine," Les says. You could tell he liked that quote. Call (870) 499-7500 for reservations, or for more information go online to pjslodge.com.

The *Wolf House,* built sometime between 1809 and 1825, is off Highway 5 in Norfork. It was the home of Major Jacob Wolf, sent as an Indian agent by President Thomas

trivia

The White River is stocked with more trout per mile than any other stream in the world.

Jefferson. For more than a half century, it served as a courthouse, post office, and stage and steamboat stop. The historic house, said to be the oldest remaining log cabin in the state, was built by black and Native American craftsmen. Handmade bricks of clay—dug and fired on the property—compose the four fireplaces and two chimneys. Half-dovetailed notched logs and original wrought-iron hinges, as well as the lock-raftered roof (no ridgepole is used), give fascinating insight into the labor and time required for the home to expand—the family grew to include the six children of two wives. To find the house, take Highway 5 south 0.25 mile past the North Fork River Bridge.

Tall Pine Resort in Norfork is 2 miles off Highway 5. It is a secluded place in the middle of a forest. The lodge sleeps as many as 10 people and has a hot tub on the back deck. There are two-bedroom cabins with spiral staircases that wind up to a loft bedroom. Owner Debra Racheter will lead guests around the property on horseback. Rates for rooms start at $120 a night. Call (870) 499-7574 or go to trailriding.net.

If trout dimpling around you in a cold stream is your idea of heaven, then Ken and Judy Epperson at the **Cotter-Trout Dock** in **Cotter,** the town just west of Gassville on Highway 345, can arrange float trips on the Buffalo, North Fork, or White River. Both single-day floats, covering 15 to 20 miles of river, and overnight camping trips are available. All trips include a guide and food. The overnight trips have a commissary boat operated by the cook and range from 2 to 6 days. You need bring only your fishing tackle and personal effects; everything else is supplied, and floats are tailored to your individual requirements. Guides with many years on the river ("We've been here as long as the trout have," says Judy) know where to fish. The cost is about $109 per person per day for day trips. Overnight trips on the White or Buffalo River (or both) start at $430 per person, with a minimum of 4 people and 2 days. Call (870) 435-6525, or (800) 447-7538 if you are outside the state, to arrange trips. Cotter-Trout Dock also has a website: cottertroutdock.com.

The dock is under the historic **Rainbow Arch Bridge** on US 62B at Cotter. Built in 1930 at a cost of $500,000, the cement bridge, with its five rainbow stands, is very rare. It was the first bridge across the White River and is listed on the National Register of Historic Places.

Cotter has been an important spot on the **White River** since the Bluff Dwellers farmed the rich bottomland there. Steamboats brought people and goods from all over the country. Lake's Ferry was here first, and there was a steamboat landing at McBee's Place upriver about 1.5 miles. Steamboats could make the trip from Batesville in about 12 hours when it took 24 to reach by land. Before the bridge was built, the citizens of Mountain Home and Yellville would meet at the ferry for picnics—stores would close in both towns, and everyone would trek to the Big Spring at the ferry in phaetons (light four-wheeled carriages), buggies, wagons, or oxcarts. A railroad bridge was built in 1904, and a tunnel was finished in 1905 for the White River branch of the Missouri-Pacific and Iron Mountain Railroad. Cotter was an exciting town.

At **Rainbow Bridge Lodge,** owner George Peters can accommodate 24 people. Rates are $30 per person per night. The lodge has a fully functional kitchen for cooking up your catch and a large commons area that is great for sharing stories, tips, and tricks with other anglers and nature lovers. For more information, visit rainbowbridgelodge.com or call (870) 404-7757. George is also the owner of **Roundhouse Shoals** fly-fishing guide service. If all this talk of trout and fly fishing intimidates you, you need to get in touch with George. He has a passion for teaching newcomers the sport of fly fishing, and especially loves the "dry fly" method. Roundhouse Shoals has all the gear needed to give fly fishing a try, from rods to waders, and even boats if you so choose. Both full and half-day services are available, depending upon your schedule and needs. Call (870) 404-7757 for more information or visit roundhouseshoals.com.

A walking trail starts in Cotter's Big Spring Park and follows the river upstream for 2.25 miles. It isn't unusual to spot an eagle or a fox as you follow the water. The best swimming hole in the Ozarks, according to the locals, is the Big Spring in the park. Rumor has it that there is a school in Cotter that has quite a reputation among anglers—you can learn to make your own fly rod there. But you will have to ask a local for information if you are interested in this unique school. The best way to spend your time around here is to float the Buffalo River. Buffalo Point is 14 miles south of Yellville on Highway 14. You can get equipment, canoes, or rafts from outfitters. Summer, when the river is tame and the bluffs are gorgeous, is a perfect time to visit this end of the river. In July or August, falling in feels good. It is a great river for first-time canoeists or families.

Trout Heaven

Fishing on the **White River** is one of the most popular things to do in this area. Here's why: There are four main trout fisheries, all tailwater fisheries fed by cold water drawn from the bottom of reservoirs and run through hydroelectric dams to generate electricity. The water runs through limestone rich in nutrients that feed aquatic insects, fish, and crawdads. This flood of nutrients makes so much food available that the trout don't have to work hard to eat, which allows them to grow as much as an inch a month. No other location in the country can produce such a growth rate. The limestone is fertilizer, and state trout biologists say that in most streams the fish stop growing because they can't get enough food. Here, they just move up the food chain and keep on growing. The brown trout reproduce naturally, but the rest are from state and federal hatcheries.

And speaking of historic places, *Whitewater*—now sometimes called "Whitewatergate" by the news media, due to President Clinton's involvement in this resort area—is here in Marion County along the White River, southeast of *Flippin* on Highway 101.

Take Highway 101 south (east of Flippin and west of the Cotter Bridge). Head for Ranchettes Access Area. The Whitewater Development is to the left, just before the Ranchettes subdivision. All you will see, though, is a gravel road and some third-growth timber. So take your fishing rod to fish at the access, because there was never much to see except a lot of reporters; now, even they are gone.

Many visitors to the Arkansas Ozarks come in search of beautiful handmade quilts, and rarely do they leave disappointed. Every little community here has active quilt guilds with hundreds of members. One place to match yourself up with their talents is at *The Curiosity Shop,* 9084 US 62 East, Flippin. Owner Paula Ross started her business here in 1994 to sell quilting supplies and handmade quilts to travelers. Paula has a large quilting machine inside the shop, and if you've never seen the process, she welcomes you to stop in and watch, for she always has a quilt on the machine. Paula says she's always in the shop, even during summer holidays, but her posted hours are Tues through Fri and Sat noon to 5 p.m. Her phone number is (870) 453-5300.

The *Old Store,* in the *Rush* historic district at the end of Highway 26, off Scenic Highway 14, is in a deserted town that was once a thriving mining community. Silver and zinc were discovered here in 1882, and in 1883 a record-setting 13,000-pound piece of zinc was excavated and shipped to the Chicago World's Fair for exhibition. Today that piece is in Chicago's Field Museum of Natural History. The remaining structures in town now belong to the National Park Service, and hiking trails, boating access, and a camping area are nearby. There are also markers to help visitors relive the past in this historic old town. Call the National Park Service for more information at (870) 439-2502 or visit nps.gov/buff.

Wild Bill's Outfitter near *Yellville* rents canoes and puts in at places with postcard-beautiful bluffs. The White River is beautiful (and icy cold), but the Buffalo National River is the best body of water in the area for canoeing. Wild Bill's also offers rustic mountain cabins that accommodate 2 to 10 people (depending on the cabin), as well as lodges and a motel that can sleep groups of 20 to 32. Cabin rates start at $75 per night, double occupancy. Call (800) 554-8657 or visit wildbillsoutfitter.com.

Buffalo River Lodge Bed and Breakfast, on Caney Road off Scenic Highway 14, sits on 62 acres of woods and meadows 14 miles south of Yellville. This 3-level log lodge with a double deck and wraparound porch has five guest rooms, all with private baths. A luscious full breakfast is served in the dining room or on the deck in good weather. You can relax in the great room, with its stone fireplace and loft library, then enjoy the hot tub on the deck or retire to one of two honeymoon suites, with in-room Jacuzzi for two. You can also have gourmet dinners on Sat with advance notice. Innkeepers Dan and Beth Powers will happily fix you picnic lunches for canoeing trips on the river. Rooms are from $79 to $124. Call (800) 733-2311 for information and reservations. The lodge website is buffaloriverlodge.com.

Harrison is called the "Crossroads of the Arkansas Ozarks" because scenic roadways to many mountain attractions meander through this small town. A visit should begin at the **Boone County Heritage Museum,** 124 South Cherry St., at the corner of Central and Cherry Streets 1 block west of Highway 7 South. The museum houses a large collection of railroad memorabilia, Civil War artifacts, Native American items, and period costumes, as well as a fine collection of Ozark Mountain rocks. The museum is open 10 a.m. to 4 p.m. Mon through Fri, Mar through Nov. From Dec through Feb, it is only open on Thurs. Admission is $2; kids are admitted free. Call (870) 741-3312 for information or visit bchrs.org.

The Hotel Seville, an authentic Spanish castle in the Ozarks, is at 302 North Main St., Harrison, and was once the most luxurious lodging facility

trivia

Yellville has hosted the annual **Turkey Trot** since 1945. The National Wild Turkey Calling Contest is held then. This is no small thing. It is the oldest wild turkey calling contest in the nation and contestants from all over the country vie for the title. Champions are determined by the judges based on demonstration of the plain yelp of the hen, kee kee run, cutting of the excited hen, adult hen assembly, and the cluck and purr. It is truly something to hear. And for the eyes, the Miss Drumsticks Beauty Contest is judged on legs only (faces and bodies hidden). The festival is held in Oct. Call (870) 449-4676.

for hundreds of miles. It is still the only full-service hotel in Harrison. Built in 1929, the hotel's interior remains like a step into 15th-century Spain and is a popular location for weddings and other social events in the area. The hotel's Seville Club is a lounge with local entertainment on Fri and Sat. You might want to spend the night; rooms range from $55 to $120. The hotel offers the European plan of bed and breakfast. Or just stop in for lunch at the hotel's Black Apple Cafe during a walking tour of the historic area of downtown Harrison. Maps for those tours are available in the lobby. Call (870) 741-2321, or visit 1929hotelseville.com.

Another interesting site is the ***Baker Prairie,*** 71 acres of America's vanishing tallgrass prairie filled with wildflowers, grasses, birds, and other creatures. It is 10 blocks west of the square on Goblin Drive. Only this section remains of what was once a 4,000-acre tallgrass prairie. (Don't you just hate to hear that phrase? It usually means something wonderful is gone forever.) Midwest prairies in Missouri and Kansas lie atop thick soil, but here in Arkansas, the prairie rests on thin soil above chert substrate. Often they were surrounded by woodlands. Somehow farmers left this little patch unplowed, and even the city built around it. Now it is cared for by various organizations and volunteers. The Goblin COPS (Caretakers of the Prairie) is made up of high school students guided by a biology and physics teacher. So life goes on in this small prairie, and plants and animals thrive just a short distance from the schoolhouse door. Carefully controlled burning in the spring or fall replicates the natural prairie occurrence and regenerates plant life. The website is naturalheritage.com. For more information call The Nature Conservancy (501) 663-6699 or check online at nature.org.

It seems as though the mountains pop up as suddenly as spring mushrooms around here once you cross the border from Missouri—everywhere a view on US 65. There can be no doubt that this is Arkansas.

If you're in the area in September, make plans to attend the *Annual Arkansas Hot Air Balloon State Championship and Festival* in Harrison. The festival features several different races, including the Hare and the Hound Balloon Race. In the Hare and the Hound, one balloon takes off first and is the hare balloon. The other balloons are the hounds. They launch after the Hare and have to chase it to where the hare has landed and set out a large target, usually about 50 feet in diameter. The hound balloons attempt to drop their markers as close to the center of the target as possible, with the closest marker earning the highest score. Other events include an evening balloon glow, where the hot air balloons inflate and light up after dark, as well as tethered balloon rides for $5 per person. It's great fun for all ages. For more information call the Harrison Chamber of Commerce at (870) 741-2659 or visit their website at arkansasballoonfest.com.

For the untethered version of a balloon ride, you can go soaring with pilot Rick Davidson between June and Nov. He and his wife Staci operate *Buffalo River Balloon Rides* out of Harrison. The flight lasts an hour, but with the time taken for inflation and for packing up after landing, it is about a 3-hour adventure. Each flight is different—the wind is the navigator—but the ending is always the same, as you'll celebrate a successful flight with a champagne toast once you're back on the ground. It's $600 for two balloon passengers. For more information, you can visit buffaloriverballoonrides.com or give Rick a call at (870) 577-7957 to set up a flight.

To get to the *Bull Shoals Lake Area,* take Highway 14 toward Yellville; then take Highway 178 North to the lake area. Each year over 100 bald eagles migrate to these shorelines, and for birders it is the place to be. Fishing on the lakes and rivers below the Bull Shoals Dam near Mountain Home makes this region popular with fishing enthusiasts. The White and North Fork Rivers provide perfect trout waters for 100 miles downstream. The silver flash glimmering in the summer sunlight is often a record-threatening catch, and all the state trout records and a former world record (a 38-pound, 9-ounce German brown trout caught in 1988) reside here.

trivia

You can cruise across Bull Shoals Lake at Peel Ferry, the only state-run ferry that still operates in the state.

That record was broken when angler "Rip" Collins caught a 40-pound, 4-ounce German brown trout in the Little Red River. The White River also produces National Fresh Water Hall of Fame line-class brown trout. Five of those fish are more than 30 pounds. So if you dream of piscatorial fame, these are the rivers to cast in.

The **Gaston White River Resort,** at 1777 River Rd. in **Lakeview,** is a good place to headquarter for the adventure because the guides are among the best on the river. Much of the fishing is done with worms and salmon eggs, so be sure to specify a guide who appreciates fly fishing. There's a landing strip here, and the resort is a popular fishing spot for celebrities like Phil Donahue, who flies in for an annual float trip. Call (870) 431-5202 or visit gastons.com for information. Prices vary from a standard room rate of $89 to $254 for an ultradeluxe cottage with a deck. Larger cottages are available for groups.

Gaston has a restaurant open every day from 6:30 a.m., so that you can get an early start on the river, to 10 p.m., from Valentine's Day to Thanksgiving. In Dec, Jan, and the beginning of Feb they are open Fri night and Sat and Sun until 2 p.m. The restaurant's view overlooking the White River makes it a popular Sun brunch destination. Pilots from as far away as Chicago and Dallas will fly in just to eat fresh fish and homemade breads. There is a private club and bar where you can have a cocktail and talk about the fish you almost caught.

The lake twists and turns for 80 miles through the Ozarks hills of north-central Arkansas and southwest Missouri. The woodsy hills and bluffs shelter the blue-green lake, leaving cool shadows. There are few boats on this lake, and you can cruise along in amazing quiet with seldom another craft in sight. Most of the shoreline is rough and undeveloped. There are no bridges, and the only way across is the Route 125 Free Ferry to shuttle people from the north to the south side and back again. The spring-fed lake is refreshingly chilly for swimming on hot afternoons.

Spelunking in the Ozarks

Arkansas is a spelunker's delight—there are more than 2,000 caves in the Ozark Mountains. Scientists call caves "our last wilderness," and those dark, yawning openings still fascinate people. Our early ancestors took shelter there, in competition with bears looking for a warm place to hibernate. The Tom Sawyer or Becky Thatcher in all of us is drawn to the mysterious holes in the mountains filled with stalagmites, stalactites, and crystal waters. Many of these caves were thought to have been discovered in the past 30 years, but there is evidence that some of them were used to hide Spanish gold and Civil War supplies and munitions. Some have petroglyphs—cave drawings—in the ceilings dating back 1,000 years. A cave is considered young if it is less than 10 million years old. So thousand-year-old petroglyphs are barely remnants of yesterday in Earth time.

Now, for the nonfishing folks along for the ride, nature gave the trout a beautiful place to live, and you can enjoy it, too. Since you will be seeing the dew-kissed mornings along with the trout hunters, drive on over to *Mountain Village 1890* and tour an authentic Ozark village unmarked by time.

See 10 historic structures moved to the village green from other towns in the state: The church stands on the highest spot in town for all to see; there's a 19th-century bank, a general store, a country school, a church, a dogtrot log cabin from Monkey Run, and the Lynch Flippin House, formerly the best house in Goatsville. Skilled craftspeople will be at work on pioneer arts and crafts.

Hear guides in old-style clothing pepper the tour with anecdotes that bring the old buildings to life. The "sinners' bench" in the church has some interesting stories to reveal.

Feel the hand-stitched quilts and rough wood of fence rails Native Americans split in 1828. Apr through Oct bring music and other special events. Visit the website at 1890Village.com or call (870) 445-7177 or (800) 445-7177.

The magnificent *Bull Shoals Caverns,* with well-lit pathways to explore the underground wonders, are located just off Highway 178 at 1011 C.S. Woods Blvd. in *Bull Shoals.* Hours are Wed through Sun 10 a.m. to 5 p.m. Mar 15 to Labor Day. Labor Day through Oct, the caverns are open Thurs through Mon 10 a.m. to 5 p.m. In Nov they are open only on Fri, Sat,

> ## Day Trip
>
> Get up early for this day trip; a number of scenic highways are involved. Drive south from Mountain Home, taking a side trip on Highway 177 at Salesville for a look at Norfork Dam and the Norfork Federal Trout Hatchery. Then return to Highway 5 and continue south through Calico Rock on the banks of the White River and on to Mountain View for the Ozark Folk Center. Huge Blanchard Springs Caverns is nearby. The western edge of this tour via Highway 14 leads to popular access points for the Buffalo National River—St. Joe, Silver Hill, Gilbert, Yellville, and others. Just off Highway 14 the historic ghost town of Rush stands near the Buffalo River.

and Sun 10 a.m. to 4 p.m. If this totally confused you, visit the website at bullshoalscaverns.com. Entry is $14 for adults, $7 for children ages 6 to 11, and free for 5 and under. Call (870) 445-7177 for more information.

If you travel down US 62, you'll find about 15 antiques, collectibles, and crafts shops, as well as several good eating places. **Bobbie Sue's Restaurant,** 2199 West US 62 East, is housed in a log cabin outside Mountain Home. This eatery is a well-kept secret—even a lot of locals haven't discovered it—and the kind of place you might pass by without noticing. But people who do know about it head there on Wed at noon for the barbecued ribs. Usually boneless, these are cut from the end of the loin and are spicy and succulent. There is homemade bread for soaking up the sauce, as well as homemade beans and potato salad. Owners Bobbie McMillan and Sue Kasinger peel potatoes and make everything from scratch. There's a daily lunch special, and breakfast draws a crowd, too. Sue says, "We give everyone a hard time so they'll feel at home." The restaurant is open Tues through Fri 6:30 a.m. to 2 p.m. and Sat until 1 p.m. Call (870) 425-2923 for information.

The Beautiful Highway 7

Scenic Highway 7 is just that, one of the loveliest drives in the state. It winds and curves and crests hills and skirts rivers. It is more than just a way to get somewhere in Arkansas, and there are some great little places along the way.

Bordering the Ozark National Forest and the Buffalo River Park, *Ozark Mountain Cabins,* about 0.3 mile off Highway 7 and 4 miles north of *Jasper,* offer a spectacular valley view, where elk and deer graze in the pastures. Each of the four log cabins sleeps six and has a gorgeous 20-mile view. The cabins are built of hand-peeled logs with pine tongue-and-groove walls and fireplaces of locally collected rock inside. Central heat makes the cabins a great place for winter vacations. The kitchens have everything you need; just bring food and drink. The cabins are about 150 feet apart, placed for the view, and with summer foliage they are hidden from one another. Summer rates for two people are $126 (less in winter) for 1 night, $106.50 per night for 2 nights, $101.50 for 3 to 6 nights, $92 for 7 nights or more. The lodge is $102 for 1 or 2 nights, $96.50 for 3 to 6 nights, and $87 for 7 nights or more. Call Connie for reservations at (870) 446-2229 or visit ozarkcabins .com/ozarkmountaincabins.

trivia

Diamond Cave, near Jasper, contains many passages. It has no diamonds, but the quartz crystals give a spectacular effect.

The annual *Fall Foliage Tour* in Oct is sponsored by the US Forest Service and leaves from the south side of the courthouse square in Jasper. It travels along a portion of the Arkansas Scenic 7 Byway and the surrounding forested area. The scheduled route is set depending on the best color opportunities. Call (870) 446-5122 for more information on this year's tour.

You might be surprised to find a herd of elk roaming the hills around Jasper. If you want to learn more about them and get an insider's knowledge on where to go to see the elk in person, stop by the *Hilary Jones Wildlife Museum.* There are kid-friendly exhibits and aquariums as well as a trove of information about the elk and other local wildlife. The museum is on Scenic Highway 7 just north of Jasper and the Little Buffalo River. Hours are 9 a.m. to 5 p.m. daily. Call (870) 446-6180 or visit arkansaselkcenter.com.

On Scenic Highway 7, just 3 miles north of Jasper and only 2 miles from the Buffalo River, *Crawford's Cabins* border the national forest with trails at the back door. The two cabins and R. R. Crawford Provisions (where you can buy the famous Mountain Man Sandwich and an ice-cold sarsaparilla as well as handmade knives, dulcimers, and camping supplies) promise to be among your fondest memories of the Ozarks. The Arkansan cabin has a native stone floor, country kitchen, and handmade willow furniture. There is a downstairs bedroom and a loft. Bear Hollow cabin boasts a cathedral ceiling, hardwood floors, and fine furnishings. The bedroom has a sleigh bed and handmade quilts. Ron and Linda Crawford are your hosts and can be reached by phone at (870) 446-2478, by fax at (870) 446-5824, or online at buffalorivercountry.com/crawfordscabins.

The Buffalo National River rushes from Ponca to the White River. This most scenic stretch is floatable only in the spring; once summer arrives, it becomes a series of quiet pools. But when it runs, it runs, and it has plenty of roller-coaster rapids to enliven the scenery.

River Spirit Retreat is a quiet place near Parthenon where Ann Lasater offers guests more than just a cabin—she provides a spiritual retreat where you can escape the world for a few days and even have an hour massage for $70. The guest cottage rents for $90 (double, $70 for one), comes with a stereo, and overlooks a beautiful garden. There's a wood-burning fireplace to take the chill off the evening and a porch swing on which to enjoy the sweet air. It's a remote place, 30 minutes from Jasper, and 7 miles down a dirt road. Most people bring their own food, but Ann does some catering, too. The Mother Lodge is for larger groups and can accommodate up to nine people. This rents for $190 (double). There's an outdoor hot tub near the Mother Lodge that everyone can use. Ann hosts workshops throughout the year on a variety of subjects. Many guests over the years have participated in an ongoing group art project called The River Hermitage/Sanctuary. Using an old, English building technique, this structure is made of sand, clay, and straw using the hands, feet, and heart of the guests at River Spirit. Right now, it's being used for meditation, but when finished it will look like an adobe hut and will be available for rent as well. You can reach Ann at (870) 446-5642. Her website is riverspirit.com.

After taking in the beauty of the Ozarks from above, try the view from underground. *Beckham Creek Cave Lodge*, on a gravel road just west of Jasper near *Parthenon,* is perhaps the most unusual lodging you'll ever encounter. Built as a bomb shelter in the 1980s for a wealthy Colorado businessman and his family, the cave is now a popular destination for weddings, honeymoons, and people wanting something "different." Deep in the crevices of a limestone cavern, luxurious accommodations are built right into the stone walls, including a hot tub in natural rock. But don't worry about bats or bugs. The bats exit the cave through another opening and eat all of the bugs and mosquitoes in the area. The cave is surrounded by 530 tree-covered acres where you can continue to enjoy the aboveground beauty of the Ozarks. The home was even featured on *Lifestyles of the Rich and Famous*. Rates for the cave per night are $450 for one room for the first night, $225 for each additional night, and $175 per night for additional rooms (there are five rooms total). Call (870) 446-6043 or toll-free at (888) 371-2283, or view the beauty of the cave rooms at beckhamcavelodge.com.

Alum Cove Natural Arch is a 1.1-mile round-trip hike from the parking area. It's an easy hike, and the reward is an impressive natural arch. But you will also see some "cowcumber trees" and "goat houses," according to the natives here. (A stand of native cucumber magnolias grows along the north side of the arch, and wild goats may have sheltered under the namesake stone arch—as did Indians on hunting expeditions—according to archaeologists.) Each season has something wonderful to see along this trail. In spring budding dogwood and redbud trees bloom; in fall vibrant colors abound. Summer has wildflowers of many colors in the cooling shade of the hardwood forest, and even winter offers interesting ice formations. Drive 15 miles south from Jasper on Highway 7, turn west on Highway 16; after 0.5 mile, turn north and go 4 miles to the parking area. There is a $3 day use fee per vehicle.

On your way back toward Jasper on Highway 7, take advantage of the opportunity to stop and see the Grand Canyon. The **Arkansas Grand Canyon,** that is. There are several overlooks that let you take in the vista and the steep drop down into the Buffalo River Valley. It is especially beautiful in the fall. Stop at **The Cliff House** to have lunch, or you can spend a night or two if the mood strikes you. The restaurant is famous for two things—the view and the "Company's Comin' Pie." This is Arkansas's state pie—a meringue crust with pecans and crackers holds up a whipped cream and pineapple filling. Their breakfasts are like grandma used to make. The lunch and dinner menus offer a variety of choices from burgers, sandwiches, salads, and home-cooking-style entrees like chicken-fried chicken or rib eye. The restaurant and gift shop are open Mar 15 through "Fall Colors," 8 a.m. to 3 p.m. Sun through Thurs and 8 a.m. to 8 p.m. Fri and Sat.

The inn has five rooms, all of which have a view of the Arkansas Grand Canyon. Rates are $80 to $98, double occupancy. There are also three cabins located a few miles to the south of The Cliff House. Rates are $115 for 1 night, $98 for 2 to 4 nights, and $89 for 5 or more nights, $15 for each additional person. Each cabin includes central air and heat, a fireplace, and a fully equipped kitchen. The bedroom downstairs has a queen bed with two more queens in the upstairs loft. For more information, call (870) 446-2292 or visit cliffhouseinnar.com.

Serious birders come to the area around Ponca, Jasper, and Boxley Valley because of its varied elevations and habitats. Wildflower enthusiasts and rock climbers flock here, too, but until recently the natural beauty of Newton County could be enjoyed only by those willing to stay in horse-camping sites or unpretentious cabins or motels. There still are very few restaurants except for a few casual spots in Jasper or other small towns in the area, and the county is dry (no alcohol), so hauling in your own food and drinks was necessary, as well. Things have perked up a bit now, and some relatively unknown new spots—guest ranches and cabins—are quite upscale and very comfortable.

If you have never tried your hand at guiding a canoe down a river, it's never too late to begin. Doing so is not difficult, and first-time-outers often come back dry as a bone, having experienced no spills (but no guarantees, either). For those of you with more experience and perhaps a canoe lashed to the car, there are several put-in points in the area. If it's later in the season and the upper Buffalo is too shallow to canoe, you can put in at Woolum on the lower river, off US 65, and take a leisurely day trip to **Silver Hill** (16.5 miles), where there's a US Park Service station, or continue for a 2-day trip (another 16 miles) to Maumee. The entire trip from Ponca takes about a week—from Woolum, about 5 or 6 days—and landings all along the river are about 4 to 20 miles apart. Canoe outfitters will pick you up where you plan to end.

The **Buffalo Outdoor Center** has 19 rustic log cabins from $129 to $329 each that are equipped with a full kitchen, a fireplace, loft bedrooms, and a front porch swing. If the swing doesn't provide enough excitement for you, you can try out the Zip Line Canopy Tour. Guides will put you in a helmet and harness and clip you onto a series of metal cables strung between the treetops in the Buffalo River Valley. As you move from platform

Falling Waters

There are some splendid waterfalls along the Buffalo National River. A spectacular 225-foot waterfall on the Buffalo River lies between Steel Creek and Kyles Landing. You can reach Hemmed-In Hollow from the river or by a trail through the Ponca Wilderness Area. Park rangers or canoe outfitters can tell you how to get there. Twin Falls is a rugged 1-mile hike from Richland Creek Campground. If hiking or canoeing are not for you, you can view the Falling Water Falls nearby without a hike. Lost Valley waterfall is part of a 3-mile round-trip hiking trail that begins at the Lost Valley Campground near Ponca.

to platform along the zipline "trail," your guide will also introduce you to the bird, plant, and animal life found in Ozark Mountain hardwood forest canopy. Of course, you'll also have beautiful vistas and the wind in your hair to enjoy. As you go along and build confidence, you might even want to try letting go of your harness and striking your best flying pose (but you don't have to). The tour takes about 2 hours to complete and is open to anyone age 10 and older. (The record for the oldest zip liner on this course is 86!) Zippers need to weigh between 70 and 250 pounds. Cost is $89 per person. Group rates are available. Tours are available Mar through Nov. To see a list of specific dates that are available for reservation, visit the website at buffaloriver.com.

Then again, if all this sounds a little too heart-pounding to you, you can stay closer to the ground and take a different kind of adventure. Put a paddle in the water on one of the most scenic stretches of the Buffalo River—the day float from Ponca to Kyles Landing is 10 miles long and takes 4 to 6 hours to complete. Buffalo Outdoor Center will outfit you with your choice of a canoe, kayak, or raft. Pack a cooler with some drinks, snacks, and PB&Js, and you'll be set for a trip that is exciting and relaxing all in one. Call (870) 861-5514 for more information, or visit buffaloriver.com.

Bill and Regena Cochrane have built *Walnut Grove Cabins* in *Boxley Valley,* Each of the three cabins are 2-stories. Across the pasture is the 1870 Boxley Community Center and Baptist church and a tree line along the Buffalo River. The interior has a native-rock fireplace, hardwood floors, and a skylight over the living area. The two bedrooms each have queen beds, plus there is a large loft with two more queen beds. One bathroom has a shower while the other features a Jacuzzi tub. The rate of $125 a night for two persons (two children under age 12 can stay free) will give you elk, songbirds, wild turkeys, and deer to watch from a rocker on your cabin's front porch. Call (870) 861-5835 for more information, or visit walnut grovecabins.com.

Rimrock Cove Ranch in Green Forest is 180 acres of Ozark beauty near the upper Buffalo River. You'll enjoy a guided horseback ride down quiet wooded trails and across meandering streams and see wildflowers in season. There is even a waterfall. If you don't ride, hayrides are excellent outings for families or groups. The 30-minute trip takes you to an open meadow for a cookout. The Suffolks, a breed of draft horse whose ancestors originated in England, are raised and trained on this small farm. Rimrock Cove is on Highway 103 about 7 miles south of Osage or 5 miles from Highway 43. Rides are by reservation only. Toni and Dennis Albers are your guides. Prices are $35 per hour. In Jan, Feb, and early Mar, you can try your hand at maple sugaring, the process of making maple syrup. After your cozy hayride through the woods to collect the sap from the resident maple and hickory trees, return to the cook site to watch it be stewed down into syrup and other treats. The Albers have added **Stonewall Cabin** for guests who want to stay awhile. The cabin is made from pine logs and sits on a hillside among several stone walls overlooking a pond and valley. It has a stone and peeled-cedar wraparound porch and stone patio. There is a fireplace and fully equipped kitchen a bedroom with a queen bed, plus a loft with a queen bed and a queen sleeper sofa. The rate is $120 a night plus $15 for each additional person in Jan and Feb, with a 2-night minimum; children under 6 stay free. Mar through Dec the nightly rate is $159. Call (870) 553-2556, or visit rimrockcoveranch.com.

There are so many places to stay around Jasper that a lodging must offer something special to stand out from the competition. For example, the **Red Rock Retreat,** a beautiful and secluded spot 12 miles south of Jasper in the Arkansas Grand Canyon, has Lipizzan horses—the famous Dancing Stallions of Vienna—that Sandy Swayne raises here on the 130 acres surrounding 2 two-bedroom log cabins. The horses, which graze in a pasture in front of the cabins, are magnificent and worth the trip to see. There are riding trails, if you bring your own horse, and Sandy has facilities for horses for $15 a day.

The cabins are crafted of local rock and hand-peeled logs with a pine and cedar interior. The rock fireplace gives a rustic feel, while central heat and air-conditioning and modern plumbing make them comfortable for all seasons. Their many windows bring the Ozarks right inside, and a quiet creek whispers in front. Ceiling fans circulate air. The Cedar Creek cabin features a red cedar bathroom and antique claw-foot tub. Both cabins have kitchens that are fully equipped for cooking. From the front porch swing, there is a breathtaking view of Red Rock bluffs and Big Creek. The cabins are about 0.5 mile from the Swaynes' house, ensuring privacy, and pets are welcome. The Cedar Creek cabin is $100 for two, plus $15 for each additional person. The Hickory Hill Cabin is $125. Call (870) 434-5316 for reservations or check the place out on their website ozarkcabins.com/redrockretreat.

Eight miles outside Jasper, the **Horseshoe Canyon Ranch** looks like a dude ranch in Colorado—boulders jutting out of the ground and open meadows. Here Barry Johnson and his father, Jerry, have 10 yellow pine log cabins scattered on one side of the valley. They all have wood-burning stoves and a western Native American theme. Often on Saturday nights, the Johnsons host horse games to liven up the evening.

This is a 350-acre guest ranch. The massive bluffs hide caves, springs, and quiet pools. Meadows and hardwood forests are home to birds, butterflies, and wildlife of all kinds. Rock climbing is a favorite activity for all ages and levels (there's even an indoor rock climbing wall for practice). But horseback riding is the real reason most stay here. Whether you are a beginner or an experienced rider, your horse will match your skill. Children have a youth program all their own, where they can learn crafts, discover wildlife and plants, ride a friendly pony, and help feed the livestock, which includes chickens, rabbits, and goats. Evenings there is a campfire and moonlight rides, or local musicians will come and play. No phones, no television, hot tubs and, of course, a pool make this a fine place to vacation with the family. In summer the minimum stay is 3 days, but a 6-day stay is best so that you can canoe or take a trek to Branson, Missouri—included in the package.

The price of $1,061 in the fall and spring—or $1,197 in the summertime—for a week includes a cottage, three meals a day, and "all the horseback riding your rear end can stand," as Jerry puts it. Family discounts and seasonal reductions apply. Rates change with the season, so call (800) 480-9635 or visit the ranch's website at horseshoecanyon.com.

"Off the beaten path" is a phrase meaning different things to different travelers. This next adventure will get you off the highways and into the forests, but the path is well traveled by hikers. The **Lost Valley Trail** begins at the Lost Valley Campground just off Highway 43 between Ponca and Boxley. It leads through the shady red cedar and sweet gum forest along Clark Creek, a tributary of the Buffalo River, to a pool below the gentle spray of Eden Falls. The creek begins about 1.75 miles up a narrow canyon of limestone bluffs and steep hills. The trail forks at a site known as Siamese Beeches, where the tree trunks have grown together high overhead. Take the right fork to Jig Saw Blocks (named for the way they fit together) and on to a clear pool fed by water slowly carving a tunnel through the outcropping. Corn Cob Cave is at the base of the cliff, so named because Native Americans left corncobs here long ago. A spur leads on to Eden Falls. The terrain becomes slightly more difficult en route to Eden Falls Cave, 170 feet higher than the pool, but if you are adventurous and have a flashlight, a bit of crawling will get you inside the cave, where you will find another 35-foot waterfall hidden inside. But the falls below are a good spot for a shower among glistening rocks in the shallow pool, surrounded by fern and moss. It's almost paradise—that's why it's called Eden Falls. For information and a map, call (870) 741-5443. For information about other trails, ask for the Arkansas Hikers' Kit from the State Trails Coordinator, Department of Parks and Tourism, One Capitol Mall, Little Rock, 772201; (501) 682-7777; rps.gov/buff.

Ozark National Forest

Due north of Kingston on Highway 21, you find **Berryville,** with lovely old homes that date back to the city's beginning. The town has a charming turn-of-the-20th-century square with a tree-shaded park, old-fashioned street lamps, and benches. There's a real five-and-ten, together with shops, restaurants, and museums, and a vintage drugstore that still has a soda fountain. The **Caroll County Heritage Center** in the 1880 Courthouse on the square contains a museum

trivia

Berryville describes itself as being "Where the Old South Meets the Old West."

whose living history displays include a schoolroom, barbershop, and moon-shine still. A working village blacksmith shop shows you how tools were forged in the 1800s; Pioneer Park features vintage log cabins and an early jail; and a restored pump station houses the city's tourist information center. Hours are Mon through Fri 9 a.m. to 4 p.m. Apr through Oct. The center is closed Mon Nov through Mar. Admission is $2 for adults and $1 for children. Call (870) 423-6312.

The volunteers at the center will direct you to the ***Saunders Memorial Museum*** at 113–115 Madison Ave. The museum has Pancho Villa's lavishly decorated Colt .45—its right grip burned brown from the Mexican sun and its handle inset with gold, jewels, and a Mexican gold coin and nameplate. The guns of Jesse James, Billy the Kid, Annie Oakley, and Wild Bill Hickok are all part of the finest gun collection in the nation. But even if you're not a gun collector, there are many other novel items in the museum, which was a bequest to the town from the late Colonel C. Burton Saunders. Among the things to see are a tent, hand-embroidered with gold thread (made by a sheikh's 200 wives); a warbonnet and battle jacket owned by Sitting Bull (and his totem scalps); and displays of antique furniture and Native American artifacts. Mrs. Saunders's closet is there, too, with clothes and acces-sories, circa 1910, as well as vases, rugs, lacework, and silverware. The museum is open from Apr 15 through Oct. Admission is $5 for adults, $2 for children ages 6 through 13; children under 6 are free. Hours are 10:30 a.m. to 5 p.m. Mon through Sat; you can call (870) 423-2563.

For a truly remote getaway, visit the ***Little Portion Hermitage*** at 350 CR 248, Berryville, near Eureka Springs. The hermitage is home to the Catholic-based monastic commu-nity wherein live both celibates and families, as well as cattle, chickens,

trivia

Berryville's original claim to fame was that its first buildings formed a circle, while most towns were laid out in a square.

More than a half-million turkeys are raised near Berryville each year.

rabbits, and the occasional pig. The large vegetable garden, apple orchard, and animal barns form an important part of the community. The garden is maintained according to organic or biointensive methods of natural growth. Bed gardens have soil sifted to a depth of 3 feet, the rock and clay replaced with compost and sand. Greenhouses prepare seeds and small plants during the colder months. The animals are organically fed in the barns and pasture. The landscaped garden is centered around a statue of the Teaching Christ. Flowers and a running stream invite you in. The bell in the cedar bell tower, through which you enter, calls everyone to worship in the Charity Chapel, the heart of the community, three times a day—at 6:45 a.m., noon, and 5:30 p.m.—for monastic chanting of the psalms, communion, charismatic or spontaneous praise, and silent adoration.

The cloister/prayer garden, a freestanding cloister-arbor in local Ozark style patterned after European monasteries, is laid out in the form of a Celtic cross, with a gazebo in the middle. The garden includes rare flowers and grasses to provide solitude at various spots. The arbor is supported by wooden monastic arches that frame occasional stained-glass windows of Franciscan saints taken from the Franciscan community that helped birth the Little Portion.

The brothers and sisters also run the Little Portion Retreat Center a few miles away, where groups can meet or individuals may spend time in contemplation.

For more information call the hermitage at (479) 253-7710 or go to little portion.org. To find the hermitage or retreat center, both of which are really off the beaten path, stop by the shop for a detailed map.

US 62 weaves from Berryville to *Eureka Springs,* which is not exactly off the beaten path. Yes, you have to look closely on the map to see it, but it is the state's premier tourist town and a must-see for any Arkansas traveler. Shops and bed-and-breakfasts come and go like cottonwood fluff in the breeze. Every year there are new and different places to see. There are some old standbys that would be a shame to miss and several small spots you might overlook. For example, the Bank of Eureka Springs on Main Street is an interesting place you might not think to visit. It is in a new building, but the interior is done in pure Victorian. The Carnegie Library has a rolling cart with photos of the town. There are 60 springs inside the city limits, and a walking-tour book will lead you along historical pathways to interesting places. There are

trivia

Carry Nation's Home is at 35 Steele St. in Eureka Springs. It is known as Hatchet Hall.

old hotels, guest cottages, tons of antiques shops, myriad art galleries, and a batch of peculiar museums (featuring bells, frogs, Bibles, musical instruments, or birds).

Perhaps the first place you'll want to stop by is the *Eureka Springs Historical Museum* at 95 South Main St. Here, you will find the story of the little town that is called The City that Water Built, The Little Switzerland of the Ozarks, and an authentic Victorian Village (the whole town is on the National Register of Historic Places). The museum is open Mon through Sat 9:30 a.m. to 4 p.m. and Sun 11 a.m. to 4 p.m. Call (479) 253-9417 for more information, or visit eurekaspringshistoricalmuseum.org.

Every day, Mon through Sat, a train pulls out of the train yard at 299 North Main in Eureka Springs, and every day people are transported not only through the beautiful Ozark woodlands but back in time as well. All aboard the *Eureka Springs & North Arkansas Railway,* a 1940s diesel locomotive from when travel was fun. There is even elegant dining and gourmet cuisine in the Eurekan Dining Car. You can walk around the train yard and the depot and the end of the line "wye" as the engine is turned on a turntable and reconnected to your excursion car. The historic depot has a gift shop as well. Rides on the 4.5-mile route are $14 for adults and $7 for ages 4 to 10. Call (479) 253-9623 or 9677 or visit esnarailway.com for reservations and times.

Gaskins Cabin

Gaskins Cabin Steakhouse, 2883 AR 23 North, Eureka Springs (479-253-5466), is a simple red log cabin that will surprise you with a menu containing grilled walleye pike and escargot in garlic butter. It also has a great wine list. The cabin formerly belonged to John Gaskins, who was one of the first settlers in the county. Living along the creek 3 miles below Eureka Springs, he would watch crowds gather around Basin Spring to take the waters. He then wrote about the many miracle cures he saw. When the Civil War broke out, he refused to serve in the Confederate army and moved to Missouri, where the Union flag still flew. After the war he returned to Eureka Springs, where he wrote his memoirs. He and his family rest in the nearby Gaskins Switch Cemetery, land he had set aside. In his memoirs he wrote: "I want to add that I believe we are raising boys here. . . who will have the brains for president." The restaurant is open Thurs, Fri, and Sat in winter; Tues through Sat in summer, 5 to 9 p.m.

You'll also find a profusion of restaurants. The **Crystal Dining Room** (at the Crescent Hotel) and **Bubba's Barbecue** ("It doesn't look famous, but it is") vie with a Czech-German restaurant (the **Bavarian Inn**) for your dinnertime dollar. You can find whatever you want at mealtime, from the most expensive to the best bargains (**Chelsea's**—the most food for the least money—don't be put off by just looking in the door; go on in, order the Macho Nachos, covered with black beans, sausage, and alfalfa sprouts, and live a little) to places like the **Oasis** (mostly vegetarian food) and **DeVito's** downtown (homemade pasta and bread and fresh trout worth the restaurant's long wait to get in). The hours vary with the season, and many places are closed in winter, so check around.

Eureka Springs is also the place where you can find unusual things to do. For example, at the **Mud Street Espresso Cafe,** 22 North Main, you can get muffin-tops for breakfast (or lunch), and downstairs in a comfortable little cellar, you can have curry or quiche and play games. The cafe will deliver breakfast to cottages in the morning if you order the night before. Call (479) 253-6732 or visit mudstreetcafe.com for more information.

The many-tiered, sprawling Victorian village dates to 1879 on the rugged, hilly terrain of the Ozark Mountains. Today, because of the collective restoration of the town, Eureka Springs offers a microcosm of late-19th-century life, making it a unique, historic tourist attraction. The streets are so steep that the entrance to **St. Elizabeth's Catholic Church** is through the top of the bell tower, and a motorized trolley roams the town's narrow ways, none of which intersect at right angles. The trolley follows the US 62 loop around town with a spiderweb of tiny culs-de-sac weaving off from it in all directions. Mr. Ripley included St. Elizabeth's Catholic Church in his famous *Ripley's Believe It or Not* cartoon. It is nestled halfway down a mountainside behind the Crescent Hotel and Spa. Listed on the National Register of Historic Places and built in 1904, this house of worship is an interesting example of the blending of three types of architectural design: Romanesque, Byzantine, and Gothic. The walkway that leads from the bell tower to the sanctuary is lined with Stations of the Cross hand-carved from marble. The dome is Byzantine in style and fashioned after the Church of St. Sophia in Istanbul, Turkey. The church and its gardens are maintained with proceeds from the St. Elizabeth Gift Shop on the lower level of the church.

More than 600 artisans live and work in the Eureka Springs area, and their crafts are sold all over town. You can find quilts, knives, baskets, Quaker furniture, stained glass—almost anything—here. The shops are crammed with fine arts and oddities. The first thing to do is park your car and buy a trolley ticket. An adult day pass costs $6. The streets are impossibly narrow, and there is never a vacant parking meter. You can get off and on the trolley as often as you want and see a lot more that way. (The secret is to ride it twice uphill and walk down, riding on the right side the first time and the left side the second time.)

The romantic setting of Eureka Springs draws hundreds of couples-in-love for weddings and honeymoons. No fewer than eight spots provide immediate, legal wedding services. One of the most romantic locations for a prearranged service is **Rosalie House** at 282 Spring St. This tour home is not only a beautiful place for a wedding but also a romantic spot for renewing your vows or having a bridal shower. Call (479) 253-7377 to make the arrangements for weddings with up to 25 guests, or you can elope for $100. You need a marriage license (but no blood work or witnesses), a photo ID, and Social Security number to make it legal.

Visit the website at therosalie.com to get a preview of the 2-story red-brick Victorian house (circa 1883 and the first brick home in the area). Tours alone of this fine home are available by appointment. **11 Singleton House** is a pretty, 2-story Victorian at 11 Singleton St. Innkeeper Barbara Gavron also has a service listing more than 30 bed-and-breakfasts and cottages in the area. She tries to match people up with the kind of place they want. Barbara is in her 21st year of business and has been in operation the longest. She knows every street and path and is a gold mine of information. (She likes to send her guests out at night with a flashlight to see the beauty of the town after dark; go to the top of the old hotels and get romantic night views, she says.)

The Singleton House has five bedrooms, all of which have private baths. A breakfast balcony overlooks the garden and pond out behind the kitchen. A full breakfast is included in the $95 to $145 price. The Gardener's Cottage is $125 to $165. The phone number for Barbara's reservation service and the Singleton House is (800) 833-3394 or (479) 253-9111. Visit them online at singletonhouse.com.

Barbara knows this town. Her guests get the inside track on goings-on in town. For example: Summer Sunday nights bring out the movie buffs on Main Street in Eureka Springs. This is not just a popcorn-and-soft-drink indoor event, though, because the screen is painted on the wall of one of the buildings and everyone brings a folding chair. What makes this weekly event so much fun is that most of the people are dressed to match the movie of the evening. A John Wayne western brings out 10-gallon hats and boots; *Gone With the Wind,* hoop skirts and Rhett Butler wannabes everywhere; and *Star Wars,* well, you get the picture—literally. It's just a have fun kinda night.

Driving on US 62E keep an eye out for **Sparky's Roadhouse Cafe,** ironically across from McDonald's at 147 East Van Buren. A big, fat juicy burger draws locals, so when in Rome. . . . Here's the thing about a place like Sparky's: It looks like a biker joint, which, if you think about it, is usually the best place to eat in any given town. Sure, McDonald's has burgers, but Sparky's has a great selection of cold beers as well. Throw in some nachos or enchiladas, and you're not in McDonald's anymore. It's a fun place for fun people. If you don't want music and laughter, take your frown to the clown across the street. Call (479) 253-6001.

Singleton Street is one of the web of streets winding off the main loop. A larger main street, Spring Street, is shaded by sycamores, colored with spring daffodils and irises, and lined with bed-and-breakfasts and shops. The springs still flow from the bluffs that line the street, and a copper-topped gazebo was recently added near one of them.

Treehouse Cottages are just that, four cottages nestled in the trees more than 26 feet above the ground. These cottages are not primitive tree houses, though; they are romantic retreats decorated with stained-glass windows, antiques, and, yes, television and a kitchen. You cross a suspended walking bridge to reach one of them, above a cascading waterfall and goldfish pond. They are located an easy 0.5-mile walk to downtown Eureka Springs. Nightly rates for these unique hideaways are $169 to $175. There are four more cottages in town with nightly rates of $149 to $155. Visit treehousecottages.com to get a look at the cottages at 165 West Van Buren or call (479) 253-8667.

When you have walked your legs off on the hilly streets of Eureka Springs, you will welcome the women waiting behind the picket fence at 31 Kingshighway. Unlike the psychologist who gives you a 45-minute hour, the massage at **Healing Benefits Massage Therapy Company** can last for more than an hour. Susan Sutherland's little pink-and-yellow Victorian house is open year-round, and she has a large following. Susan and her staff are all reflexologists as well, so service is from your face to your feet. Soothing music and aromatic lotions relax you and silken your skin while you receive a first-class massage. Call ahead for an appointment at (479) 253-6751.

Smith Treur and Deborah Sederstrom have the **Rogue's Manor at Sweet Spring** at 124 Spring St., Eureka Springs, where seafood—especially from the Northwest (they are from Oregon and Alaska)—and custom-cut steaks as well as vegetarian dishes are beautifully served. The Manor is open for dinner 5 to 9 p.m. Wed through Sun. The inn has four suites, all with room service, at $85 to $200. Call (800) 250-5827, or visit roguesmanor.com.

As the name implies, Eureka Springs was once a spa. The **Palace Hotel and Bathhouse,** at 135 Spring St., is a restored Victorian hotel that has the only bathhouse in town and a staff of licensed therapists. Ask for "the works" and get a mineral bath, steam treatment, clay mask, and 30-minute massage for $80. Call (479) 253-8400 for an appointment. The eight hotel suites contain king-size beds; a bar, sink, and refrigerator; and a whirlpool unit to bring a modern touch to the comfort of the antique furniture. A continental breakfast of juice, coffee, and pastries and an evening snack tray are included in the price, which ranges from $155 to $185. Call (479) 253-7474 for a room. For a preview of the Palace, check out palacehotelbath house.com.

Like every historic town with lots of old buildings, some of them are considered haunted. If seeking out the supernatural is your thing, or if you just like the idea of haunted houses, you have two options.

Nightly tours of "America's Most Haunted Hotel" begin in the lobby of the **Crescent Hotel** at 8 p.m. The Crescent was built in 1886, so there are plenty of stories to be told. You'll have the opportunity to meet some of the hotel's most permanent guests and learn about the hotel's storied

trivia

The 18-inch-thick limestone-marble walls of the Crescent Hotel in Eureka Springs were fitted without mortar. In 1886 the "Castle in the Wilderness" opened with a gala ball attended by 400 prominent and wealthy social elite from several states. The hotel had its own orchestra for nightly dances, along with a bowling alley, swimming pool, riding stable, and fresh springwater on every floor for drinking and bathing.

past. Find out about secret underground passageways and visit the basement morgue that still remains from when the hotel was a cancer hospital. Tour tickets are $21.50 for adults and $8 for children under the age of 12. Group rates are available with 10 people or more. To purchase ghost tour tickets call (877) 342-9766 or visit americasmosthauntedhotel.com.

At the Crescent's sister hotel, the **Basin Park Hotel**, you can also go on tour nightly starting at 8 p.m., Mar through Nov. Tickets for this tour are $16.50 for adults and $8 for children under the age of 12. Group rates are available for groups of 12 or more. For more information, visit eurekaghost tours.com.

Both hotels have lodging packages that include the ghost tours so that you can have an even greater opportunity to experience paranormal activity. Or, you can just take the opportunity to enjoy the interesting architecture and historical significance of these two stately hotels. You can check room rates for the Crescent Hotel online at crescent-hotel.com, or call (855) 725-5720. For Basin Park, go online to basinpark.com or call (877) 456-9679.

Stone fences, old farmhouses, and creeks make for a lovely drive along Highway 187 north of Eureka Springs. If you want to take a nostalgic drive across one of the last single-lane swinging bridges left, take Highway 187 Northwest toward Holiday Island to the town of **Beaver.** Built in 1949, the bridge is known as the "Little Golden Gate Bridge" because of its shape, but also because it is painted yellow. As you cross the bridge into Beaver, look to your right. You'll see the remnants of a railroad trestle bridge crossing the lake. It has its own claim to fame, as it was used in the filming of the miniseries *The Blue and the Gray.* You can also reach these two bridges by driving 4.5 miles back from the US 62/Highway 187 junction after you have visited these interesting places.

Outside Eureka Springs on US 62 West, down a wooded trail, stands **Thorncrown Chapel,** a tall and glittering glass chapel tucked into the Ozarks woods. In May, when the spring canopy of leaves hasn't yet eclipsed the light, wildflowers carpet the forest floor. It is a peaceful spot, dedicated to God by a dreamer named Jim Reed and his wife, Dell, who hired E. Fay Jones, a nationally honored and recognized architect, to design the chapel of glass and two-by-fours that sits on 8 acres of woods. The chapel, surrounded by blue sky and filled with sunlight, is just 60 feet long, 24 feet wide, and 48 feet tall, with 11 rows of bench seats. It holds only about a hundred people.

Where Shoes Come From

Tarantulas and armadillos dot Highway 187, but an even more interesting thing will appear along the roadway as you swing by Inspiration Point. Be sure to watch for the **Shoe Tree.** You will see brake lights come on and cars backing up and turning around. This huge tree has somehow grown thousands of shoes, boots, sneakers, slippers, and roller skates. It gets heavier each year with the strange crop. There are no signs leading up to it and no gift shop under it. It is one of nature's mysteries. So when the kids ask, "Mom and Dad, where do shoes come from?" you can take them here and show them one of the wonders of nature. It is an ever-bearing, year-round crop—not at all seasonal. But you have to watch for it, or you will drive right on by.

The base was made from the roughly cut sandstone of the surrounding hills. To avoid using building materials too large to carry down the path, cross-braced, hand-rubbed timbers 2 by 4 feet and 2 by 6 feet and in-filled with glass were used. The more than 6,000 square feet of glass in the walls and central skylight reflect the sunlight in patterns that change with the time and the seasons and let the chapel blend into surrounding timber as though it had grown there. It is called "Ozark Gothic"—Gothic in reverse, in that darkness becomes light. The chapel has seasonal hours: daily 9 a.m. to 5 p.m. Apr through Oct, closed Sat in Nov, and 11 a.m. to 4 p.m. Dec and Mar. It is closed in Jan and Feb. Sun services lasting 1 hour are at 9 and 11 a.m. Apr through Oct. In Nov and Dec, there is only the 11 a.m. service. The church is nondenominational, and the Reverend Doug Reed, son of the founders, is minister. Call (479) 253-7401 for information or visit thorn crown.com.

The area around Eureka has been an artists' colony since the 1930s and today is a fine arts center. Galleries are everywhere, and hundreds of artists live and work in the area.

No one around here laughs when you refer to opera in the Ozarks. They are not talking about Opry or country music at **Inspiration Point Fine Arts Colony** on US 62. This summer opera workshop consistently gives exceptional performances of such operas as *La Bohème* and *Die Fledermaus* (performed at the Walton Arts Center) in the 300-seat theater on Rock Candy Mountain. "This," says Jim Swiggart, former general director, "is

Trail of Tears

You will notice splashes of lavender paint on trees and fence posts along Highway 187. This marks the *Trail of Tears,* the path from Echota, Georgia, to Parkhill, Oklahoma (near Tahlequah), walked by 13,000 Cherokee who lived at Chota Valley for 500 years. They were a settled people who, in September 1838, were uprooted and forced to march to a new land to make way for white settlers. After a cruel winter march of privation and grievous loss, only 7,000 lived to see their new home. They camped at Blue Spring for several days, resting and waiting for stragglers to catch up. This portion of the trail is held as a memorial to a staunch and valiant people.

all about young people." The group has a long history of giving aspiring young artists the push needed to pursue a professional career (one young singer calls it "the boot camp of opera") and giving patrons and guests an outstanding musical experience. People from both coasts call and request seats, and many performances are sold out well in advance. The group works in repertory style, so there is a different opera every night. All seats are reserved, so be sure to call ahead. Performances are at 7:30 p.m. during the season from mid-June to mid-July. Call (479) 253-8595 for information and reservations. The colony also sponsors a barbershop quartet weekend, as well as blues and jazz festivals. Their website is opera.org.

Blue Spring Heritage Center at 1537 CR 210 (5.5 miles out of Eureka Springs off US 62) spans 33 acres of hardwood trees, flowers, and plants. The main floral season of this native garden begins in spring with displays of flowering bulbs followed by dogwood, redbud, and azaleas. Summertime is alive with stunning perennials and annuals native to the area. The fall brings a blaze of foliage along with chrysanthemums by the thousands. The garden is fitted with ramps as well as stairs, making it accessible to the physically handicapped, but to enjoy the best of the garden, wear comfortable shoes and take your time walking the trails.

The visitor center features a film of the area as well as artifacts from an archaeological dig. Other attractions include a tepee, and the kids can feed fish in the river. Hours are 9 a.m. to 6 p.m., and the center is open from Mar 15 to Thanksgiving. Admission is $9.75 for adults and $6.50 for ages 6 to 17; children under 6 are free. The Bluff Shelter is on the National Register of Historic Places. Two new gardens have recently opened in honor of the Native American tradition. Visit the Medicine Wheel Garden, a planting of healing herbs, and the Three Sisters Garden. There are also many beautiful spots for weddings. Visit the website at bluespringheritage.com or call (479) 253-9244 for more information.

Begin, if you are able, on the soft mulch path that descends the bluffs of the gardens on the series of stairways, allowing about 2 hours for the walk. The alternative route on raised wooden walkways is engineered for the handicapped and is good for the return trip up the bluffs for everyone.

At the foot of the stairs, you will see the Spring Lagoon, where the waters from Blue Spring mark the beginning of the White River. **Blue Spring** is the star of the show; it bubbles up 38 million gallons of water a day and is the natural source of the White River. It is a deep cobalt blue, but at times it appears as different shades of green. After heavy rains the surface water is picked up in local recharge areas, making Blue Spring brown for a couple of weeks.

The spring is dedicated to the Cherokee people who camped here along the Trail of Tears, but in 1971

trivia

The four divisions of the Ozark National Forest total more than a million acres in the Ozark and Boston Mountains of the northwest part of the state.

a University of Arkansas archaeological dig uncovered a great number of artifacts, some dating back to 8000 BC. The cliffs are marked with hieroglyphs (crude markings, not pictures) from 8000 BC to AD 1500 etched into the overhanging bluffs and show that Native Americans have lived near this water since prehistoric times.

During the Archaic period (810 to 500 BC), mobile hunters and gatherers depended on native plants and animals. During the Woodland era (500 BC to AD 900), the people here tended gardens and domesticated barley, sunflower, squash, and maize, and by the Mississippian era (AD 900 to 1541), they were agriculturists growing crops. Translations of the hieroglyphs appear near the crude markings.

Following the softly mulched path, you will pass through the Wild Flower Gardens, Meadow Gardens, and along the crushed limestone path to the dam. After crossing the dam (here is the archaeological dig), the

Rock Garden appears—an area simply planted in a rock garden created by nature.

At the end of the trail, the **Trading Post Gift Shop** is surrounded by benches where you can relax and enjoy the butterflies and hummingbirds. Call (479) 253-2126 for more information.

On a nice day look for the **Horizon Restaurant** just off Highway 187 at 304 Mundell Rd. Chef Nate Seymour offers a seasonal menu that includes steak, fish, vegetarian, and gluten-free choices. The open deck, where a cool breeze makes it comfortable, is the place to eat. You'll enjoy stunning views of Beaver Lake and a unique fine dining experience. The Horizon is open Wed through Sat 5 to 9 p.m.; call (479) 253-5525 for more information or visit horizoneurekasprings.com. To find the Horizon, follow US 62 West to Beaver Lake, then turn left again on Highway 187, then left on Mandell Road, and go 0.25 mile.

While you are near Beaver Lake, you might want to ride the **Belle of the Ozarks,** which departs from Rocky Branch Marina and covers miles of splendid shoreline and clear water. Cruise around a 200-acre island wildlife preserve (see deer swimming) and Ozark Bluff Dweller burial grounds. All of the rides are narrated, but the trip is especially fine when the leaves turn and in Jan when the annual Eagle Watch Weekend happens. Departures to view bald eagles in their natural habitat on the lake go out three times a day with expert guides to help spot eagles. Cruises are $22 for adults and $8.50 for children under the age of 12. Call (800) 552-3803 and visit estc.net/belle.

What to do with a lion cub that keeps growing beyond the "kitty, kitty" stage and begins wreaking havoc around the house? Well, rambunctious felines—some weighing more than 300 pounds—have a home here at **Turpentine Creek Wildlife Refuge.** Hilda Jackson and her daughter Tanya Smith call it a labor of love: a nonprofit home for unwanted or abused big cats. The ranch is 7 miles south of Eureka Springs on Highway 23 and is a USDA-licensed refuge for large carnivores. With 120 big cats, this is possibly the largest collection of these magnificent creatures open to the public. Saying "120 big cats" doesn't even begin to prepare you for the experience of actually seeing them.

When asked how it began, Hilda said simply, "We've always been pet owners," but this collection of felines is beyond that. Hilda traded a motorcycle for a lion cub named Bum, who was a house pet the first 300 pounds of his life. Bum liked to lie around and watch television. Then a woman showed up one day with a horse trailer full of big cats, and the Jacksons couldn't say no.

Tanya talks to people about dying breeds, such as the Siberian tiger and the Sumatran tiger, which is now extinct in the wild. Some of the cats are most unusual—a lion-tiger mix called a liger, for example. Many of the cats are from abusive backgrounds. They come in cowering, sometimes starving, often covered with sores. In time they settle in and lie in the sunshine eating chicken and becoming gentle. The cats make a "chuffing" sound, a sort of big-cat greeting. Tanya can walk up to any of the fences and a giant kitty will stroll over to rub against her, just like a house cat. But she emphasizes to the 2,500 schoolchildren who visit the ranch each year that these are not playthings. She shows them the cute, young tiger cubs, then shows them the mature Siberian who weighs more than 800 pounds and eats 20 to 40 pounds of raw meat every night. Although the love she feels for these cats seems to be returned by them—many turn their faces to her to be kissed— she always remembers they are wild animals and their moods may change suddenly. She takes no chances. Bum lived to be more than 20 years old, and Tanya says her father would often sleep in Bum's cage toward the end, he was so devoted to the cat.

Taking care of the cats is expensive, and it could not be done without dedicated volunteers, many of whom live on the property, and donors who provide chicken and vegetables whenever possible.

Lodgings are available on the site, too, at the **Suites at Turpentine Creek.** Seven suites are available—decorated in various safari themes—and are $150 per night, with a continental breakfast. **The Tree House Cabin** is another option. Located high in one of the property's oak trees, the cabin sleeps four, and one of the bedrooms looks right into a lion's den. The Tree House costs $150 per night, double occupancy. Additional guests are $20 per night. There are also RV and tent spots available for $25. These lodgings are at 239 Turpentine Creek Ln., and there is a website: turpentinecreek.org. Call (479) 253-5841 for information.

Because the meat bill around here is about $1,500 a day, donations from visitors are happily accepted. The refuge is open 9 a.m. to 5 p.m. in the winter and until 6 p.m. in the summer. The best time to get a good look is at feeding time, which is 4 p.m. in winter and 5 p.m. in the summer. Tours run daily on the hour 11 a.m. to 3 p.m. in the winter and until 4 p.m. in the summer. Tour tickets are $20 for adults, $10 for children age 4 to 12, seniors, and veterans. There is a shop to browse in, too.

Off US 62 north of Rogers, the National Park Service has rebuilt the historic Elkhorni Tavern on the eastern overlook of *Pea Ridge Battlefield* (giving a good view of the western portion of the battlefield) and has fixed up the battle site with a visitor center for history buffs. A taped slide show and lecture every half hour and a walk-through museum or a drive-through tour (accompanied by recorded messages) of the battlefield make it possible for visitors to get both the Yankee and the Rebel perspectives on one of the only major battles fought in the state—but it's the battle that saved Missouri for the Union. Admission to the battlefield is $5 per person, or $5 per motorcycle, or $10 per vehicle. The visitor center is open 8:30 a.m. to 4:30 p.m. daily. Call (479) 451-8122 for more information, or visit nps.gov/peri.

The second of architect E. Fay Jones's crystal chapels is in *Bella Vista.* It is a nondenominational chapel just off Highway 340, east of US 71. The *Mildred B. Cooper Memorial Chapel* has similar dimensions to those of the Thorncrown Chapel, 24 feet by 65 feet and 50 feet high, but this chapel uses steel, whereas Thorncrown is made of wood. The dominant pattern is curved, like a Gothic arch, rather than triangular, as is Thorncrown. It is open 9 a.m. to 5 p.m. 7 days a week; call (479) 855-6598 for more information.

Bentonville is south of Bella Vista on US 71. Bentonville's town square has what looks like a 1950s five-and-dime—it even has a red-and-white awning—but it is the *Wal-Mart Visitor Center,* at 105 North Main St. Inside is a tiny office with a low ceiling and a room the size of an elevator, with an upturned apple crate for a chair. Here Sam and Helen Walton did accounting with wooden pegs stuck in the wall for hanging receipts and invoices. It is the American Dream: a five-and-dime called Walton's that changed business in the US forever. It traces the phenomenal growth of the giant discount store chain—today's general store—from its beginning right through today. There are relics from such companies as Procter and Gamble, Johnson & Johnson, and Kimberly-Clark. This is a real "local boy makes good" story. At the time of his death in 1992, Sam Walton was one of the richest men in America. The center is open 8 a.m. to 9 p.m. Mon through Thurs, 8 a.m. to

10 p.m. Fri and Sat, and noon to 9 p.m. Sun. Call (479) 273-1329 for more information.

The square is the hub of the town, of course, and every other weekend beginning in April there is a farmers' market where you can pick your favorite fresh produce. This is a clean, lovely town, with many well-kept old houses. It is also the home of the annual Phillips Celebrity Golf Classic. Enjoy the camaraderie of the townsfolk at Cecil and Betty Turner's *Station Cafe* on the square at 111 North Main, where most everyone passes through at one time or another. Hours are 8 a.m. to 8 p.m. Mon through Sat. Call (479) 273-0553 for information.

Let's do a little sightseeing around Bentonville. Begin with the Italianate 3-story villa tower *Peel Mansion,* 400 South Walton Blvd. It is made of brick, embellished with stucco, trimmed in white, and topped with rose-colored roof tiles. A covered front porch wraps around the side, runs the length of the house, and is surrounded by flowers and plants commonly found in this country during the 1800s. This home was built in 1875 by Samuel West Peel, a Confederate colonel, Indian agent, attorney, and the first native-born Arkansan to serve in the US Congress. The 180-acre farm and apple orchard was known as The Oaks. A massive renovation program using local artisans and craftspeople has restored the home to its Victorian grandeur. The library has a rare Anglo-Japanese mantel. Gardening teams did months of detailed research to replicate the historic plantings in the five gardens surrounding the Peel home. One garden is filled with wildflowers; another has plants and flowers taken from the 1842 lists of a Fayetteville nurseryman. A pioneer garden has been added in recent years. Visitors enter the property through a log cabin that serves as a welcome center and gift shop. The cabin is a two-room structure that was dismantled log by log and moved from Brightwater to its current location. A map discovered in an attic in California, drawn by a Civil War army officer during the Battle of Pea Ridge, depicts the cabin as early as 1862. The Peel Mansion and Garden is open Tues through Sat 10 a.m. to 3 p.m. Admission is $5 for adults and $2 for children age 6 to12. In Dec the home is decorated for Victorian Christmas. For more information call (479) 273-9664 or visit peelcompton.org. You don't even need a ticket to take advantage of the archival library in the carriage house.

When it's time to eat, *Fred's Hickory Inn,* at 1502 North Walton Blvd., Bentonville, is the place to try if you like lots of noise and table-hopping.

Fred and Lou Gaye feature Italian recipes handed down in Lou's family. Hickory-pit barbecue was Fred's passion, and so with fine seasoning and quality meat he went into the business. Silver-haired Fred has lots of regulars who call if they are not coming in. He loves to tell jokes, and his place is usually filled. Call (479) 273-3303 for information or reservations. Hours are 11 a.m. to 10 p.m. Mon through Sat.

Even though the **Crystal Bridges Museum of American Art** just opened in 2011, it appears to have inhabited the valley it is nestled in for a very long time. Designed by architect Moshe Safdie, and built by Wal-Mart heir Alice Walton, the museum houses sculpture and paintings that rotate in an ever-changing display. There is a gallery for "visiting" exhibits as well. You can eat lunch or just have a drink at the full-service restaurant and bar, Eleven. One of the pavilions houses the museum gift shop.

The grounds of the museum are just as beautiful as the works you'll find on the inside. There are over 3 miles of trails meandering through the 120 acres that surround the main museum buildings. Here you will find more sculpture, wildflowers, and several art installations intended to connect visitors with nature. One of them, *Skyspace*, designed by world-renowned artist James Turrell, is located where two trails intersect. Step inside, and you will find yourself in a circular stone room that serves as a viewing chamber for the sky. A round oculus in the roof allows contemplation of the heavens at any time, but sunrise and sunset is when the magic really happens. A programmed LED light display begins inside the *Skyspace*. These colors on the ceiling of the room change visitors' perception of the color of the sky viewed through the oculus.

The museum offers year-round programming for all ages, including lectures, art-making workshops, films, gallery talks, and special events. Hours are Mon and Thurs 11 a.m. to 6 p.m., Wed and Fri 11 a.m. to 9 p.m., and Sat and Sun 10 a.m. to 6 p.m. The museum is closed Tues. Trails and grounds are open from sunrise to sunset daily. The *Skyspace* is open for viewing every evening for the sunset display, and one morning a month for the sunrise display. There is no admission to visit the museum, although there are fees to view some special exhibits and for some programs. You can find the museum and all its treasures at 600 Museum Way in Bentonville. For more information, call (479) 418-5700, or visit crystalbridges.org.

If you stay on US 71, you will be in the Rogers area. And, no, **Rogers** wasn't named for Will Rogers, although Will Rogers was married to a local woman (Betty Blake) here in 1906. The **Rogers Historical Museum**, at 322 South 2nd St., was formerly the Victorian 1895 Hawkins House. Guides will give you a taste of the history of the area with old photos, handmade furnishings, and forgotten tools. A barbershop, bank, and dry goods store are assembled in great detail, right down to the clipped hair on the floor by the broom. The "Attic" is stocked with antique toys, clothes, and tools to peruse. Rogers was a boomtown in the 1880s, when the railroad established a depot and apple orchards began to be planted; this was called the "Land of the Big Red Apple." A red Frisco caboose is parked 4 blocks from the museum for children to climb aboard. Hours are 10 a.m. to 5 p.m. Mon through Sat. Call (479) 621-1154, or visit rogersarkansas.com/museum.

The **Rogers Daisy Air Gun Museum**, 202 West Walnut, has hundreds of interesting displays on the history of these popular toys beginning in the late 1800s. The company relocated to Rogers in 1958, and the corporate headquarters are still around, although the air guns are no longer manufactured here. The museum is open 6 days a week 9 a.m. to 5 p.m. Call them at (479) 986-6873, or check out daisymuseum.com.

Downtown Rogers has been restored to what it was when the town was young. Returning to Rogers and looking for that old soda fountain on 1st Street that you remember will lead you now to **The Rabbit's Lair** at that address, 116 South 1st St. in Historic Downtown Rogers. This grand old building—the old Applegate Drug Store with its original marble soda fountain—is as it was both inside and out. Now, though, the oak woodwork, glass shelves, and a marble soda fountain are covered in wide variety of fabric, wool, yarn, stitchery supplies, and more—it is a quilter and crafter's heaven. The building was constructed of marble from nearby Carthage, Missouri. The shop contains solid mahogany fixtures, and the marble soda fountain has a mahogany back bar and room divider that offers a fine example of the cabinetmaker's craft of the time. A large mahogany clock with brass movement hangs to your left as you enter the store; its enamel face has kept time since 1907. The tile floor and pressed-tin ceiling tiles are original. The porcelain drawer pulls are inscribed with the names of various drugs—in Latin—and pharmaceutical supplies. (If you pull one open today, it will likely be full of fabric.) The Rabbit's Lair also offers classes in sewing, crochet, quilting, and more for beginners as well as more experienced folks. For more information call (479) 636-3385 or visit therabbitslair.com. The shop is open 9 a.m. to 5 p.m. Mon through Fri and until 3 p.m. on Sat.

Poor Richard's Art, at 101 West Walnut, is another downtown point of interest. The gallery bills itself as the "Northwest Arkansas Premier Art Collective," and it surely deserves the title as it showcases the work of over 45 artists. In fact, the artists volunteer their time to keep the gallery open and running, so you'll have the opportunity to meet the folks behind the art. Paintings, jewelry, mission furniture, photography, fused and stained glass, wood turning, fiber, and polymer clay are all on the list of what you might see when you visit. You can check out the website at poorrichardsart.com to see examples of each artist's work. Gallery hours are Mon through Fri, 9:30 a.m. to 5:30 p.m. and Sat 9:30 a.m. to 4 p.m. Call (479) 636-0417 for more information.

The *Iron Horse Coffee Company,* at 220 South 1st St., is open Mon through Fri 6:30 a.m. until 9 p.m., Sat 8 a.m. to 9 p.m., and Sun 8 a.m. to 5 p.m. This locally owned shop serves coffee, tea, and frozen drinks as well as sandwiches and a wide selection of desserts. Try their signature sandwich, the Numan, which comes in four different variations. Call (479) 631-9977 or visit ironhorsecoffee.com.

Local legend *Smokin' Joe's Ribhouse,* at 803 W. Poplar, (479) 621-0181, is the place to go for perfectly smoked fall-off-the-bone ribs or a giant chicken-fried steak with real mashed potatoes and excellent creamy white gravy, Smokin' Joe's is the stop for delicious down-home dining at a reasonable price. Hours are Sun through Thurs 10:45 a.m. to 9 p.m. and Fri and Sat 10:45 a.m. to 9:30 p.m. You can visit their website at smokinjoes ribhouse.net.

War Eagle is the site of the huge *War Eagle Fair,* 11045 War Eagle Rd. (crossroads of Highway 12 and Highway 303)—a 4-day event that brings thousands of visitors each May and Oct to see handmade, one-of-a-kind Ozarks crafts in tents covering acres of ground. The fair always

trivia

Because of the large crowds drawn by the War Eagle Fair in the fall, other fairs are held at the same time, and in order to take advantage of the traffic, many handcrafted items are displayed on porches, antiques placed in yards, and quilts hung on clotheslines. The area becomes a shopper's dream.

begins on the first Fri in May and the third Thurs in Oct. Across a 1-lane rusty steel bridge (with a 2-ton-limit sign), the War Eagle Mill Arts and Crafts Fair is on the mill side of the river, and what seems to be more than 2 tons of traffic and pedestrians flows back and forth. Call (479) 789-5343 for information.

War Eagle Mill is a reproduction of an 1873 gristmill, powered by the War Eagle River, with three sets of buhr stones and an 18-foot redwood

War Eagle Tales

War Eagle Mill is well known around these parts. It's a bit out of the way, but the path is well beaten because of the annual crafts fairs held here. We went to War Eagle during the off-season, which is the best time to visit most of Arkansas's attractions.

I was fascinated with the products of the mill: cracked wheat and seven grains of flour to give a crunchy texture to breads; pastry flour, which is low in gluten to make a delicate, flaky crust; and, of course, bread flour, which is higher in gluten to allow bread to rise up high and proud. I love to bake, as you may have gathered. Since most of the products will keep in the freezer for a year or so, my poor husband found himself hauling 20-pound bags of various grains to our car. There was one product with which I was not familiar: yellow corn grits. I am not a Yankee, being from Missouri's southern Ozarks, and grits are not commonly served in Kansas City, so I had never seen yellow grits. So I bought a 5-pound bag.

Well, I loved those grits. They had texture—not all cream-of-wheaty like white grits—flavor, and color. I made cheese-grits casseroles and fried patties for breakfast or just enjoyed a hot bowl with butter in the morning or late at night. They were gone as fast as a greyhound after a rabbit, and I yearned for more. I searched the War Eagle catalog for yellow corn grits, to no avail. I assumed they quit making them and sadly returned to white grits.

Two years later we returned to War Eagle Mill, and I once again searched for yellow corn grits. I read every package on the shelves and was now certain they had stopped making my favorite food. I approached a woman working behind the counter and asked her about it.

"Oh," she said, "They're right ova' there," pointing to a shelf I had just searched. I looked again. All I could find was a package of something called Yankee Grits. "That's it, honey," she said.

"Why," I asked, "do they call it Yankee Grits?"

"Well," she drawled, looking me dead in the eye, "'cause they're yellow."

undershot waterwheel. First built in 1830, the mill washed away in 1848. The second mill was burned by order of a Confederate general to prevent the Union army's using it. This undershot waterwheel is the only one of its kind still operating. Inside is War Eagle

Mercantile, an old-fashioned general store with all manner of jams, honey, herbs, mixes, rugs, toys, clothing, pottery, and dozens of other things. The working water powered gristmill is still making buhr stone-ground cornmeal, whole-wheat flour, rye flour, and yellow corn grits.

In the same building the **Bean Palace Lunchroom** serves War Eagle buckwheat waffles and biscuits and sausage gravy for breakfast. For lunch there are always beans and corn bread, smoked ham and turkey, and home-baked cakes, tarts, and cookies—all with apple cider and all made right there at the mill. The Bean Palace is open 7 days a week for breakfast 8:30 a.m. to 11 a.m., lunch 11 a.m. to 4 p.m., and tea and dessert 4 p.m. to 5 p.m. The mill is open 7 days a week 8:30 a.m. to 5 p.m., Mar through Dec. It is closed in Jan, and in Feb it is open Fri through Sun only. Take CR 98 from Highway 12, or call (479) 789-5343. The War Eagle website is at wareaglemill.com.

Traveling south on US 71 makes it easy to detour over to **Tontitown** on US 412 West. This is an Italian community separated from nearby Fayetteville by vineyards. Settled in 1898 by Father Bandini, Tontitown was named after the first Italian to explore the state, Henri de Tonti. The neat white **Tontitown Historical Museum,** on US 412 West, features an early grape press and wine bottling and spaghetti machines. It is open June through Oct, Sat and Sun 1 to 4 p.m. or by appointment. The museum tells the story of the settlement of the town (for example, a huge churn that stumped the Smithsonian and an antique pipe organ that could be electronic or manual). Call (479) 361-2700 for information or visit tontitown.com/museum.

To get the true feeling of the community, try to be there for the **Tontitown Grape Festival**. It has been happening annually for over 115 years and is one of the state's oldest continual festivals. Held the first weekend in Aug, the festival features homemade spaghetti and sauce, a pageant, a fun run, and of course, grape stomping. It is held at the St. Joseph's Church and school that Father Bandini founded. For more information, visit tontitown grapefestival.com.

There are three old Italian restaurants in town. **Mama Z's Cafe** has been around for years. The original Mama, Edna Zubo, left her daughter, Julie Bowling, to make homemade pastas just like in the old country. This relaxed family restaurant turns out great Italian food, freshly baked bread, and tops it off with homemade pies and cobblers Tues through Sat 7 a.m. to 2 p.m. and 5 to 9 p.m. It is about 2.5 miles west of US 71 Bypass on US 412 West. Call (479) 361-2750 for information.

The **Venesian Inn**, at 582 Henri de Tonti, is owned by Johnny and Linda Mhoon and has been here since 1947, in the same brick building in which it began. It is always busy, but the service is immediate—the salad (just lettuce covered with a strong garlic and oil dressing that everyone seems to love) is brought right away; fresh warm bread served with honey, basic Italian fare (spaghetti or ravioli), and chicken or steak entrees follow. The restaurant is open for lunch Mon through Fri 11 a.m. to 2 p.m. and for dinner Tues through Thurs 5 to 9 p.m. and Fri and Sat 4 to 9 p.m. Call (479) 361-2562 for information or visit thevenisianinn.com.

The third Italian restaurant in the area is quite different. Tablecloths, soft lighting, and a good wine list make **Mary Maestri's**, on the other side of Highway 540 at 669 E. Robinson, more upscale. A more complete selection of homemade pastas and sauces, including excellent lasagna and tortellini, join Italian entrees like chicken piccata (a favorite—cooked on the grill with lemon butter), the best steaks in the region, and, of course, homemade spumoni, pies, and New York cheesecake for dessert. Owner Daniel Maestri is Mary's grandson, and the restaurant and its traditions have been here for about 70 years, since a poor grape harvest left Aldo and Mary Maestri looking for ways to increase their income. Mary, using her mother-in-law's spaghetti sauce, opened a restaurant in their home, and the place was such a hit that more and more tables were squeezed in. At one point even the beds were used as chairs, with small tables between them, and when that wasn't enough, customers often used their laps as tables. The fried chicken and spaghetti dinner was the favorite and still is. All the spaghetti you want with any entree is still traditional, so you will never leave hungry. Hours are 5 to 9 p.m. Tues through Thurs and 5 to 9:30 p.m. Fri and Sat. Call (479) 756-1441 for information or visit marymaestris.com.

Yesteryears Antiques Mall at 548 Henri de Tonti Blvd., is considered the largest antiques mall in the state. It is open 10 a.m. to 5 p.m. Mon through Sat and noon to 6 p.m. Sun. Call (479) 361-5747.

Stay on US 412 west of Tontitown to the Oklahoma border, where Sugar Creek flows through the town of **Siloam Springs.** The 100-year-old town grew up around mountain springs. Restored Victorian homes and buildings dot the place, which is filled with art galleries, crafts shops, and picture-book parks. It is the home of John Brown University and the Sager Creek Arts Center for the performing arts.

North of Siloam Springs on Highway 59 is the town of **Gentry.** Here, you'll find an interesting attraction—the **Wild Wilderness Drive-Through Safari.** There is a 4-mile drive-through trail on the 400-acre park, plus petting parks and walk-through areas for interaction with the animals, which include big cats, foxes, wolves, monkeys, hippos, bears, kangaroos, zebras, and much more. In warmer months, you can even ride a camel (but you'll have to use your own car for the drive-through part of the visit). Hours are 9 a.m. to 5 p.m. daily, but the staff recommends visiting between 10 a.m. and 3 p.m. to see the animals in action. Admission is $10 for adults age 13 and up, and $8 for children age 3 to 12. Don't forget to bring cash, because they do not accept debit or credit cards. There is a snack bar, but you can also bring a lunch to eat at the picnic tables so that you can make a day of it. The safari is at 20923 Safari Rd. in Gentry. Call (479) 736-8383 for more information or visit wildwildernessdrivethroughsafari.com.

Southwest of Fayetteville off of Highway 62 is one of the nation's most intact Civil War battlefields, **Prairie Grove Battlefield State Park.** On December 7, 1862, the Confederate and Union armies fought a battle here that resulted in about 2,700 casualties. It was the last major Civil War engagement in northwest Arkansas. Today you can walk the 1-mile Battlefield Trail and motor along the park's 5-mile Driving Tour. The Ozark village has historic structures that you can tour. Tour rates are $5 for adults, $3 for children age 6 to 12, or $15 for a family pass. The visitor's center is Hindman Hall. Here, interactive exhibits detail the Battle of Prairie Grove. In December of even-numbered years, Arkansas's largest battle reenactment is held here. The park is open 8 a.m. to 5 p.m. daily. For more information, call (479) 846-2990 or visit arkansasstateparks.com/prairiegrovebattlefield.

Springdale is the home of Tyson Foods, and driving on US 71 behind trucks filled with chicken crates feels like riding in a ticker-tape parade of chicken feathers. If all those flying feathers put you in the mood for a good chicken dinner, stop in at **AQ's Chicken House,** 1207 North Thompson, about 2 miles north of town on US 71. AQ's is in a lovely Victorian ginger-bread house and has been serving up the best batter-dipped chicken since the 1940s. They are open 7 days a week beginning at 11 a.m. and closing at 8:30 p.m. Call (479) 751-4633 or visit aqchickenhouse.net.

While you are in Springdale, you might want to visit the **Shiloh Museum,** at 118 West Johnson Ave., and see the history of families like the Tysons and Waltons. But most of the museum's space is dedicated to the people who turned the northwest wilderness into a state. The walls and furnishings from the 1843 cabin of Elizabeth McGarrah and the collected works of more than 130 area photographers, as well as more than 50,000 tintypes, prints, postcards, and stereo cards, are displayed here. The museum is open 10 a.m. to 5 p.m. Mon through Sat year-round. There is no admission charge. Call (479) 750-8165 for information, or visit online at shilohmuseum.org.

The **Arkansas and Missouri Railroad** operates from the Springdale depot, which is based on the design of the city's original depot. The train leaves at 8 a.m. for an all-day adventure. Between two and five trains a week make the trip, and the bright-red locomotive pulls as many of the turn-of-the-20th-century mahogany-lined and perfectly restored passenger cars as required from Apr to the last weekend of Oct.

Passengers travel through the most rugged portion of the Ozarks—a 7-mile ride from Winslow, through the 1,700-foot Winslow tunnel, and across the three highest trestles on the line. After the 117-foot-tall trestle, the trains begin a series of steep grades and end in the town of Van Buren, where a 3-hour layover gives you time to browse the historic town or take a ride on the **Frontier Belle** riverboat. During the layover the train

trivia

The town of Winslow was made famous in 1971 when *Smoke in the Wind*, a Civil War movie starring Walter Brennan, was filmed here. Churches and stores built almost 100 years ago can still be found in Winslow.

makes a 3-hour, nonstop trip to Winslow. The cost of the trips is reasonable. Call (479) 725-4017 or (800) 687-8600 for reservations. You can also find fare information at amrailroad.com.

The Rodeo of the Ozarks has been putting on events in Springdale since 1944. You'd expect to find bull riding and barrel racing here, and you will, but depending on your timing, you might be able to catch a demolition derby (with cars, not horses) or a monster truck rally. The kids can don padded vests and helmets to try their hand at mutton bustin', which is essentially a contest to see who can ride a sheep for the longest period of time. There are also cowboy quick draw competitions and barbecue cook-offs. The "season" for all this entertainment runs Apr through Oct. Check the website at rodeooftheozarks.org for a calendar of events, or call (877) 927-6336. You can find the Rodeo of the Ozarks at Parsons Stadium, 1423 E. Emma, Springdale.

Highway 23—from Highway 16 to I-40—leads into **Fayetteville** and is known as "The Pig Trail" to Razorback fans who travel north through a canopy of forest toward Fayetteville for home games. In Fayetteville you can wine and dine and shop till you drop and still be only minutes away from the unspoiled mountains, lakes, and streams of the surrounding countryside. It is home to the state's largest university, the **University of Arkansas.** Old Main, the most famous building on campus, rises on a hill with its massive redbrick walls and mansard roof. Its twin towers stand watch over the campus and the Razorbacks who call it home. You will probably see groups of people walking along looking at their feet near Old Main, because the names of every graduate since 1876 are etched into the sidewalks radiating out from the famous old building. You can choose an atmosphere to suit your whimsy: the laid-back, anything-goes attitude on Dickson Street; the beer-and-boots cowboy scene south of downtown; several college hot spots that mix hard rock with huge dance spaces; the disco crowd on the square; and a couple of fine listening clubs for the quieter set.

If you are a sports fan, while you are strolling the campus you might want to duck into the **Tommy Boyer Hall of Champions,** in Bud Walton

trivia

Fayetteville was on the Butterfield stage route and was developed early as an important trade center.

Arena at 1207 LeRoy Pond. Glass cases hold glittering trophies and stories of athletes' performances. There are interactive stations in each section and touch-screen displays to help you relive great seasons. Exhibits show off star performers in many sports: Miller Barber in golf, Kevin McReynolds in baseball, and Mike Conley in track, as well as a basketball section devoted to Coach Nolan Richardson's 1994 NCAA championship team. Be sure to head over to the *Hog Heaven Gift Shop* to the left of the exhibit where you can purchase all sorts of Razorback souvenirs. The *Jerry Jones and Jim Lindsey Hall of Champions Museum* in the Frank Broyles Center

trivia

Driving south from Fayetteville along Scenic Highway 71, the signs read "Very Crooked and Steep," an accurate description. The trip is almost worth ruining your transmission. You will find old cemeteries, abandoned log cabins, and an ostrich farm.

covers the history of Razorbacks football. Hours for both halls are 8 a.m. to 5 p.m. Mon through Fri. The admission is free. Call (479) 575-8618 for more information.

The *Inn at Carnall Hall* provides a unique lodging and dining experience right on the university campus. Carnall Hall was originally built to be a women's dormitory in the early 1900s, which makes each of its rooms a bit different from the next. Many feature sitting areas and workstations. The building was named after a distinguished associate professor of English and modern languages, Miss Ella Howison Carnall, who was the first female faculty at University of Arkansas. For more information on this historic inn, visit the website at innatcarnallhall.com or call (479) 582-0400. The inn is at 465 North Arkansas Ave. and is within walking distance of Dickson Street and the square.

Ella's Restaurant, on-site at the Inn at Carnall Hall, provides a fine dining experience featuring nouveau cuisine made from regionally grown and seasonal ingredients. It is open for breakfast Mon through Fri 7 a.m. to 10 a.m. and Sat and Sun 7 a.m. to 11 a.m. Lunch is Mon through Sat 11 a.m. to 2 p.m. with a Sun brunch at those same hours. Dinner is Mon through Sat 5 p.m. to 10 p.m. Locals give rave reviews for all of these meals, plus cheese and wine tastings. You can see Chef Michael Wilson's menus at ellasrestaurant.com, or give them a call at (479) 582-1400 to make a reservation.

The Handmade Market, at 1504 North College Ave., is where Mim Wynne has the most eclectic shop you will ever find. This spot, just off the square, is filled with very fine-quality handmade European, Japanese, and American soaps. There is jewelry produced by craftspeople across the country and other gift items as unique as cotton or canvas couch throws, handmade ceramics, tea and teapots, and even exotic bugs. Yes, bugs. You just have to come in and see for yourself. Gifts you won't find anywhere else and things you want for yourself are all here *and* Mim's own handwoven rugs, which are sold around the world and have been featured on the cover of the Neiman Marcus catalog. Hours are Mon through Sat 10 a.m. to 6 p.m. Call (479) 582-5731 or visit ourhandmademarket.com for more information.

If eating's your thing, Fayetteville is your town. Colorful taverns and restaurants surround the campus, and there's even an old-fashioned farmers' market every Tues, Thurs, and Sat morning May through Oct, 7 a.m. to 1 p.m., on the vibrant town square that's alive with flowers and trees, produce, and crafts. A leisurely walk through the Washington-Willow historic district is a fine way to spend some time, get some exercise, and see sensational old homes. The opportunity to browse through the farmers' market and the stores along the downtown square or catch the scenic view from Mount Sequoyah makes the town a quiet oasis. You can attend a concert at the Walton Arts Center or take home a treat from the Ozark Mountain Smokehouse.

The first local brewery and pub in the northwest part of the state is the *Hog Haus Brewing Company* at 430 West Dickson St. A half-dozen varieties of beer, brewed on the premises, are available to try.

The old buildings have held businesses since 1880. The pub serves traditional food, such as bratwurst, pizza, chili (made with their own beer), and sandwiches, as well as an eclectic mix of pastas, salads, and desserts.

The restaurant's heavy post-and-beam construction is similar to the timber framing of 18th-century New England barns, using massive 12-inch beams and wooden dowels. Beer styles from all over the world—Czech Bud and German Koenig and Jeverpils—can be brewed in the stainless steel tanks visible from the glass-walled elevator carrying people to the second-floor restaurant. It is open Sun through Thurs 11 a.m. until 10 p.m. and Fri and Sat 11 a.m. until 11 p.m. Call (479) 521-2739 for information or visit hoghaus.com.

In 1999 interior designer Chris Bronson joined forces with high school French teacher Renee Hunt and began traveling to France and throughout Europe to buy antiques for their shop, **French Quarters Antiques** at 11 North Block Ave. They are a good team. Renee's fluency in the language and Chris's eye for design and 20 years of experience allow them to be direct importers of fine French antique furniture and accessories, all personally selected from Paris to Provence.

Scenes from a French village cover the walls, and the atmosphere is perfect to show off the cafe umbrellas, *Provençal pots de confit* (chamber pots), and marble-top tables. Hand-carved armoires stand by custom-made chairs crafted in a family-owned workshop in France. From small items—a collection of majolica plates or dainty Limoges boxes—to large items like a handpainted fountain or a pair of iron gates, you can take things home in a bag or a truck. There is a great selection of antique French baskets, including wine presentation baskets, trunks both small and large, market baskets, laundry baskets, baguette baskets, and grape gathering baskets used in the Burgundy region of France. Their husbands, Terry Hunt and Storm Carr, are also partners in the venture. You can find great buys here at a fraction of the cost of big-city antiques shops. Call (479) 443-3355 for hours, or shop online at french-quarters.com.

Inn at the Mill, between Fayetteville and Springdale at 3906 Johnson Mill Blvd. (the Johnson exit off US 71/62), is only minutes outside of the city but a world away. You are greeted with coffee, tea, or wine (sometimes hot apple cider). A complimentary continental breakfast is served in your room, in the parlor of the historic mill, or on the deck overlooking the pond and waterwheel. The comfort of a country inn with the amenities of a first-class hotel—turndown service and a cookie by your bed—makes this place most pleasurable. Rates are $99 to $229. Call (479) 443-1800 for information. Visit online at innatthemill.com. The cherry on this sundae is the restaurant next door.

The "James" of **James at the Mill,** is Chef Miles G. James, who serves Ozark plateau cuisine next to the beautiful spring-fed waterwheel in the glass-enclosed restaurant. The entrees are unusual and unbelievably good: try the citrus marinated and hickory grilled pork tenderloin ($26) or dry onion–crusted chicken ($19). An excellent wine list, cited by *Wine Spectator* (the only one in Arkansas to receive that distinction), accompanies the menu. The wine list contains some unusual liquors as well. The white chocolate crème brûlée with fresh fruit and espresso anglaise is the best thing on the dessert menu. Call (479) 443-1400 for reservations. Hours are Mon through Sat 5 to 10 p.m. It is closed on Sun. To get a sneak peak at the full menu, visit jamesatthemill.com.

If you are driving along US 62, at a mile west of its intersection with US 71 in Fayetteville, you can probably follow your sniffer to the *Ozark Mountain Smokehouse,* 1725 Smokehouse Rd., in a stone-and-wooden barn tucked into the base of Mt. Kessler. Free tours are offered 9 a.m. until 4 p.m. Mon through Sat. Apron-clad guides put a paper hat on your head and lead you into the smokehouse. Through picture windows you can watch the meats and cheeses being cured and flavored with mixtures of herbs and spices. The pungent, sweet aroma of smoke coming from four dark smoking chambers, where racks of hams and turkeys hang, will stir the desire for a taste—and you can taste the smoked products (and fruit preserves) as well. Owner Frank Sharp has come a long way from the barn his father, Roy, burned down nearly 50 years ago while perfecting the art of smoking. It's not fancy—wooden tables and stone floor and walls—but it's comfortable, so stay for lunch. Call (800) 643-3437 or (479) 267-3339 for information.

The historic district at Washington and Willow Streets between Dickson and Davidson is filled with Victorian mansions and large shade trees. Tours of the district and of Headquarters House, an 1853 frame structure that served both sides during the Civil War, along with many of the town's historic homes, are included on a walking tour. A tour can be arranged through the *Washington County Historical Society*, 118 Dickson St., Fayetteville; (479) 521-2970.

The *Arkansas Air and Military Museum,* located in the vast, all-wood White Hangar of Fayetteville's Drake Field on US 71 South (4290 South School), houses everything from famous racing planes of the 1920s and '30s to an early airliner. Music of the 1940s plays in the hangar to help you drift back in time. But this is no ordinary museum; here the colorful displays take off and soar. The planes are maintained and licensed and can be seen in the air, earning the name "The Museum That Flies." There are open-cockpit biplanes and closed-cabin monoplanes all up, up, and away at various times. The volunteers who run the museum 10 a.m. to 4:30 p.m. Sun through Fri and 10 a.m. to 4:30 p.m. Sat are lifelong pilots and mechanics whose love of airplanes and sense of humor keep the hangar full of life. A free movie, *Aviation Oddities,* shows many of the bizarre contraptions people have built to try their wings. You can also watch antique airplanes being restored in the museum's restoration shop. Admission is $10 for adults, $9 for military, $5 for children over 6, or you can get a family pass for two adults and two kids for $20. A gift shop sells model airplanes and T-shirts. Call (479) 521-4947 for information. The website is arkansasairand military.com.

The house at 930 West Clinton Dr. is where Bill and Hillary Clinton lived while they taught at the University of Arkansas Law School in Fayetteville. The couple was married in their home with just a few close friends. Now it is the **Clinton House Museum.** You can visit the living room where they were married, see a replica of Hillary's wedding dress, learn more about their early political careers, and tour the garden which features flowers dedicated to several different first ladies. Hours are Mon through Sat 8:30 a.m. to 4:30 p.m. Admission is $8 per person. Call (877) BIL-N-HIL or visit clintonmuseum.org for more information.

Highway 16 between the "Pig Trail" and Fayetteville shows the beauty of the prairies and woodlands colored by the wildflowers that grow in the hollows and along the creeks. Digging these plants is not encouraged because of the delicate balance of the ecology.

The **Holland Wildflower Farm,** at 290 O'Neal Ln., **Elkins,** on Highway 16, is where Bob and Julie Holland have another way to fill your yard—with the reds of cardinal flowers, the blue of phlox, the purple of coneflower, or the dramatic burst of color of the orange butterfly weed. The farm offers wildflower seeds and native plants. A visit to the farm is like a nature walk, abloom with native color. The gardens and flower beds, together with the fields of wildflowers and native plants, offer wild columbines, irises, and other native perennials—all nursery propagated. Bob has a degree in wildlife research and plant pathology, Julie is a biologist, and the two have plenty of helpful advice to offer on how to raise the plants you select. If you plan to visit, call ahead for an appointment (479-643-2622). They have no retail help on the property. The farm is 0.5 mile from Highway 16 off 1st Street. All sales are through their website at hwildflower.com.

You can find your Bluebird of Happiness at **Terra Studios,** 12103 Hazel Valley Rd., 16 miles southeast of Fayetteville on Highway 16. The newest thing at Terra Studios is glassblowing. You can watch the famous little glass bluebirds being made by skilled glass craftspeople—or learn to blow glass yourself. There is a large stoneware pottery showroom, too. Rita Ward's clay-sculptured "Terrans," tiny elf-like creatures who live at Terra, are popular with collectors of gnomes and such, and John Ward's unusual large urns are displayed out front. Classes in pottery are also available. The Ward family has produced elegance everywhere. This is one of the few working family studios in the nation. It has two complete pottery studios and a 5,000-square-foot hot-glass studio. The lovely grounds include a picnic area under the cedars, an arched bridge, and a garden; visitors picnic in the hand-built clay gazebo beyond the arched bridge. The facility is open 7 days a week 10 a.m. to 5 p.m. Call (800) 255-8995, or visit terrastudios.com.

An absolute *must* if you really want to get the feel of the Ozarks is the **Little O' Opery** in downtown **West Fork.** Dan Wiethop celebrates genuine Ozark homegrown music every Sat night beginning at 7 p.m. It is the finest collection of real Ozark music anywhere, performed by real Ozark folks— a nonprofit gathering of musicians offering "good, honest, natural music" grown on the banks of the West Fork of the White River. The staff band is made up of an acoustic flattop guitar, steel guitar, fiddle, bass, and drums, and it backs up singers from around the Ozarks. Call (479) 839-2992 for information or visit littleoprey.org.

West Fork is also home to one of the Arkansas State Park system's gems—**Devil's Den State Park.** Nestled deep in Lee Creek Valley and surrounded by the Ozark National Forest, Devil's Den provides a bevy of outdoor activities as well as a chance to experience the legacy of the Civilian Conservation Corps (CCC). The park is a designated National Historic District and holds what has been called the most complete example of CCC park architecture.

Rental canoes and pedal boats are available if you want to explore Lake Devil, formed by a CCC-built natural stone dam. There's also plenty of trails for hiking, backpacking, and mountain biking. The park provides guided hikes at various times throughout the week, and you can also go on a scavenger hunt through the park using a GPS unit or smartphone. Family-friendly programs and activities are scheduled daily during summer and on weekends in spring and fall.

Seventeen fully-equipped cabins featuring kitchens and fireplaces are available throughout the year. These cabins were built by the CCC using wood and stone taken right from the Lee Creek Valley. There's a park cafe, convenience store, and swimming pool (both open in summer only) near the lake.

To reach Devil's Den State Park, travel 8 miles south of Fayetteville on I-540 to West Fork, then go 17 miles southwest on AR 170. For more information, call (479) 761-3325 or visit arkansasstateparks.com/devilsden.

More Places to Stay in Northwest Arkansas

BELLA VISTA

Inn at Bella Vista
1 Chelsea Rd.
(479) 876-5645
iabv.com
Moderate

BENTONVILLE

Holiday Inn Express
2205 SE Walton Blvd.
(479) 271-2222
Inexpensive

EUREKA SPRINGS

Best Western
US 62 & Highway 23
(479) 253-9551
eurekabw.com
Inexpensive

FAYETTEVILLE

Holiday Inn Express
1251 North Shiloh Dr.
(479) 444-6006
Inexpensive

MOUNTAIN HOME

Comfort Inn
1031 Highland Circle
(870) 424-9000
Inexpensive

SILOAM SPRINGS

Hampton Inn
2171 Ravenwood Plaza
(479) 215-1000
Inexpensive

SPRINGDALE

Travel Lodge
1394 West Sunset
(479) 751-3100
Inexpensive

YELLVILLE

Eagle's Nest Lodge
109 Hwy. 235
(870) 449-5050
eaglesnestlodgeyellville
.com
Inexpensive

More Places to Eat in Northwest Arkansas

BULL SHOALS

Village Wheel Restaurant
1400 Central Blvd.
(870) 445-4414
Inexpensive

CHAMBERS OF COMMERCE IN NORTHWEST ARKANSAS

Eureka Springs Chamber of Commerce
Box 551, Eureka Springs 72632
(479) 253-8737
eurekaspringschamber.com

Fayetteville Chamber of Commerce
Box 4216, Fayetteville 72701
(501) 521-1710, (800) 766-4626
FayettevilleAR.com

Harrison Chamber of Commerce
621 East Rush St., Harrison 72601
(870) 741-2659, (800) 880-6265
harrison-chamber.com

Jasper Chamber of Commerce
(800) 670-7792
theozarkmountains.com

Mountain Home
(800) 822-3536
mountainhomechamber.com

Ozark National Forest
Bentonville Advertising and Promotion
(800) 410-2535
nwanews.com/bbvchamber

Springdale Chamber of Commerce
Box 166, Springdale 72765
(479) 872-2222
springdale.com

Yellville Area Chamber of Commerce
Box 369, Yellville 72687
(870) 449-4676
yellville.com

FAYETTEVILLE

José's Mexican Restaurant
324 West Dickson
(479) 521-0194
Inexpensive

HARRISON

DeVito's Restaurant
350 Devito's Loop
Highway 62/65 Junction
(4 miles north of Harrison)
devitosrestaurant.com
(870) 741-8832
Inexpensive

Neighbor's Mill Bakery and Cafe
1012 Hwy. 62/65 South
(870) 741-6455
Inexpensive

ROGERS

Prairie Creek Steak & Seafood Co.
14340 Hwy. 12 East
(479) 925-3158
Inexpensive

SILOAM SPRINGS

Cathy's Corner
1910 US 412 East
(479) 524-4475
Inexpensive

West Central Arkansas

In Kansas the Arkansas River is called the *Ar-KANSAS* River, but when it crosses the state line, its name changes, because in 1881 the legislature appointed a committee to ascertain the right pronunciation of the word, and the result was a resolution declaring it to be *AR-kan-saw*.

The western Arkansas River Valley glides from Fort Smith to Little Rock and is quilted with pastures, vineyards, forests, and rice fields. Rocky, towering mountain ranges line both sides—the Ozarks to the north, with lakes and hardwood forests, and the Ouachitas to the south, with pine forests and waterfalls.

The river crackles with life. Locks and dams divide the river into long lakes (dotted with sails, skiers, boats, and barges). A bouquet of small towns cluster around Fort Smith and lie sprinkled along the 160-mile valley with old depots, stagecoach stops, a frontier fort, and a monastery.

Scenic highways connect the towns. Highway 22 rolls east from Fort Smith to Dardanelle through farmland nestled between the river and steep slopes of the mountains. Highway 7, of course, is one of the nation's most scenic drives, wandering through both the Ozark and the Ouachita Mountains from Harrison to Hot Springs.

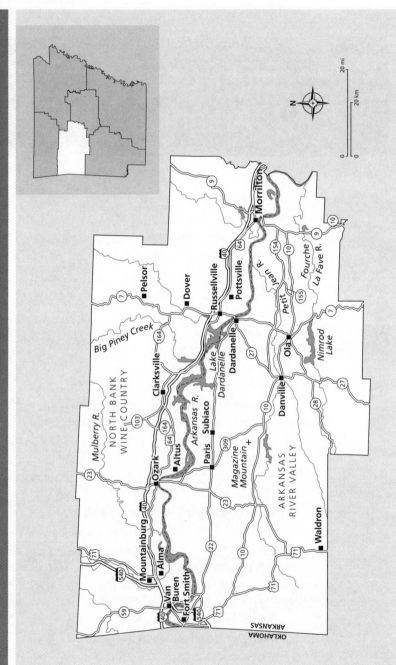

20 mi

20 km

N

Morrilton

9

10

9

154

Fourche

La Fave R.

Petit Jean R.

155

7

Pelsor

Dover

Russellville

Pottsville

64

40

7

Big Piney Creek

164

Clarksville

Lake Dardanelle

Dardanelle

27

Ola

Nimrod Lake

27

NORTH BANK WINE COUNTRY

103

Mulberry R.

164

Altus

Ozark

64

Arkansas R.

Subiaco

Paris

309

Magazine Mountain +

10

Danville

28

23

ARKANSAS RIVER VALLEY

23

Mountainburg

40

Alma

22

10

71

Waldron

71

540

71

Van Buren

Fort Smith

40

540

71

59

OKLAHOMA

ARKANSAS

Arkansas River Valley

When **Fort Smith** was founded at the confluence of the Arkansas and Poteau Rivers, it was frontier America at its worst. Outlaws, bushwhackers, and gunrunners heading southwest joined whores and men seeking gold. This place had it all. It was a tough boomtown known as "Hell on the Border," where a federal judge and a band of US marshals sent 79 outlaws to the gallows. (Judge Isaac Parker, "The Hanging Judge," is famous for saying, "I never hung a man; it's the law.")

The fort was built at Belle Point on the Arkansas River in 1817, and the Butterfield stage line stopped here on its way to San Francisco. This was also the Arkansas terminus of the Trail of Tears, which sent the remnants of the five great civilized Native American tribes to the Oklahoma Territory.

BEST ATTRACTIONS IN WEST CENTRAL ARKANSAS

Arkansas-Missouri Scenic Railway
Van Buren
(800) 687-8600
arkansasmissouri-rr.com

Cedar Falls at Petit Jean State Park
Dardanelle
(800) 264-2462 or (501) 727-5431
petitjeanstatepark.com

Grapevine Restaurant
Paris
(479) 963-2413

Museum of Automobiles
Petit Jean
(501) 727-5427
museumofautos.com

Post Familie Winery
Altus
(479) 468-2741
postfamilie.com

Subiaco Abbey
Subiaco
(479) 438-9115
countrymonks.org

Taliano's
Fort Smith
(479) 785-2292
talianos.net

Tanyard Springs
Morrilton
(501) 727-5200 or (888) TANYARD
tanyardsprings.com

Wiederkehr Village
Wiederkehr
(479) 468-2611 or (800) 622-WINE
wiederkehrwines.com

The Victorian-era Belle Grove Historic District, on the banks of the Arkansas River off Rogers Avenue, dates back to the boomtown days. This charming time capsule has some of the best antiques shopping around. The **Fort Smith Museum of History,** at 320 Rogers Ave., is housed in the former Atkinson-Williams Building, which is listed on the National Register of Historic Places. The museum depicts the growth of the town and contains a circa 1900 pharmacy, including a working soda fountain and a steam-powered fire pump. It's also believed to be haunted and has been investigated for paranormal activity. It's open Tues through Sat 10 a.m. to 5 p.m. Admission is $5 for adults and $2 for children. Age 6 and under are free. Call (479) 783-7841 for information or visit fortsmithmuseum.com.

The **Trolley Museum,** at 100 South 4th St., includes three gasoline locomotives and other railroad memorabilia. They now have a Frisco steam engine and a turn-of-the-20th-century trolley that has been restored. The museum is open 10 a.m. to 5 p.m. Mon through Sat and 1 to 5 p.m. Sun. From Nov through Apr the museum is open only on weekends—Sat 10 a.m. to 5 p.m. and Sun 1 to 5 p.m. Call (479) 783-0205 for information or visit fstm.org.

Now pay $2 ($1 for children) and climb aboard the restored electrified trolley, the last one to run downtown. The half-mile ride to the national cemetery is accompanied by the clanging of the trolley bell as the worn brick buildings slide past. When the ride ends at the **Fort Smith National Historic Site,** at 3rd Street and Rogers Avenue, the driver walks down the aisle, flipping the seats over for the return trip—the car can't turn around, so the seats do.

The Fort Smith National Historic Site preserves 80 years of national history. Start at the visitor center, which is within the imposing redbrick building that was formerly the barracks, courthouse, and jail at Fort Smith. Here you'll find exhibits about the military and the Trail of Tears. You will also find the jails and the courtroom of Judge Isaac Parker, who is known as "The Hanging Judge" due to his record of sentencing over 150 people to death by hanging. A paved, accessible trail will take you to a replica of the gallows that helped Judge Parker earn his nickname. Admission to the historic site is $4 for adults (kids age 15 and under get in free), and it is open 9 a.m. to 5 p.m. daily. Call (479) 783-3961 for information.

Looking for a bed-and-breakfast? Then go up the hill and into the driveway of **Beland Manor Inn,** at 1320 South Albert Pike, and fall in love with the colonial manor wrapped in a porch. The winding, open staircase leads to suites with such amenities as a Jacuzzi for two and four fireplaces. Innkeepers Mike and Suzy Smith almost always have something baking, so the scent of bread or chocolate will wake you in the morning. Down the hall from the suites, the refrigerator in the great room is stocked with beverages and ice, and the sofa invites you to stretch out. Big pine rockers give you a peaceful spot from which to enjoy the view from high up in the trees. Dinner is an experience in elegance: candlelight, soft music, fine china, and a table for two. Everything is made from scratch—pasta, continental cuisine complete with salad, French bread, and a very indulgent dessert. You can imagine what breakfast is like in the sunny blue dining room, or have it served in your room. Sun breakfast features dessert! Suites are $109 and $185. One is on the first floor if stairs are a problem. Call (800) 334-5052 or (479) 782-3300 for information and reservations, or check the website at fort-smith.net.

trivia

Fort Chaffee Military Reservation, south of Fort Smith, is famous among rock-and-roll trivia fans. It was here on March 25, 1958, that Elvis Presley was inducted into the US Army and received a GI haircut. The photo of that event is one of the most requested from military archives. Four days later, Elvis shipped out to Fort Hood, Texas, where he spent the majority of his military career.

Fort Chaffee continued to make international news in the 1970s when it became home to more than 25,000 Vietnamese refugees, many of whom have now made their homes and businesses in the area. In the 1980s Cuban refugees from the Mariel Boat Lift were housed temporarily at Fort Chaffee. The post has been deeply scaled back by the US Army, but for more than 75 years, it held a significant role in the history of western Arkansas and the US.

The ***Fort Smith Regional Art Museum***, also known as RAM, is housed in a renovated bank building at 1601 Rogers Ave. It displays the work of artists from around the world as well as area artists and hosts numerous art competitions throughout the year. They also host a variety of lectures, workshops, and special events for both adults and children. Admission is free. Hours are 9:30 a.m. to 4:30 p.m. Tues through Sat and 1 to 4 p.m. Sun. Call (479) 784-ARTS (2787).

The ***Clayton House,*** at 514 North 6th St., in the historic district, is an example of Italianate-style architecture from 1882. Originally the home of

William Henry Harrison Clayton, who was appointed US attorney for the western district of Arkansas by Ulysses S. Grant in 1874, it has been restored and refurbished in period furnishings and contains original belongings. Hours are Wed through Sat noon until 4 p.m. and Sun 1 to 4 p.m. Admission for the 45-minute guided tour is $6 for adults, $5 for seniors, $3 for children ages 6 to 12. The Clayton House also hosts afternoon teas, which feature a variety of presentations on aspects of Victorian-era life, tea and desserts from local bakeries, and a guided tour of the home. Reservations for the afternoon teas can be made online at claytonhousefortsmith.com.

Many of the volunteers at the Clayton House also volunteer at *The Darby House,* 311 General Darby St. This was the boyhood home of William O. Darby, who grew up to be a military general and leader of the US Army Rangers in World War II. Darby was killed in action in northern Italy just 2 days before the armistice was signed. His home is decorated in that time period and filled with great history of the Army Rangers and the European theater of World War II. The house is open Mon through Fri 8 a.m. to noon. Call (479) 782-3388 for more information.

BEST ANNUAL EVENTS IN WEST CENTRAL ARKANSAS

Annual Native American Heritage Festival
Fort Smith; first weekend in Apr
(479) 782-5074

Old Timers Day
Van Buren; first weekend in May
(479) 474-8112

Butterfly Festival
Mount Magazine; last weekend in June
(479) 963-8502 or (877) 665-6343
mountmagazinestatepark.com

Altus Grape Festival
Altus; last Fri night and
Sat in July
(479) 518-1963

Johnson County Peach Festival
Clarksville; last weekend in July
(479) 754-9152

Fall Festival
Van Buren; first weekend in Oct
(479) 471-8112

Annual Mount Magazine Frontier Day
Paris; first weekend in Oct
(479) 963-2244
parisaronline.com
Admission free

Ed Walker's Drive-In is certainly not fancy—you would probably drive right by. But it probably has the only curbside beer service in the state (maybe in the country) to go with its famous French dip or huge hamburger steak, which is smothered in onions and oozing brown gravy. Remember to flash your lights for curbside service, or go inside to enjoy the race car memorabilia on the walls. You can drive in 10 a.m. until 12 a.m. daily. You'll find the eatery at 1500 Towson, Fort Smith (479-783-3352).

Miss Laura's was once a bawdy Front Street "social club." Well, to be truthful, it was a brothel. Actually, Miss Laura Zeigler ran the best whorehouse in town, they say. Now the historic building (you bet it's historic—if walls could talk!) is the Fort Smith Visitor Center, where volunteers will show you around the upstairs bedrooms furnished as they were in their heyday. You can buy a T-shirt in the gift shop telling the world that you visited a, um, social club in Fort Smith. It is the only (former) bordello on the National Register of Historic Places, and it is open Mon through Sat 9 a.m. to 4 p.m. and Sun 1 to 4:30 p.m. Just follow B Street clear down and across to the wrong side of the railroad tracks to the river park. You can hear the lonesome whistle as the trains pass the colorful house, which sits alone by the river at North B Street and the Clayton Expressway. Call (479) 783-8888 for information. A website will show you everything in town: fortsmith.org. Donations are appreciated.

Taliano's, at 201 North 14th St., was born when childhood friends Tom Caldarera and Jim Cadelli wanted to start a restaurant. Across the street from Caldarera's home stood an old building, the Sparks Mansion, built in 1887, that Caldarera had made into apartments. The mansion, shaded by grand old magnolia trees, has been reborn. The chandeliers, the stained glass, the hand-carved wooden dividers, and the rest of its original Renaissance revival beauty were restored, and it has since been placed on the National Register of Historic Places. Now the two men, whose families were from northern Italy (Jim's) and Sicily (Tom's), serve handmade pastas and sauces that reflect those heritages.

There are five dining rooms on the first floor. The original brass chandeliers have been converted to electricity, and the marble fireplaces were imported from Carrara, Italy. A white stone porch surrounding one side has been glassed in, and there white wrought-iron tables and chairs also seat guests. For a quarter of a century Caldarera and Cadelli have done all the cooking, at first with the help of their Italian parents, and the recipes are still the same family favorites. The pastas are all homemade, as are the sauces, of course. Even the sausages are specially made. Prices range from $11.75 for the classic spaghetti and meatballs to $18.25 for veal dishes and $20.95 for seafood entrees, but everyone's favorite is Jim's lasagna. Taliano's is open for dinner Mon through Sat 5 to 9:45 p.m. Call (479) 785-2292 for reservations, then visit talianos.net to start drooling over the menu.

Drive along Highway 22 from Fort Smith. The highway parallels I-40 along the south banks of the Arkansas River. The river valley has mountains sloping up on both sides, creating rich bottomland for small farms along the roadway, where horses graze in the pastures.

Cowie Wine Cellars, at 101 Carbon City Rd., is east of Fort Smith on Highway 22 in Paris. The stone and cedar building is owned by Bob Cowie. A great-great-uncle of the Cowie family came from Switzerland to Altus, where he spent his life propagating new varieties of grapes—nine of them, to be exact. Today's bottles of Cowie wine have artist labels—pen-and-ink sketches of a ridge scene near the winery—and an annual series with limited edition prints is available.

Robert Cowie is the artist of the Arkansas wine industry, and the wines produced here reflect his art tempered with science. Old-world traditions and modern wine-making skills combine to produce some of the best wines in Arkansas. Tour the winery and enjoy a complimentary wine tasting. A good time to visit is during the Arkansas Wine Competition held the last Sat in Apr. The winery is open Mon through Sat 10 a.m. to 6 p.m. For further information or to place an order, call (479) 963-3990 or visit cowiewinecellars.com.

The *Arkansas Historic Wine Museum,* adjacent to the winery, is the first museum in the nation devoted to the wine history of an entire state. It displays the area's finest collection of wine-making equipment, artifacts, and documents from the 19th century. A special collection highlights the life and works of Professor Joseph Bachman, an internationally known developer of grapes in the early years of the 20th century. The museum exists to preserve the state's ethnic and wine-making traditions that led to the federal bonding of 147 wineries in Arkansas since the end of Prohibition. All but a few of these are no longer in operation. The museum is open Mon through Sat 10 a.m. to 6 p.m. and Sun noon to 6 p.m.

The newest addition to the Cowie winery is the *Winery Bed and Breakfast,* a romantic hideaway for two. It has a private entrance and a nice balcony view and is quiet and secluded. Visit with the vintner and owner of the winery, stroll through the pine trees or relax in the grape arbor with a glass of wine and some cheese, learn about Arkansas's interesting wine history, and see how wine is made—even help if you like. A new chapel and four bell towers have been added to the property. The largest tower is 45 feet tall, and there are over 33 bells total. The chapel is dedicated to St. Ann because the property used to be the home of the St. Ann School.

There is a large double whirlpool to relax in and a complimentary continental breakfast. You can even get a licensed masseuse by appointment to take the kinks out of you. All this for $90 a night. Another, larger suite ($125 per night) has just been added. It opens onto a romantic inner court. A wine and snack basket will welcome you. For reservations call (479) 963-3990 or (800) 419-2691.

Vineyards begin to appear along the roads outside Paris. The scenery is *très bien,* as peaceful as a day in France, and there's even an old monastery looking down from a hill. This is wine country, and wine country is the same all over the world, *n'est-ce pas?* Rolling east on Highway 22 is like a drive in the Provence region of France, with low stone walls curving beside the road.

Paris is the gateway to **Mount Magazine State Park** in the Ozark National Forest, the highest point between the Rockies and the Appalachian Mountains. Hang gliders and rock climbers practice their daring sports on these great sandstone bluffs watched over by an Ozark National Forest ranger station. Dramatically rising about 2,750 feet above the view—which is, of course, spectacular—the mountain lures scientists, naturalists, and explorers. Like the rest of the Ozark Mountains, this was once part of the vast floor of an ancient sea and is home to several rare and endangered

What's on Mount Magazine?

Mount Magazine, at 2,753 feet, is the highest elevation in Arkansas and a popular destination for rock climbers (and hang glider pilots, astronomers, and others looking for places to get high).

The *Mesodon magazinen* is a snail found only in rock streams beneath Cameron Bluff. There are 23 other species found only on Mount Magazine. Ecologists call it "The Galápagos of Arkansas."

Butterflies of Mount Magazine

Mount Magazine is home to 80 of the 127 known species of butterflies in the world. One, the Diana Fritillary butterfly, is unique to Mount Magazine. It is simply beautiful, and entomologists travel here to see the richly colored creatures. The male is a deep shade of rust and black, while the female is several shades of blue with black markings. *National Geographic* published an article about the butterflies of Mount Magazine in 1997, and the Logan County Chamber of Commerce had the first annual Butterfly Festival in August of that year. The festival is now held during the third weekend of June. For more information see mountmagazinestatepark.com.

trees, including the Ozark chinquapin, the maple-leaved oak tree (not found anywhere else), and the yellowwood tree, noted for the large, impressive clusters of flowers that hang from its branches in springtime. The state park's 60-room mountain lodge and 13 cabins all offer incredible views of the Petit Jean River Valley and distant Blue Mountain Lake below. Inside the lodge, you'll find Skycrest Restaurant, which is open daily for breakfast, lunch, and dinner (call 479-963-8502 for exact hours). The mountain boasts miles of scenic trails ranging from easy to strenuous. There is an 8,000-square-foot visitor center with exhibits, a wildlife observation deck, and a native plant garden. Start here to gather information on things to do in the area as well as the schedule for programs and events. Call (479) 963-8502 or visit mountmagazinestatepark.com to get more information and make lodging reservations. Highway 309 leads to the top of Mount Magazine and connects with Scenic Highway 10. Blue Mountain Lake is hidden in the mountains between the Ozark and Ouachita National Forests, just off Highway 10 west of Danville and is a great spot for fishing and swimming.

The area along the Arkansas River was settled by German Catholics, who were reminded of their homeland and had brought along wine-making skills when they immigrated. Vineyards have prospered and produce some fine wines, using both imported and native grapes. A restored jail in Paris houses a small museum that depicts more of the region's history.

The first stop in Paris should be *The Grapevine Restaurant*, owned by Kenneth and Lisa Vines, a husband-and-wife team cooking great food there on Highway 22. Smoked meats, fresh-baked bread and cinnamon rolls, and sinfully delicious desserts join healthful fresh vegetables. Handwritten menus announce the daily specials. Lisa seems to know everyone in town and can direct you to the wineries and other interesting places to visit. The restaurant is open 6 a.m. to 8 p.m. Tues through Thurs and until 9 p.m. on Fri and Sat. The Grapevine is at 105 East Walnut; call (479) 963-2413 for information.

Three clothing shops and a shoe store make it easy to buy Paris fashions in the shopping area downtown on the square. You can also send postcards from Paris to impress your friends. Tell them you are about to enter wine country—they'll be green with envy.

Then seek forgiveness for the little white lie at the graceful *Subiaco Abbey* in the tiny town of *Subiaco*, 3 miles east of Paris on Highway 22. The stone and red-tile-roofed abbey is a Benedictine academy built in 1878 and the only monastery in the state. It was constructed of locally quarried sandstone by monks. Fifty-two tons of German, Italian, and Spanish marble and stunning stained glass imported from Europe accent the fine rockwork. The massive dome over the altar is supported by 20-foot white marble columns with a canopy made of balsam wood covered in gold leaf. From the canopy hangs a huge crucifix of carved wood with silver overlay. The abbey church has more than 175 stained-glass windows. The abbey rises dramatically from the farmlands surrounding it, and the 70 monks welcome visitors to tour the church and courtyard and see the museum of local history.

The Coury House at the abbey offers guests a retreat wherein you can take time to meditate and relax without the distraction of even a telephone. The abbey's reputation isn't just built on its academic record, beautiful location, or spiritual life. It is also the perfect place to find peanut brittle. What began as a fund-raiser has become a best-selling regular industry. The delicious recipe was given to the abbey by a kitchen staff member's mother. Made by the monks and staff in the kitchen's big cast-iron skillets, the brittle costs $24 for a 2-pound tin. Or if you like pepper sauces, try the new Monk Sauce, 5 ounces of hellfire for only $9. Rooms are $30 for one, $40 for two, with private baths; meals in the guest dining hall are available for $6. The academy is a boys' prep school for grades 9 through 12. According to Brother Mel, a monk at the academy and director of Coury House, there are also organized retreats: marriage encounters and prayer retreats with monks or different denominational groups who use the facility throughout the year. The monks' Mass is at 6:30 every morning and open to the public; Mass on

Sat night is at 7:30, and Sun Mass is at 10:45 a.m. Call Jean Rockenhaus, the Coury House secretary, at (479) 438-9115 for a schedule of retreats or for room reservations, or visit countrymonks.org.

Scenic Highway 22 running along the river connecting Paris and Dardanelle is a beautiful side trip to get you off the freeway and into the countryside. It cuts across some of the coves of Lake Dardanelle and through the Ouachita National Forest.

Dardanelle is a historic old river town on the banks of the Arkansas River and Lake Dardanelle at the crossroads of Scenic Highways 7 and 22. Steamboat passengers landed at Dardanelle a century ago. The road climbing Mount Nebo's steep slopes was narrow, with hairpin turns, but the scenery and cool breezes made the trip worth the effort. Arkansas summers can be hot, and this was a great escape. It still is. The town sits at the hub of three state parks.

Mount Nebo State Park, on Highway 155 South, up gorgeous Mount Nebo, is a fine spot to get the feel of the Arkansas wilderness. This is the state's highest state park, with panoramic views of the valley. Ten rustic cabins dating from the Civilian Conservation Corps era, as well as five modern A-frames, are scattered around the top of the mountain above the Arkansas River Valley. Many of the cabins are very secluded and quiet, while others are very, very secluded and quiet. All are fully equipped and have fireplaces. The park is lovely, containing a large lake with the pine forest coming right down to the shoreline. The beautiful lake is spotted with islands and surrounded by softly wooded land. The park commands a terrific view from a plateau 1,800 feet above the river. Cabins rent for $109 to $229. Call (479) 229-3655 or (800) 264-2458 for information or visit arkansasstateparks.com/mountnebo.

Lake Dardanelle State Park, on Highway 326, allows campers to stake out shoreline sites at the campgrounds. Skiers and sailboats crisscross the water, while anglers anchor in coves, casting for bream, crappie, and bass. Record-making monster catfish weighing in excess of 40 pounds are caught here under the dam. The oldest state fishing record was set in 1964, when someone caught a 215-pound alligator gar on the Arkansas River near Dardanelle (he was using a minnow). The river here has sandy beaches and access for boats on Highway 22 West. There is also a marina that rents kayaks. Call (479) 967-5516 for information, or visit arkansasstateparks.com/lakedardanelle.

Beyond the city of Dardanelle lies flattopped Petit Jean Mountain near Morrilton. **Petit Jean State Park,** on top of the mountain, has eight rustic cabins and nine modern duplexes. These are not as secluded as the ones at Mount Nebo. In fact a couple of them are near the highway, but there's little traffic at night. They rent for $115 for two people. Honeymoon Cabins with a hot tub go for $185, with a 2-night minimum. *Mather Lodge,* inside the park, has 24 rooms and a restaurant. This was Arkansas's first state park and still perhaps the best. Breakfast in the Mather Lodge is made even better by the Petit Jean ham and the panoramic view of the Arkansas River Valley. The cozy lodge, built in the 1930s by the Civilian Conservation Corps, is poised on the rim of Cedar Creek Canyon, and hiking paths weave more than 24 miles throughout the park. Call (800) 264-2462 or (501) 727-5431 for information, or visit petitjeanstatepark.com. Rooms in the lodge are quite reasonable in-season and slightly less in Jan and Feb.

Trails lead to the picture-perfect, 95-foot-high *Cedar Falls* within Cedar Creek Canyon, to delicate sandstone monoliths, and to Rock House Cave, containing ancient pictographs etched into stone by early inhabitants of the area. The falls are spectacular and worth the trip to see. The best time to photograph them is in late afternoon, when the sun shines directly onto the falls and reflects sunlight in crystal sparkles. (During morning hours the mighty falls are shaded and dark.) The falls are created by rainwater caught in the saucer-shaped mountaintop.

The park gets its name from the legend of Adrienne DuMont, a French girl who disguised herself as a boy (calling herself Jean) and accompanied her sailor sweetheart to America. She died before the return trip and was buried on the mountain. There is an unmarked grave on the mountain, and the legend begins there.

Learn survivor skills used by Arkansas pioneers at the annual Mountain Rendezvous in the fall at Petit Jean State Park. At the mountain man camp there are demonstrations of muzzle-loading rifles, tomahawk throwing, and more, all done by members of the Early Arkansas Re-enactors Association. Call the park (501) 727-5441 for times and details or visit petitjeanstatepark.com.

The *Museum of Automobiles,* on Highway 154 near the eastern edge of Petit Jean Mountain, displays privately owned antique and classic automobiles from collectors throughout the country and abroad. The museum was founded by former governor Winthrop Rockefeller and features some of his personal cars. The 1929 Rolls Royce Phantom I coupe is worth the price of admission, which is $10 for adults, $9 for seniors, and $5 for children 6 through 17. The Museum of Automobiles is also home to the only car former president Bill Clinton ever owned (since he was in public service his whole career, he was provided with transportation). The 1967 six-cylinder, light blue Mustang convertible waits there for his return to Arkansas. The place is in a constant state of change, so you can visit it again and again if you are an auto buff. About 20 cars are in the permanent exhibit, but another 40 or so cycle through throughout the year. There are memories here in chrome and leather, as well as cars you've only heard about. Several Harley-Davidsons from 1913 to 1946 are in the motorcycle section. The facility is open year-round 10 a.m. to 5 p.m. and has a gift shop on the premises. The museum is situated 15 miles southwest of Morrilton via Highways 9 and 154. Call (501) 727-5427 for information or visit museumofautos.com.

Tanyard Springs, at 144 Tanyard Springs Rd., *Morrilton,* on Highway 154 on the west edge of Petit Jean Mountain, calls itself "The Un-Resort"

Tanyard Springs Memory

The Arkansas River wound below. My husband and I sat on the edge of a cliff early in the morning enjoying the crisp air and warm sunshine. I know others have enjoyed this vantage point—perhaps Native Americans looking for campfire smoke in the distance or the French explorers who also wandered here.

Except for the electricity, the cabin we walked from on this particular morning was reminiscent of those built in the early 1800s. The 13 cabins in the *Tanyard Springs* compound are scattered around the historic springs named for the tanning pits that used to be on the site. Forty acres of trees and the magnificent Cedar Falls are tucked into the nearby 8,500 acres of pine-oak woodlands of Petit Jean State Park. A 1.5-mile trail loops among the cabins, and 20 miles of serious hiking trails interconnect in the park.

It was early winter, off-season at the resort, but for us it was the best possible time. We flew into the area in our Navion airplane, a huge beast of a plane—single engine, slide-back canopy—and landed at the airstrip here, which even though it is a daylight-only strip is more than a mile long. We stepped out of the cockpit and onto the wing of the plane and felt the cool breeze on our faces. We had come in just ahead of a rain shower.

Winter was always our favorite time in the Ozarks. We lived on the Missouri side. The quiet is intense, and the occasional call of a hawk or crow is clear and sharp. This was going to be a beautiful weekend.

and lives up to that billing with 13 rustic-looking but handcrafted cabins, each different and each designed to fit the setting. None of the natural beauty of the area has been changed; the cabins are tucked into the woods near a stream or a pond. Big porches with swings and rocking chairs allow the sounds of the woods to penetrate even the most stressed-out soul. Each cabin is perfectly reproduced in incredible detail, with wood carvings, handcrafted antique furnishings, and accessories to ensure historical accuracy. Each is also decorated around a theme. The most unusual, The Stagecoach, has a full-size Butterfield stagecoach as a bed in the loft (the kids will love it). The kids will also get a kick out of the Woodsmen, where they climb a ladder to their loft room. Rates at Tanyard Springs are $150 Sun through Thurs and $175 Fri and Sat during the season. From Dec 1 through Feb 28, they are $125 and $150. Each cottage features an interior as comfortable as any fine city hotel's, with cleverly hidden appliances

Our cottage was the most romantic one in the compound, the Adrienne DuMont. When we arrived, a Crock-Pot of beans and a chilled bottle of muscadine grape juice, locally bottled, waited for us. You can't call these cottages "cabins." Ours had a queen-size bed and a walnut headboard with a hand-carved lover's knot. Even with no telephone or television, we found enough to do to pass a very pleasant afternoon listening to the sound of the rain dripping among the dry oak leaves.

That night we had reservations at the splendid restaurant on the grounds, where we were offered a menu of continental specialties and a good wine list. It is sad that the restaurant is no longer there. The other option was to eat at Mather Lodge in the park, which is an easy mile-long hike away. The next morning we awoke to find a breakfast of croissants, fruit, and orange juice waiting on the steps. Hidden inside the rustic kitchen were a microwave and coffeepot. The romantic feeling of stepping back in time was not at all lessened by not having to split wood—there was a neat stack by the front door. We poured a cup of hot coffee to warm our hands and built up the fire to take the chill from the room. My husband was from Michigan and firmly believed that sleeping with the windows open was the only healthy thing to do. That night we cooked steaks on a grill. The last day we had breakfast at Mather Lodge and enjoyed the spectacular view from the bluff over the canyon as much as the famous Petit Jean ham and eggs. This is, without a doubt, the most romantic and beautiful memory I have of Arkansas. It is not surprising that reservations are made a year in advance for summertime at Tanyard Springs.

and large, comfortable beds. Each cottage has a complete kitchen and an outdoor grill.

The resort is not a mom-and-pop operation, obviously; it is owned by Winthrop Paul Rockefeller, son of the late governor, and the cottages are all carefully tucked behind a security gate. A conference center is available for weddings or large family gatherings. Sometimes getting off the beaten path costs a little more—in this case it's worth it. The resort complex also has a stocked fishing pond, miniature golf, basketball, horseshoe pits, and a hiking trail with scenic overlooks and easy access to nearby Petit Jean State Park. It is about an hour northwest of Little Rock. From I-40 take exit 108. Go south about 10 miles on Highway 9 and turn right onto Highway 154 in Oppelo. At the top of Petit Jean Mountain, stay on Highway 154. The gated entrance is about 9 miles on the left. Call toll-free (888) TANYARD or (501) 727-5200 for reservations or visit tanyardsprings.com.

South of Petit Jean Mountain on Highway 9 and about 40 miles west of Little Rock off Highway 10, **Heifer Ranch** is a working ranch that serves as a demonstration and training ground for many of the methods that Heifer International uses to provide support to villages and rural areas in developing countries. During your visit, you will have a chance to learn how sunlight can be harnessed, bricks made of earth, and weeds thatched for roofing; how livestock can be raised in poor areas of the world; and how poor soil can be made to produce food. Water harvesting and biogas fuel are a few of the innovative processes. The 1,225-acre ranch includes Katahdin hair sheep, water buffalo, camels, and llamas. There are hands-on teaching units of swine to be slopped, goats to be milked, and poultry, rabbits, and bees to be tended. Informal visits can be made anytime and a guided tour of the small-farm project can be arranged as well.

If you want to go more in-depth, there are special programs and work-shops available for all ages ranging in duration from 2 hours to several days. One unique experience at Heifer Ranch is a visit to the **Global Village,** which is situated around a small lake. Each section of the village represents a different part of the world, from an Appalachian shack set in the woods, to a Taiwanese stilt house, to an urban slum. Participants are divided up into groups, assigned to a village "home," and equipped with the resources that someone in that home would typically have access to. Then, they spend between 24 and 48 hours experiencing what life is like in less fortunate parts of the world. If you choose to take part in this program, you probably won't come away refreshed or relaxed, but you will have expanded your world view immensely.

Maybe the Global Village is a little too "off the beaten path" for you. In that case, the ranch also offers much more comfortable lodging options up the hillside in three different lodges. There's also a dining hall that features meals made with meat and veggies harvested right there at the ranch. It's a neat place to plan a family reunion or a ladies retreat. Call (508) 886-2221 for more information on accommodations.

Long-term working visits, internships, and volunteer experiences can also be arranged by calling (855) 343-4337. Signs will lead you to the center at 55 Heifer Rd. from Highway 10. The gift shop, which features earth-friendly and fair trade wares from around the world, is open 9 a.m. to 5 p.m. Mon through Sat. Take a look at what's going on by visiting heifer.org.

North Bank Wine Country

Cross to the north side of the Arkansas River at Morrilton and head back west on US 64, which parallels I-40. You will be following the same route the Butterfield Overland Mail took. There's an old stagecoach at 9th and College Streets in **Pottsville,** one of many that used to be headed for **Potts Tavern,** now a museum downtown. The beautifully restored antebellum house was a stagecoach stop and tavern on the Butterfield route. But there's more, if sombreros are your fetish: It is also one of the only two hat museums in the country. Five log cabins have been moved onto the property—one is the caretaker's home.

One of the cabins shows off a collection of about 75 dolls, all dressed in the inaugural gowns of all of Arkansas's first ladies and the first ladies of the US. Hours at the Potts Inn museum complex are Wed through Sun 10 a.m. to 4 p.m. Admission is $3 for adults and $1 for children. Call (479) 968-8369.

Russellville, on US 64, is small-town friendly, maybe because it's a college town, home of Arkansas Tech University.

River Valley Arts Center, at B and Knoxville Streets (1001 East B St., Russellville) in a natural stone building erected by the Civilian Conservation Corps in the 1930s, is a former swimming pool and bathhouse that is now a gallery and more. There are two galleries, actually: the Artists' Gallery, which displays the work of 10 or 12 local artists every month; and the Main Gallery, which features one-person shows of well-known artists, such as Ansel Adams or Leonard Baskin, Works Progress Administration artists of the 1930s whose output changed art in America. The gallery displays work from every medium—two- and three-dimensional art, weaving, sculpture, and photography. But there is more: Truly a center for the arts in the area, it has a community theater, a band, and a chamber chorus. There are educational arts programs, as well as the only pottery program in the state that is staffed year-round, for both children and adults. Associations like the River Valley Writers' Club, a songwriters' group, and an artists' support group meet here. The center is open Mon through Thurs 10 a.m. to 5 p.m., Fri until 4 p.m. Call (479) 968-2452 for information. The website, which lists a calendar of events, is arvartscenter.org.

Ready for a sandwich? **Stoby's** is a one-of-a-kind place—a 1941 Rock Island dining car parked at a redbrick and stucco depot, a replica of the real thing across the way. It's open for breakfast, lunch, and dinner with a menu that is both ordinary and extraordinary. They've received numerous awards for their meals from the statewide newspaper, the *Arkansas Times*. Take the Stoby's sandwich, for example. The number of meats, cheeses, breads, and toppings totals 3,000 possible combinations, according to the computer. Besides the full breakfast menu, there are homemade pies and cakes, since Stoby's opens at 6 a.m. and closes at 9 p.m. every day except Sun. *Casual* is the key word here. The place offers an unusual mix of familiar things. It's just the right combination of quick food and full service, with prices in the very comfortable zone. You'll find Stoby's 2 miles south of I-40 on Highway 7, at 405 West Pkwy., Russellville. Call (479) 968-3816 for information.

Everybody's favorite restaurant seems to be the **Old South Restaurant** at 1330 East Main St. (US 64 East). This mom-and-pop place has been here in this building forever, and although the building has been renovated, it is still the same wonderful structure it was when it was constructed in 1947. Owners Mary and Jim Austin are proud of the diner, and their Old South cooking is in a league all its own: fried chicken with all the trimmin's and the famous Old South salad dressing. They even cut their own steaks and clean their own shrimp. You can eat there just about any time because it opens every day at 6 a.m. and doesn't close until 9 p.m. Call (479) 968-3789.

Big Piney Creek, near Russellville, is a small stream flowing from the wilderness of the Ozark National Forest to the Arkansas River. Canoes and whitewater rafts float on gentle tributaries like Big Piney and the Illinois Bayou. You can take a trip down Big Piney, winding along spectacular granite bluffs from Fallsville through the mountains and into Lake Dardanelle. Short afternoon floats or several-day trips can also be arranged. Although the Big Piney's 67-mile route has Class II and Class III rapids—the first, Split Decision, to the grand finale, Haystacker Rapid—it can be enjoyed by both the beginner and the experienced whitewater paddler (areas containing Class III rapids need whitewater experience).

The Big Piney Creek outpost at **Moore Outdoors** is 10 miles north of **Dover** on Highway 164 West and Long Pool Road. Kerry and Debbie Moore have canoes, rafts, wet suits, helmets, throw lines, dry bags, and other whitewater accessories (for experienced people), as well as camping equipment and kayak lessons. The Moores will also shuttle hikers to the Ozark Highlands Trail by the Ozone or Richmond campground. The creek is at its finest from Mar through May and, in wet years, sometimes as late as Thanksgiving. If you want to make a weekend or longer of it, the Moores offer Indian Creek Cabin for rent for $125 per night for two adults, with a 2 night minimum. The cabin is located in the heart of the Ozark National Forest, so it's a great honeymoon or anniversary getaway. It has a queen-size bed, Jacuzzi tub, and a small kitchen with full-size appliances—everything you need to comfortably "rough it." Call (479) 331-3606 for information, or check out the website at mooreoutdoors.com.

Looking for a great collection of handmade quilts? Head up Scenic Highway 7 to just south of the little town of **Pelsor.** There you will find **Nellie's Gift Shop** and more than 100 quilts made by Nellie Dotson and her friends in area quilting guilds. She also carries handmade oak and cedar chests to store your quilts or other valuables and myriad ceramics and other collectibles. Nellie lives right behind the shop and says she's open just about 7 days a week or any other day you stop by. Hours are 8 a.m. to 5 p.m. Her phone number is (870) 294-5317.

Also along Highway 7, about 5 miles north of Pelsor, you will find Anna Lee Hampton's shop, **The Triple O,** which carries a fine collection of hand-made split-oak baskets. Anna is there from 9 a.m. until about 5 or 6 p.m. ("depends on the traffic," she says) weekdays and 1 to 5 p.m. on Sun during summertime. In winter she is just there "whenever," because there isn't much traffic then. Call her at (870) 294-5290 or visit ozarkmountaincrafts.com.

Looking for a remote spot in the mountains near the **Mulberry River,** one of the state's premier whitewater streams? Well, this may be the place for you. It was for James and Sandy Wright. A few years ago they bought 53 acres 8 miles from the nearest highway and 5 miles from their home. On that property stood an old house. They decided to renovate it, and as they began to peel off old wallpaper, they discovered layers of newspapers with dates showing the house to be at least 100 years old. As they continued to gut the house, they found a layer of boards, and under the boards was the original log structure, a double-pin log cabin with a dogtrot. It turned out to be one of the first homesteads built in this valley in the late 1800s. Now the cabin has been completely renovated and has become **Lizard Springs Lodging on the Mulberry,** 3431 Cass Oark Rd., near Ozark. The original hand-hewn timbers still show in one of the rooms, as they did a century ago. The dining room table, which sits over an old well in the west part of the cabin, has a glass top. With a flashlight you can see the bottom of the well. There is an old root cellar on the property. The cabin is available to canoeists ready to float the Mulberry, which is just a stone's throw from the front porch—you can hear the rush of water as you fall asleep at night. It is surrounded by woods with trails for hiking and mountain bikes. Ask the Wrights about the one behind the house. It will lead you to the graves of two Civil War deserters who hid out in these hills. They were killed by locals who accused them of raiding and looting the area. The Ozark Highlands Trail is within hiking distance, about a quarter of a mile as the crow flies. Two bedrooms are available in the cabin. On either side of the dogtrot, each has two double beds and a fold-out bed. Sandy provides a continental breakfast your first morning. There are certainly no restaurants around here, and the nearest store is at Turner Bend, 10 miles away, but that is fine with hikers and canoeists looking for a wooded hideaway.

To get to Lizard Springs, take Highway 103 from Clarksville to Highway 215. After it crosses the Mulberry River, Highway 215 turns west. Go approximately 6 miles, and you will see the sign. The office is James and Sandy's home, which is 7 miles farther up the road (west) on Highway 215. The price is $85 per two plus $15 for each additional person. Call (479) 667-4398 for reservations. The drive to the cabin is through the beautiful valley, past farms where cattle graze beside the roadway. There's even an old-fashioned country general store down the way a bit for odds and ends you might need. The twisting road curves up the Boston Mountains and tops out near Batson, then starts downhill again to the valley. It's about a 40-minute drive.

The *Ozark Highlands Trail,* running through the remotest and most scenic wilderness in the Ozarks, has several access points nearby. It is a well-marked trail, and you can choose easy and short sections or longer hikes that could take several days.

The center of wine country on the north bank of the Arkansas River lies along US 64. *Altus* (which means "altitude") is the highest point between Little Rock and Fort Smith. Swiss and German settlers arrived during the 1880s and blanketed the valley with grapevines. Wineries dot the valley today and continue the tradition. Although not as well known, the 12,000-acre Altus region is a registered wine-producing region like Napa and Sonoma. There are tours and tastings year-round, together with festivals celebrating the harvest and barefoot grape-stomping contests among the families who own the wineries.

Post Familie Winery, 1 block north of US 64 on Highway 186 (1700 St. Mary's Mountain Rd., Altus), was founded in 1880. Wine-making tours take visitors through the process from grape to cork. The prolific Post family has 12 children, all grown now and, for the most part, all in the wine business. The patriarch is Mathew Post. Seven of his children are in partnership with him in the winery. A variety of grapes, both those native to the state and those harder to grow here, are produced in the vineyards. The French Cabernet grape is handpicked and lovingly cared for; it is at risk this far east, as a hard winter could destroy the root stock. But so far it is growing well, producing a wine that will surprise even connoisseurs. The Cynthiana grape, with its bright color and distinctive flavor, is native to the valley. A must-try is muscadine wine, a traditional southern drink.

The winery has a gift shop that carries local crafts, as well as clever handmade gift items like wooden airplanes and trucks designed to be used as wine bottle holders. Quilts, grape leaves brushed with gold and made into earrings and pendants, and even smoked trout make the gift shop and tasting room worth a stop. Hours are 9:30 a.m. until 6 p.m. Mon though Sat and 10:30 a.m. until 5 p.m. Sun. Call (479) 468-2741 for information, or go to postfamilie.com. To order winery products, call (800) 275-8423.

Continuing up the mountain on Highway 186 will bring you to *Wiederkehr Village,* a Swiss Alpine–style village, home of the *Wiederkehr Winery.* The Weinkeller Restaurant is in the winery's original wine cellar, dug by Johann Andreas Wiederkehr in 1880 and listed on the National Register of Historic Places. A romantic little candlelit spot, it offers German food—the grandfather was from the German-speaking region of Switzerland—such as schnitzel, German fried potatoes, cheese fondues, and wines carefully aged in oak. Hours Mon through Sat are 11 a.m. to 3 p.m. for lunch and 5 to 9 p.m. for dinner; Sun hours are 11 a.m. to 9 p.m.

Tours of the winery itself are every 45 minutes 9 a.m. to 4:30 p.m. Mon through Sat and starting at noon on Sun. The huge winery covers 350 acres and produces 50,000 cases of wine a year. The annual wine festival, held the last weekend in Sept, is worth a trip, with polka bands and a grape-stomping contest among the winery families of the valley. Call Linda Wiederkehr at (479) 468-2611 or (800) 622-WINE for more information, or visit wiederkehrwines.com.

Atop St. Mary's Mountain at Altus is *St. Mary's Catholic Church,* one of the most remarkable buildings in Franklin County. It was constructed by Germans who fled the Franco-Prussian War. The church is made of native sandstone in Roman basilica style and known for its 29 striking stained-glass windows, bells, pipe organ, and original paintings by German artist Fridolin Fuchs. What makes these paintings unique and memorable are the gold leaf murals that feature the faces of local residents who served as models (many folks here recognize great-uncles and aunts and grandparents). The church was dedicated in 1902 and is on the National Register of Historic Places. It underwent a half-million-dollar renovation. It's open 8 a.m. to 6 p.m. so that visitors can see the famous murals inside. Call (479) 468-2585 for a tour or service times.

The trip up to Wiederkehr isn't the last of the wineries, though. *Mount Bethel Winery* is 0.25 mile east of Altus on US 64. Eugene and Peggy Post and their eight grown children are the current owners. At harvest time,

15,000 gallons of wine are made here. Mostly sweet wines and fruit wines like blackberry and wild plum, these screwcap wines make no pretenses to greatness. But the Golden Muscat Port is similar to the Lagrima ports of Portugal, a very light and fruity wine, fortified with brandy to keep in a decanter for slow sipping. Hours are 8:30 a.m. to 6 p.m. Mon through Sat and noon to 5 p.m. Sun. Call (479) 468-2444 for information. Their website is mountbethel.com.

Continue west on US 64 to the town of *Ozark*. *The Lamplighter Bed and Breakfast* at 905 West River St. is the circa 1945 home of Albert and Carol Sneath. This neat 2-story home sits on 3.5 quiet acres. The 6,800 square feet of house has four bedrooms, each with private bath. Carol will serve a full breakfast to guests and fill you in on what to see and do in Ozark. Call (479) 667-3889.

The *Ozark Bridge,* which spans the Arkansas River on Highway 23, is listed as one of the 16 most beautiful long-span bridges in the US, according to the American Institute of Steel Construction. If you can, be in this area at night. The lights on the bridge reflecting into the breadth of the river water at this point make a spectacular photograph or memory.

If you are in Ozark during business hours, stop by the *Bank of Ozark* at 601 Commercial St. The 56-foot-long wall behind the tellers' windows is a 10-panel mural telling the history of the area, beginning in the 1880s. The mural is made of redwood but was sandblasted with Arkansas River sand. It took 30 months to complete. The folks at the bank welcome tourists all the time, and you don't even have to open an account. The bank lobby is open 9 a.m. to 4 p.m. Mon through Thurs, Fri until 5:30 p.m. Call them at (479) 667-2181.

If you have time for a side trip, turn north on Highway 282 (it parallels US 71) near Van Buren and drive to *Mountainburg.* The route is steep and winding, with sharp turns, and provides glimpses of genuine log cabins—the kind with mud between the logs—hidden in the trees. The housing may not be modern, but folks living in these cabins have the kind of view out the back window that people in other parts of the country pay millions for. There is a spectacular vista of Lake Fort Smith, Lake Shepherd Springs, and the river that makes them.

The White Mountain Wildlife Management Area is nearby, and 8 miles north of Mountainburg you will find *Artist Point,* on scenic Saddle Canyon off US 71 (19924 US 71 North) with an overlook that offers a view of the Boston Mountains that is a photographer's dream. The tiny gift shop there (479-369-2226) has a bit of everything, including homemade jams as well as a historical Indian museum. There's a four-bedroom lodge upstairs ($90) and a new hiking trail to that beautiful view. Hours are 10 a.m. to 4 p.m., closed Wed.

The little town of **Alma,** population 2,900, is known as the Spinach Capital of the World. Area farmers produce tons of spinach that is packed by the Popeye Spinach Company. An 8-foot statue of the cartoon character keeps watch over the downtown square, and the city's water tower is a huge can of Popeye Spinach. The Saturday morning farmers' market on the downtown square is a good place to purchase—you guessed it—fresh spinach. The market runs from about mid-Apr to mid-Oct.

The **Ozark Highlands Trail** begins at Dockery's Gap, which is deeply nestled in a wooded valley of the Boston Mountains. (Take US 71 to Highway 348 East and turn onto FR 1007 to find the trailhead.) This trail offers hiking and backpacking through the Ozark National Forest, a 187-mile adventure as challenging as any you will find in the country. The scenery along the trail is outstanding, with hundreds of streams and more than 200 waterfalls and pools. Rambling through remote and rugged land, the trail is dotted by access points with parking and passes through eight campgrounds. There are several ways to go: A short day hike up White Rock Mountain will give you a pretty sunset, or begin at Shores Lake and take the 6-mile spur trail up to White Rock and spend the night. Hare Mountain lets you explore the remains of an 1800s homesite via a 6-mile hike from Highway 23 or a 2-mile walk from Hare Mountain trailhead. One of the most beautiful spots, however, is the Marinoni Scenic Area, where the trail hugs a steep hillside and overlooks a creek. The Hurricane Creek Wilderness Area has deep green pools connected by whitewater and surrounded by towering bluffs. Swimming in the pools; lying on the large, smooth rocks; playing in waterfalls; going hunting, fishing, and camping—all are there. The *Ozark Highlands Trail Guide*—a 104-page handbook with maps, elevations, and mileage logs; information on scenic spots and campgrounds; a weather guide; and an animal and insect guide—is available through the National Forest Service at (501) 667-2191. The Evans Point Loop, a 6-mile trail circling the lake, is there for those who don't want to go overnight on the trail but still want to see waterfalls and caves. From I-40 take exit 13 at Alma and go 12 miles north on US 71 to just north of Mountainburg.

Fort Smith and *Van Buren,* founded in 1818, are next-door neighbors. But there is so much to see in Van Buren's beautifully preserved Main Street Historic District that you can just plan to spend a day there. The town was once called Steamboat Landing or Phillips Landing and was a stop on the Butterfield stage line from St. Louis to California. The name Van Buren was to honor Martin Van Buren, but, interestingly enough, the change occurred before he was president—he was just a friend of Phillips then. Main Street in Van Buren is a restored delight, bustling with shops and restaurants and some of the best antiques shopping around. It retains its original 19th-century charm and has been used as the location for filming such movies as *The Blue and the Gray, Biloxi Blues,* and *Main Street Van Buren.* Stay on Main Street and sample what Van Buren has to offer.

A vintage train excursion on the *Arkansas-Missouri Scenic Railway* takes visitors on day trips from the Old Frisco Depot (1901), at 813 Main St., to the beauty of the Ozark Mountains. The 70-mile round-trip to Winslow takes 3 hours. You will pass over three high trestles and then go through a mountain tunnel surrounded by the lush Ozarks. Now a new first-class parlor car has been added, so you can go in old-time luxury. Fares are from $30 to $90, children are half price, and seniors get a 10 percent discount. Visit the website at arkansasmissouri-rr.com. Reservations can be made by calling (800) 687-8600. Trains run on Fri and Sat. The train leaves Springdale at 8 a.m. and Van Buren at 10:30 a.m.

The *King Opera House,* in Van Buren's historic district at 427 Main St., is home to the King Opera House Players and, they say, the ghost of a traveling actor who was shot and killed by the father of a young lady about to run away with him sometime in the 1880s. You can hear a performance schedule (for the opera, not the ghost!) by calling (479) 474-2426.

Janean Saunders is also the proprietress at *Carter Trading Company,* 412 Main St. in downtown Van Buren. They carry a variety of antiques as well as Arkansas-made baskets of every variety. Their phone number is (479) 471-7182.

If you have a sweet tooth, stop by *Main Street Candy and Fudge* at 512 Main St. As the name implies, they have the cure for what ails you.

Ghostly!

Jackie was alone in the **Crawford County Bank** building. It was dusk, and the doors were locked because the restaurant and bed-and-breakfast she owned in that old Victorian showplace was closed and she had no guests that evening. She decided to use the time to clean. She was bent over a table dusting in the dim light of evening when she looked up into the mirror above the table and saw him. "I screamed and whirled around, but there was no one there, just the empty room. I have never been so frightened," she said. "I turned on every light in the house and was whistling and singing and trying to convince myself that it was just a reflection of something that looked like a man.

"It took me a good fifteen minutes to get up the nerve to look into that mirror again, and when I did, of course, there was nothing there but the double doors of the wardrobe behind me."

But for Jackie it wasn't just a momentary apparition. "I can still see him. Our eyes were locked, and he was staring deep into my eyes. He was clean shaven, about thirty-six years old, blond."

"Jackie," I said, teasing her a bit, "he sounds like a very nice-looking man. Was he well dressed?" Her answer was fast: "He was wearing a white shirt with a high-button starched collar and a black jacket," she said without missing a beat. "I can close my eyes any time of the day or night and see him. He left an indelible impression on my mind."

Jackie can tell other stories that make this one all the more believable. She once had two guests who loved old buildings. She chatted with them in the restaurant one night about the bank. They asked if they could see other rooms, so she took them upstairs and showed them around. When they went into the Green Room, the woman kept talking but the man became silent and stared into a corner of the room. When his wife realized what was happening, she fell silent, too. "They are here, you know," he said to Jackie. "The man and his wife are in the corner over there." He pointed to an empty corner. "He was the president of this bank. They are lost and confused. They can't move on because things keep changing here."

"The gentleman said he was a psychic or a channel or something," Jackie explained. "I don't know anything about that kind of thing, but he was sure impressed with the place. He said the room was alive—that they lived there and he could see them."

Hours are Mon through Sat 10 a.m. to 5 p.m. and Sun 1 to 5 p.m. Call (479) 410-3026 for more information.

A Little Bit of Mexico is found at 614 Main St., where you can buy trinkets and silver jewelry, tapestries and tiles, and all other kinds of south-of-the-border delights. Dave and Barbara will welcome you 7 days a week from 10 in the morning until 5 in the evening. Call (479) 474-5155 or visit their website at littlebitofmexicoimports.com.

Big Jake's Cattle Company, at 1702 Fayetteville Rd., not only has really good steaks of any kind (they own a meat-processing plant, so you know the steaks are right) but pretty good pasta, too. Kids and adults love watching the elevated toy train circle the 2-story dining room. Big Jake's is open Sun through Thurs 11 a.m. to 9 p.m., Fri and Sat until 10 p.m. Call (479) 474-5573.

After checking out the shops on Main Street and the rest of the historic district, walk down toward the river, across the tracks, to the wall that protects the town from the Arkansas River. There, overlooking the river is a park, a relaxing spot where you can enjoy the soothing sounds of running water. While contemplating the river, turn around and look at the back side of the wall. You will see a mural depicting the history of Van Buren, painted by local high school students.

The Drennen-Scott Historic Site, which overlooks the river at 222 North 3rd St., provides a window back in time. John Drennen is considered to be the founding father of Van Buren. His circa 1838 home and surrounding 31 acres was purchased and underwent a five-million-dollar restoration beginning in 2005. Inside the antebellum style home, you'll find many original artifacts and artwork from the Drennen family. The visitor center features exhibits and demonstrations, and the surrounding grounds have been landscaped as they would have been 150 years ago. The home is linked to the Trail of Tears, the Underground Railroad, and the Civil War, so its history is not just about local development. Admission is free. The museum is open Mar through Nov, Thurs 1 to 5 p.m. and Fri and Sat 10 a.m. to 5 p.m. Call (479) 262-6020 for more information.

More Places to Stay in West Central Arkansas

FORT SMITH

Holiday Inn
700 Rogers Ave.
(479) 783-1000
Inexpensive

RUSSELLVILLE

Best Western
Highway 7, exit 81
2326 North Arkansas Ave.
(479) 967-1000
russellvillearkansas.org
Inexpensive

VAN BUREN

Holiday Inn Express
1637 N. 12th Ct.
(479) 471-7300
Inexpensive

RUSSELLVILLE

Italian Gardens Cafe
315 West Main
(479) 967-1707
Inexpensive

More Places to Eat in West Central Arkansas

FORT SMITH

Calico Country Restaurant
2401 South 56th St.
(479) 452-3299
Inexpensive

CHAMBERS OF COMMERCE IN WEST CENTRAL ARKANSAS

Fort Smith Chamber of Commerce
612 Garrison Ave., Fort Smith 72901
(479) 783-3111
fortsmithchamber.org

Paris Area Chamber of Commerce
301 West Walnut, Paris 72855
(479) 963-2244
parisaronline.com

Russellville Chamber of Commerce
708 West Main St., Russellville 72801
(479) 968-2530
russellvillechamber.org

Van Buren Chamber of Commerce
510 Main St., Van Buren 72956
(479) 474-2761
vanburenchamber.org

Southwest Arkansas

Western Arkansas's mountains, caves, and rolling hills provide the perfect terrain for those who enjoy rappelling, spelunking, serious hiking, biking, or just general messing around outdoors. The upper Ouachita River is a boulder-strewn stream with plenty of riffles and gravel bars. As the river turns south, it gets slower and deeper and forms three lakes: Ouachita, Hamilton, and Catherine.

The Diamond Lakes region covers five counties and contains five surprisingly uncrowded lakes, as well as the Caddo, Ouachita, and Saline Rivers. Water babies will revel in the lakes, streams, and rivers, loaded with bass and catfish and perfect for fishing, boating, waterskiing, canoeing, rafting, or just wading.

The Cossatot River crashes through here. It is called "Beauty and the Beast" because of its Class V rapids of crystal-clear whitewater—definitely not for beginners.

Don't be tempted to take the easy way through the southwest corner of the state on I-30—try some back roads. This dense, piney woodland area is alive with natural attractions and some of the state's most exciting history. The old Southwest Trail passed through here, as did men as famous

SOUTHWEST ARKANSAS

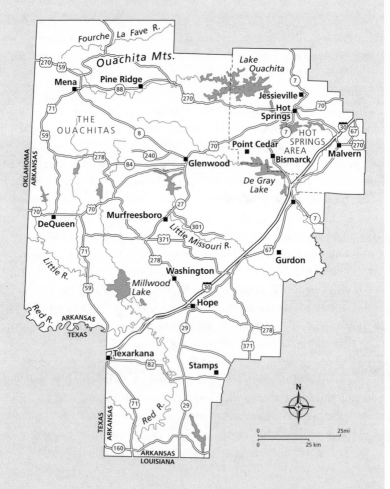

BEST ATTRACTIONS IN SOUTHWEST ARKANSAS

"Beauty and the Beast,"
Cossatot River State Park
Langley
(870) 385-2201
arkansasstatepark.com

Crater of Diamonds State Park
Murfreesboro
(870) 285-3113
craterofdiamondsstatepark.com

Fox Pass Pottery
near Hot Springs
(501) 623-9906
foxpasspottery.com

Garvan Woodland Gardens
Hot Springs
(501) 262-9300 or (800) 366-4664
garvangardens.org

Mountain Thyme Bed and Breakfast
Jessieville
(501) 984-5428 or (888) 820-5424
mountainthyme.com

The Owl Prowl
DeGray Lake Resort State Park
Bismarck
(501) 865-2801 or (800) 737-8355
degray.com

Queen Wilhelmina Lodge
Queen Wilhelmina State Park
(479) 394-2863
queenwilhelmina.com

as Colonel James Bowie, Stephen F. Austin, Davy Crockett, and Sam Houston on their way to Texas.

Hot Springs Area

The mystical qualities of the clear quartz crystal gemstone have intrigued humanity for years. Millions of years ago silica-rich fluids and gas here in the southwest part of the state were subjected to high temperatures and fluid pressures. What was created is specimen-quality crystal, also used in electronics. Only a couple of mines allow visitors to dig for their own gems. *Coleman Crystal Mine* in *Jessieville* is one of them.

Ron Coleman, owner of the mine that bears his name, has found hefty chunks of good crystal, some of which he values at $80,000. Only two areas of the world—this one and one in Brazil—have this quality of quartz crystal, according to experts. Arkansas crystal is on display in a Zurich

The Blue Goofus

Traveling on Arkansas's scenic highways can create the illusion that just over the next hill there will be a town. I call it an illusion because often there is nothing but more scenic highway, and more and more. I mention this as fair warning to carry a bag of trail mix or some cookies to quiet the growling of your stomach as the miles of evergreen forests pass by.

My husband was the real traveler in our family. He enjoyed cruising Arkansas's roadways and would choose curving scenic routes and spend hours pointing out little waterfalls and hand-mudded log cabins. I tried, in vain, to explain that I was a travel writer—that is, we were here not to enjoy the scenery but to find someplace to eat! I can only take so many notes about rolling hills and evergreen forests, no matter how beautiful they are.

But restaurants, ah, now there is something I can write about.

He would say, "Patti, I remember this road. When we [he and his golf buddies] drove to Hot Springs last year, there was this really great restaurant. It served the best fried chicken, had a fireplace, wonderful desserts,. . . " and on and on. "It had a funny name. The Blue something. It's right over this next hill, I think."

museum. Visitors leave with keepers every day. For a price per pound or set time limit (here it is $20 for all day, $5 for students ages 7 to 16, $15 for seniors—or if it's your birthday!—and free for children 6 and under), visitors are handed digging tools and buckets and head off into the red dirt to find treasures—because crystals you find yourself are more powerful than those bought in gem shops, some say. The mines are open 8 a.m. to 5 p.m. 7 days a week, but hours are seasonal, so call (800) 291-4484 for information or visit colemanquartz.com.

At Jim Coleman's **Miller Mountain Crystal Mine,** also in Jessieville, the charge is $10 for all day; kids 9 and under get in free. Jim is Ron's brother. Call (501) 984-5752 for information. The other mining area is near Mount Ida, 35 miles west of Hot Springs on US 270. The gift shop opens at 8 a.m. and closes at dusk, as does the mine.

Highway 7 squiggles through the mountains. Distances are deceiving on the map, so allow plenty of time if you want to get in before dark. Come into the Ouachita Mountains on Scenic Highway 7, and slow down about 3 miles north of Jessieville. Polly Felker and her daughter and son-in-law,

And I believed him. The next hill came and went. Several more slipped by. Still no Blue Something with great fried chicken.

"Bob," I pleaded, "are you sure this Blue Something place is on this highway? I am starving." I was eyeing the roadkill along the highway, and some of it was beginning to look appetizing—maybe deep-fried—and I was getting crabby. "I don't believe in this Blue Goofus," I grouched.

Then we crested a hill, and sure enough there it was: a smoky stone chimney surrounded by blackened grass and trees. Bits of broken glass caught the last light of day and winked in the fading sunlight. Charred boards leaned against the beautiful stone fireplace, and a broken sign announcing the Blue Goofus, or whatever it had been called, swung creaking on a chain over stone pillars. I could have wept.

But ever after that, when the going got tough and I got grouchy, Bob would say that there was sure to be a Blue Goofus over the next hill, and that would always make me laugh.

He was usually right. Arkansas is full of wonderful Blue Goofi, and I promise you, we found most of them and put them in this book.

Rhonda and Michael Hicks, built the eight-bedroom **Mountain Thyme Bed and Breakfast** here.

You can get a really good look at this bed-and-breakfast online at mountainthyme.com, where you can tour each room of this pretty Cape Cod at your leisure. Rhonda and Michael wanted this to be the "perfect B&B" and looked to every detail to make it so. The sheets are soft, the towels thick, and the breakfast gourmet. Once you get settled in, you won't want to leave. Cozy up on the porch and listen to the woodland creatures—this bed-and-breakfast is on the edge of a national forest. It is no wonder that instead of just signing the guest book in each room, people write a page about how relaxed they are. Some rooms have a fireplace or Jacuzzi and all rooms have books to read and perfect lighting to do it by. Prices range from $125 to $225 for the honeymoon suite. Call (501) 984-5428. The toll-free number is (888) 820-5424.

The great burger search continues, and former president Clinton would be happy with the results. The latest find is **The Shack,** at 7901 North Hwy. 7, Jessieville. The quarter-pound Shackburger—or the half-pound

Super Shackburger—arrives wrapped snugly and fastened with toothpicks. Unwrap it carefully, because the wrapper also serves as a plate. When the weather is good, you can take in the sunshine at tables around the Shack while enjoying a thick milk shake. Shoestring potatoes come flavored in Cajun or ranch, and both are great. You can get a grilled chicken if you are weight conscious, but the fried catfish and shrimp are very popular with the rest of us. The Larry Special, named after a family friend, is two beef patties topped with grilled onions and comes with fries and coleslaw. The owners of The Shack are Bill and Glenda Cockman. Hours are 10 a.m. to 9 p.m. Mon through Sat. Call (501) 984-5619 for information.

Fox Pass Pottery is also the home of Jim and Barbara Larkin and their son, Fletcher. To visit the studio, take Highway 7 out of town 2.5 miles and go 0.5 mile down Fox Pass Cutoff. They have lived in the stone house attached to the studio and surrounded by national forest for 31 years. The Larkins use local quartz for glazing and silica sand from the White River in their creations. This business is a family affair. Barb's work is hand built from coils and slabs of clay. She does bud vases, trays, and other sculpture. Jim creates more functional items, such as dinnerware sets. His colanders, mugs, and vases are fired in the kilns he built himself. The bisque kiln is the first step. It goes to 1,800 degrees, then cools. Then the "car kiln" reaches 2,400 degrees for the glaze. This kiln takes 16 hours to heat and 2 days to cool. Jim has also added a large two-chamber wood-fired kiln, which reaches a temperature of 2,400 degrees. In the second chamber they do salt glazing. Their son, Fletcher, does much of the creative work here. Their daughter, Erin Larkin, visits the shop from time to time, and her field of expertise is costume design. She does wonderful work with fabric. Visit this unique shop online at foxpasspottery.com. Hours are Tues through Sat 10 a.m. to 5 p.m. Call (501) 623-9906 for information.

As it enters **Hot Springs,** Highway 7 is lined with big old homes set back on deep lots high on hills. The highway becomes Central Avenue and Bathhouse Row when it gets into town. Here's a city where you can have your palm read, enjoy a bath and massage, get married, go to the races at Oaklawn—or all of the above. And there are plenty of good restaurants for a city so small.

Even though former president Bill Clinton calls himself the man from Hope, his formative years he spent in Hot Springs, and it's hard to miss that information, with huge banners declaring "Hot Springs—Boyhood Home of Bill Clinton" flying across most main streets and signs in plenty of windows stating that Bill Clinton ate here.

Hot Springs was the hot spot in its day, no question. People came from miles around for the mineral water baths (health seekers, they claimed to be). To fill the time between baths, gambling houses were run by the underworld of Chicago, New York, and Miami. Certainly not off the beaten path then, nor is it now. It is the nation's smallest, yet second most visited national park in the US. During Prohibition, the Valley of the Vapors had bathtub gin, clanging electric trolley cars, speakeasies, and

trivia

You can find brochures detailing every single facet of former president Bill Clinton's life as a dorky teenager: boyhood homes, high school prom locations, senior party (Class of '64), his church; where he bowled, went to movies, and ate ice cream. And of course at the *Josephine Tussaud Wax Museum*, where both he and Hillary are in living color.

painted women. It was an odd combination of shady entertainment along Central Avenue: One side was shady as in illegal; the other side was shady as in a tree-filled national park managed by federal rangers.

People have been bathing at the spa since Hernando de Soto did in 1541. But he was just doing what the Native Americans had always done. According to legend, the Indians soaked in steaming pools when they talked peace with warring tribes. Through the years traders, trappers, politicians, and gangsters have soaked in these waters. By the 1900s Bathhouse Row's most elegant establishment was the Spanish Renaissance revival–style Fordyce Bathhouse, where water bubbled up from deep in the Earth's center, reaching the surface at 143 degrees Fahrenheit, whereupon it was cooled for bathing. Fordyce Bathhouse visitor center was restored by the National Park Service at a cost of $5 million; the elegant bathing facility is now open to the public—although you can't have a bath there today.

The 4,800-acre **Hot Springs National Park** visitor center in the restored bathhouse has the decadent legacy of that bygone day. The only gambling done now takes place at Oaklawn Park during the spring Thoroughbred racing season, although dinner in the circa 1875 Arlington Hotel's

BEST ANNUAL EVENTS IN SOUTHWEST ARKANSAS

Annual Tea for Poets & Lovers
DeQueen; second weekend in Feb
(870) 642-6642

Annual Hot Springs Fishing Challenge
Hot Springs; May through July
(501) 321-2277 or (800) 543-2284
Tagged fish are released into the lake and merchants sponsor prizes in value from $10,000 to $500.

Annual Lake Catherine Tag Fishing Derby
Malvern; May through Dec
(501) 332-2721
Tagged fish are released into the lake and merchants sponsor prizes in value from $10 to $550.

Watermelon Festival
Hope; third weekend in Aug
(870) 777-7500
hopechamberofcommerce.com/
festival_info.htm

Four States Fair and Rodeo
Texarkana; 9 days beginning the second weekend after Labor Day
(870) 773-2941
Rodeo, carnival, demolition derby, exhibits, and live entertainment

Hot Springs Documentary Film Festival
Hot Springs; Oct
(501) 538-2290
hsdfi.org
One of the first and the oldest documentary film festivals in the world

Annual Boo Grass Picking Around the Campfire
Texarkana; Halloween weekend
contact Church and Billie
(903) 255-0408
Picking, grinning, crafters, quilting, food, Halloween party; RV hookups available for $10 and $14 Oct 20–25

Annual Christmas at the Ace of Clubs House
Texarkana; all of Dec
contact Ina McDowell at
(903) 793-4831
Victorian Christmas decorations throughout this historic home built in the shape of a playing card club; music and readings; admission $3.50

Venetian Room might help you replay some of that feeling under glimmering chandeliers, with jazz drifting in from the lobby bar.

This is the very place where Al Capone headquartered his gang during Prohibition days. Veined Italian marble, wrought iron, and hardwood railings are everywhere, as are classical sculptures and ornate ceramics. The third-floor sunroom is the true showstopper, with its stained glass, vaulted ceiling, grand piano, and wicker furniture. And the promenade behind Bath-house Row is a nice place to stroll. The visitor center is open 9 a.m. until 5 p.m. daily. Call (501) 624-2710 for information.

Visit the **Buckstaff Bath House** on Bathhouse Row to experience a spa Hot Springs style. It's easy to spot by the blue and white awning. You can get the whole enchilada, with thermal bath, whirlpool, Swedish mas-sage, and loofah mitt, for $64, or a 1-hour facial for $75, Mon through Sat 7 to 11:45 a.m. and 1:30 to 3 p.m. On Sat in Dec, Jan, and Feb the bathhouse closes at 11:45 a.m. for the day. Call (501) 623-2308 for an appointment.

The **Hot Springs Visitor Center,** at 629 Central Ave., is a good place to start a walking tour of the city. In addition to a computerized kiosk to help you find what you're looking for, the center has maps, discount cou-pons, and the latest information on shows and exhibits in the city. Hours are 8 a.m. to 5 p.m. 7 days a week. Call (501) 321-2277 or (800) 543-2284 or go to hotsprings.org.

Hot Springs is still a resort town, so there is more entertainment here than in other cities this size. There are many live music places in town, and as for eating, well, you've come to the right place.

Another interesting building on Bathhouse Row is the **DeSoto Min-eral Springs building,** which is now the headquarters and visitor center for **Mountain Valley Spring Company** (they sell bottled water). At 150 Central Ave., the building was built with classical revival style architecture. It was constructed in 1910 right over a spring that can still be seen today on the first floor. In 1921, a Japanese-styled ballroom was added. Mountain Valley Spring Visitor Center hours are Mon through Fri 9 a.m. to 4:30 p.m., Sat 10 a.m. to 4 p.m., and Sun noon to 4 p.m. If you like to tour factories, you can also tour the Mountain Val-ley Spring Company's historic spring site and bottling facility, about 20 minutes outside of Hot Springs at 283 Mountain Valley Water Place. Tours are Tues at 9 a.m. and 10 a.m. or

trivia

The fully restored Quapaw bath-house shows the splendor of what it was like to sit on the veranda in the bathhouse era. Visitors can enjoy a variety of spa services including massage, body treat-ments, thermal baths, and even a visit to the "steam cave." There is also a cafe serving sandwiches, satisfying smoothies, soft drinks, coffee, iced and hot tea.

by appointment for groups. Call (501) 624-1635 or (800) 828-0836, or visit mountainvalleyspring.com/mountain-valley-visitors-center.aspx.

A favorite place with the cognoscenti is **McClard's,** at 505 Albert Pike St. This is an unassuming place with bright lights and, according to locals, the best barbecue in the state. The 1950s diner is always crowded, and with good reason: Not only is the barbecue great, but the tamale spread is fiery hot and, with a cold beer, hard to beat. It hasn't changed much since Bill Clinton and his buddies hung out here. It's open Tues through Sat 11 a.m. to 8 p.m. Call (501) 623-9665 for information or visit mcclards.com.

Steinhaus Keller is more than off the beaten path, it is *under* the beaten path. Located below street level in Spencer's Corner in downtown Hot Springs, this interesting restaurant takes a little extra effort to find. The reward for your effort is an authentic German menu featuring specials like apple stuffed pork and German surf and turf. Chef and owner David McGuire cooks with locally sourced fresh ingredients. The ambience is also interesting, as it's been described as both cave-like and cozy. Steinhaus Keller is open for dinner Tues through Thurs 3 to 10 p.m., Fri and Sat 3 p.m. to 2 a.m., and Sun 3 to 9 p.m.

trivia

The water that flows from the springs in Hot Springs is naturally sterile. It is rainwater that is absorbed into the mountains and carried 8,000 feet underground, where the Earth's heat raises the temperature to 143°F. The purified water makes its way back through pores and cracks in the rock in the form of hot springs.

But "man does not live by bread alone." Hot Springs has recently become a fine arts center for the state. A Gallery Walk, held the first Fri of each month, is gallery open-house night to meet with artists whose works are being shown. About 20 fine arts galleries and arts-related businesses participate in the walk; refreshments are served, too. The **Hot Springs Arts Center,** at 405 Park Ave., is the heart of the city's art renaissance. Call (501) 625-3992 between the hours of 10 a.m. and 2 p.m. for more information about the walk.

The **National Park Aquarium,** at 209 Central Ave., is home to a 90-pound snapping turtle that could take off your arm. You and your children can learn that it is part of the Chelydridae family and inspect the fresh and saltwater fish, frogs, tortoises, lizards, and other turtle inhabitants in residence. The cost is $5.75 for adults, $4.50 for seniors, $4 for children ages 4 to 12. Hours vary, so call them at (501) 624-3474 or go to national parkaquarium.org to get a sneak peek at what you'll see during your visit. Just down the block, the **Arlington Hotel and Spa,** at 239 Central Ave., will take you back in time. Enjoy the unique lobby with bright green leather sofas, and have a drink in the bar. You might even decide to make a day of it in this grand old southern hotel. Have a Day of Beauty in the full-service Beauty & Facial Salon, or try the spring-fed waters in the Bath House, where a staff of skilled attendants and massage therapists will pamper you with thermal whirlpool baths, hot packs, and massages. The outdoor mountain-side hot tub and 50 of the sleeping rooms also have the thermal waters piped in. Rates run from $60 for a bath and massage called "the works," to a full-day package at the Beauty & Facial Salon, which could cover the Paris Moor Black Mud face and body masque or the Deluxe Rejuvenation Package, which includes a 2-night stay in the hotel, two manicures, two pedicures, and body treatments tailored for a couple or two friends—there is even a credit for food and beverages. Call (501) 623-7771 or (800) 643-1502, or visit arlingtonhotel.com for information about spa packages.

Complementing the art scene in Hot Springs is great food. One restaurant that draws a crowd is **Belle Arti,** at 719 Central Ave. Owners Joseph and Penny Gargano were attracted to the city's reputation and moved here from New York in 1998. Belle Arti already had an established reputation for authentic Italian cuisine, and the Garganos continue the tradition of home-made pastas, ravioli, and tortellini, but their most requested menu item is the stuffed portobello mushroom ($10). Hours are 11 a.m. to 11 p.m. Mon through Sat; until 10 p.m. Sun. Reservations are suggested for dinner, which begins at 5 p.m. To make reservations or ask for information, call (501) 624-7474.

A beautifully restored Queen Anne at 808 Park Ave. is the home of **1884 Wildwood Bed and Breakfast Inn,** owned by Wayne and Tink Walker. Their daughter and son-in-law, Rebecca and David Hall, are the resident innkeepers. It is a magnificent 3-story home with five guest rooms and two cottage suites, each with private bath. Three of the rooms have their own porches. There is original stained glass and many original furnishings and photographs. It is, of course, on the National Register of Historic Places.

Breakfast is served in the dining room or morning room. You can preview the rooms at wildwood1884.com or call (501) 624-4267 for more information. Prices range from $139 to $199.

There are so many lovely old homes in Hot Springs, and many of them are now bed-and-breakfasts. Another is the elegant *1890 Williams House,* a Victorian brownstone and brick mansion with a carriage house at 420 Quapaw Ave. Nine guest rooms all have private baths. This one is also on the National Register. Innkeepers Karen and David Wiseman have shown attention to detail that will make your stay comfortable. Breakfast is served in the dining room between 7:30 and 9 a.m. Complimentary chocolate chip cookies and snacks with springwater are served to guests on arrival. Prices range from $159 to $229. Call (501) 624-4275 or visit 1890williamshouse.com.

To get an overview of the town, go up to the 216-foot *Hot Springs Mountain Tower* in Hot Springs National Park. Taking the glass-enclosed elevator to the open-air deck is a treat. The elevator operates 9 a.m. to 5 p.m. Admission is $7 for adults, $4 for children, and $6 for senior citizens. Children under 4 are free. Call (501) 623-6035. From the top of West Mountain, there's an equally good view; you can even see the tourists in the tower on the other mountain. The view is especially pretty at night. Pull your car off on the turnouts and enjoy the scene below—downtown Hot Springs glittering like the fabled spa it once was.

trivia

Treatments at the bathhouses in hotels were interesting. Spa visitors were prescribed needle showers and sessions in steam-and-chill chambers, and syphilis sufferers had mercury rubbed on their genitals. Quack devices (the Zanda machine) were also used. The treatment rooms contained not only showers and lockers but also ornate stained glass and sculpture—locker rooms for the wealthy leisure class.

Going down from West Mountain onto Prospect Street, you will see a Russian villa at 634 Prospect. The fairy-tale house is vivid in red and yellow, with intricate decorations on the detailed shutters in the style of a northwestern Russian summer home, or dacha. It was designed and built by a former officer of the czar's army in 1930. Once abandoned, the house has now been restored.

The Promenade, a paved path behind Bathhouse Row, is a pleasant stroll that offers a hint of the natural beauty of Hot Springs National Park.

For the more adventurous, several paths lead to the top of Hot Springs Mountain. It's about a mile round-trip to the top.

A longtime feature at Hot Springs is **Dryden Pottery,** at 341 Whittington Ave. and offering pottery made of native clays and crystal quartz. For more than 50 years, members of the Dryden family have made their living at the potter's wheel. The showroom is filled with examples of the finished product. A mural painted on the building tells the story of Native Americans and their pottery. Dryden is now listed in the *Antiques and Collectibles Price Guide* for its one-of-a-kind original pieces. Call (501) 623-4201 for tour information. Hours are 9 a.m. to 3:30 p.m. Mon through Fri and 10 a.m. to 3 p.m. Sat. Check them out online at drydenpottery.com.

Hot Springs Country Club Golf Course, 101 Country Club Dr., is open to the public. Its tree-lined fairways and hilly 45 holes draw golfers from all over the five border states. Midwesterners vacation here in February and March, when the weather is usually golfable but snow still covers the rest of middle America. (The fact that it's racing season doesn't disappoint anyone, either, if the weather is less than perfect.) Eighteen holes with a cart cost $95. For tee times call (501) 624-2661; hotspringscc.com.

Any tour of former president Clinton's hometown should include a drive past the two homes in which he lived—the 2-story white house at 1011 Park Ave. and the brick house at 213 Scully St. You can get a presidential self-guided-tour booklet at the visitor center and see places like the Malco Movie Theater (where Clinton liked to sit in the middle of the front row) and the Park Place Baptist Church.

If you are looking for a quiet spot, you will want to check out **Garvan Woodland Gardens,** 550 Arkridge Rd., near Carpenter Dam at the eastern end of Lake Hamilton. The handsome 5,100-square-foot welcome center is made of cypress, stone, and glass. Inside you'll find a gift shop and the Magnolia Room, which hosts monthly art exhibits. After paying your admission and picking up a self-guided tour map, you'll venture out the back door and into the gardens. Make sure you have your eyes open wide, because there is much to see.

The two large peninsulas with more than 4 miles of shoreline on Lake Hamilton are all native forest and contain sweet gum, maple, redbud, and dogwood, as well as pine, oak, and hickory. The garden, which is more of an arboretum, has the best flowers in the spring and fall. It was donated by Verna Garvan, who inherited the 232 acres from her father and wanted it preserved.

You will see Three Sisters of Amity Daffodil Hill, where several thousand daffodils bloom with blue French-Roman hyacinths, blue *Anemone blanda,* and 235 varieties of narcissus each Spring. Walk the Camellia Trail surrounded by *Camellia japonica* and more than 50 sasanqua, interplanted with English laurel, *Euonymus sarcoxie, Osmanthus heterophyllus,* and hardy evergreens for winter protection. Old Brick Hill is a road of solid red brick from the fuel house of a turn-of-the-20th-century lumber company. The bricks were made at the historic Atchison Brick Company in Malvern. There is plenty of shade and water here, too; rocky streams and bubbling brooks splash throughout the park. A 12-foot waterfall, four pools, two springs, and a half-acre pond set it apart from most other botanical gardens.

One of the most striking features of the garden is the Verna Garvan Pavilion, designed by architect E. Fay Jones (designer of Thorncrown Chapel near Eureka Springs) in the Border of Old Roses near the end of the tour. The roof includes a glass skylight in the center shaped to resemble a flower opening. The garden has 110 varieties of old roses dating back to *Rosa gallica* from about AD 1300. The best view is from the top of Singing Springs Gorge, accessible by way of the Millsap Canopy Bridge, which is 2 stories high.

There are several spaces within the gardens that children will especially enjoy. The Sugg Model Train Garden features a G-scale railroad with 389 feet of track and 259 trestles. Three independent operating loops carry a passenger train, a freight train, and a logging train. The Greater Hot Springs Garden Railway Society constructed the train garden's buildings, trestles, and tracks.

Down the hill to the northwest of the visitor center, the interactive Evan Children's Garden features a favorite with the 10 and under set—rocks. Over 3,200 tons of native Arkansas boulders are stacked and assorted here to form a man-made cave, complete with a 12-foot waterfall at the entrance and "ancient" fossils inside. Kids can climb over a bridge constructed from tree branches and find their way through a rock maze. Be prepared for them to get wet as they explore a series of wading pools. A 20-foot-tall elevated walkway provides great views of the Adventure Garden as well as Lake Hamilton and the surrounding woodlands.

Do not miss the Garden of the Pine Wind, an award-winning Japanese garden. The 4-acre space features two bridges, a 12-foot waterfall and several other smaller cascades, and a half-acre koi pond. It makes a beautiful setting for quiet contemplation or family photos.

Garvan Woodland Gardens also host a wide variety of educational programs as well as special events throughout the year. If you visit around the holidays, the walk-through light display is a popular attraction.

You can see a list of events and classes offered, and also plan your visit to the gardens at their website: garvangardens.org. You can also call (501) 262-9300 or toll-free (800) 366-4664. Hours are 9 a.m. to 6 p.m. daily. Admission is $10 for adults and $5 for children age 6 to 12. Dogs are $5 and golf cart tours are $10. Wear good shoes for walking. If you look to the far end of the parking lot of Garvan Woodland Gardens, you will notice a 6-story structure that both stands out with architectural interest and blends in with its natural surroundings. You have found the **Anthony Chapel**, which is open to the public at no charge. However, if you're there on the weekend, there's a good chance the chapel will already be in use—it hosts over 160 weddings each year. From the inside, the floor to ceiling glass walls give you the feeling that you are standing under a canopy roof being held up by very symmetrical trees. Take a few moments to take it all in—it is truly a beautiful blend of Mother Nature and man-made architecture.

You can get a closer look at Lake Hamilton and its beautiful shores from the deck of the **Belle of Hot Springs** riverboat. The 1.25-hour narrated sightseeing cruise includes million-dollar mansions, panoramic views of the Ouachita Mountains, and historical information blended with humorous stories and interesting anecdotes. There are also lunch and dinner cruises available. Cruises leave the dock at 5200 Central Ave. off of Hwy 7 South

trivia

The *Arkansas Alligator Farm and Petting Zoo,* in business since 1902 at 847 Whittington Ave., Hot Springs, is stocked with more than 200 alligators of different sizes. Visitors may take a self-guided tour past the four ponds in which they live. You can watch the alligators as they are fed Thurs, Sat, and Sun at noon. Open daily 9:30 a.m. to 5 p.m. Call (501) 623-6172 or go to arkansasalligatorfarm.com for information.

each day at various times. Rates start at $9.50 for children and $18.99 per adult. Call (501) 525-4438 or visit their website at belleriverboat.com for cruise times, rates, and more information.

The riverboat company also has two lake houses available to rent nightly or by the week. The Shore House is a two-bedroom, two-bath cottage that sleeps four. Rates start at $175 per night (2 night minimum) or $1,050 per week. The two-bedroom, one-bath Captain's Cottage sleeps six starting at $125 per night or $750 per week. Both are right on Lake Hamilton and have swimming docks and child-friendly swimming areas. Call (501) 276-2546 for more information and availability, or visit belleriverboat.com/gilligan_s_dockside_cafe for photos and rate details.

The **Mid-America Science Museum,** 500 Mid-America Blvd., is in a heavily wooded, 21-acre site about 6.5 miles west of Hot Springs off US 270 West. The 50,000-square-foot building is divided into two wings, connected by a glass-enclosed catwalk over a stream. This is a hands-on museum, where the exhibits are designed to be touched. Here the arts and sciences come together with playful contraptions like the Featherstone Kite Open-Work Basketweave Mark II Gentleman's Flying Machine—the work of Rowland Emmett, who designed the mechanical creations in the movies *Chitty-Chitty Bang-Bang* and *Those Magnificent Men in Their Flying Machines.* The lighthearted tone of the museum delights visitors.

The museum is dedicated to featuring internationally renowned traveling exhibits that captivate the imagination, instill creativity, and cultivate a lifelong hunger for learning on a year-round basis. Upon crossing the bridge

trivia

Kellar Breland, a pioneering animal behaviorist, lived in Hot Springs during World War II and directed workers in top-secret research. Dolphins were trained to attach mines to Axis warships, crows to carry listening devices behind enemy lines. Breland opened the IQ Zoo, which became a popular attraction. One hundred twenty performers waited in cages for their part in the ongoing show. A telepathic raccoon read your mind and shot baskets; a rabbit who played the piano and a duck plucking a guitar provided music; and there was a rabbit ready to fire a cannon at the audience. It got even better. There was Andy, a pig who drove a Cadillac.

to the west wing, visitors can explore hands-on opportunities to understand the science and technology of our modern world. The Balance Challenge alters your equilibrium with mirrors, the Walk-In Camera allows you to see how a camera lens views the world, and the Sun-Earth Scale shows how much you would weigh on the sun. The museum is also home to the world's most powerful operating Tesla coil, producing 1.5 million volts of electricity in the Caged Lightning Exhibit.

The Virtual Reality Simulator allows you to experience the thrills and excitement of death-defying high-speed adventures without ever leaving the building. With more than 100 exhibits, a trip to the museum is an all-day adventure that children will not forget. Hours are 10 a.m. to 6 p.m. 7 days a week from Memorial Day to Labor Day, Tues through Sun 10 a.m. to 5 p.m. after Labor Day. They are also open on Mon in Mar for spring break. Tickets are $10 for adults; $7 for children (3 to 12 years old), seniors, and the military; free for children 2 and under. Call (501) 767-3461 or (800) 632-0583. The website is midamericamuseum.org.

On the north side of DeGray Lake near **Point Cedar,** Gabe and Dawn Rubio are building two private and secluded Adirondack cabins in the 40-acre woods they own. "We are definitely off the beaten path!" says Dawn. You can pitch your tent—right back in the closet—and stay in one of the **Lone Cedar Cabins.** The first was completed in 2006 at the foothills of the Ouachita Mountains. "Rough it in comfort" is their motto. High ceilings and tall windows allow the view and the breeze, but there is central air for warm days and a gas log fireplace for cool nights. There are no phones or computers, but there are hiking trails, a stocked catfish pond, and nearby stream as well as a fire pit and barbecue grill. There are indoor and outdoor showers (secluded, remember? Sound like fun?) and a TV with movies for evenings in the queen-size bed. Children are welcome, too, of course. They will enjoy the chickens, guineas, sheep, and an Australian shepherd named Cedar. Sleeping in the loft or on the army cots outdoors will be fun for them, too. You can spend sunsets swinging on the large front porch with ceiling fans stirring up the air. The cabins rent for $135 to $165. A cute little camp trailer nestled on a knoll with a beautiful view is called "The Pine Cone" by Gabe and Dawn. "It's cute as a button," she says, and it goes for $60 a night. Dawn is a talented artist as well. Her studio, **Paintings by Dawn,** features oil paintings on antique metal, barnwood furniture, and antique collectibles.

For reservations, a map, and directions, call (501) 865-6782 or virtualcities .com/ar/lonecedarcabins.htm.

The drive along Scenic Highway 7 is the most beautiful way to travel south in this part of the state. ***DeGray Lake Resort State Park*** covers 13,800 acres in the foothills of the Ouachita Mountains. You can find not only clear water, scuba diving and snorkeling, and all the water toys you could ever want (party barges, sailboats, WaveRunners, and luxury house-boats), but also a luxurious lakeside lodge with a view. In October the park hosts the Arkansas Storytelling Festival with workshops and story swaps. Rooms with a view are only $85 to $100 and a bit less for a view of the woods. So if you prefer a bed to a bedroll, call (800) 737-8355 or (501) 865-2851, or visit degray.com.

Birders especially seek out this area because the park hosts many events for them. Night owls will like ***The Owl Prowl*** on Fri and Sat nights in summer (and in Jan); this event lets you see and hear barred owls, screech owls, and great horned owls by using taped calls to attract them. The annual ***Eagles Et Cetera*** in Jan is a weekend offering numerous opportunities to see bald eagles in the wild. You will learn how to identify birds or how to photograph them with some of the best birders in the state. The 90-minute tour by barge—which can be chilly—offers more than a 95 percent chance of seeing bald eagles. The barge runs year-round on weekends and 7 days a week spring through fall. Tickets are $5 for adults and $3 for children ages 6 to 12. Call (501) 865-2801 for information about the events.

The Eagle and Raptor Rehabilitation Program has these birds in tem-porary captivity. Other bird hikes continue throughout the day. Some other wildlife you might see include the common loon, great blue heron, raccoon, and gray and red foxes. All programs at the lodge and the bird hikes are free, but advance registration for hikes and barge tours is necessary because of limited space.

There are other special events here, too. March brings early-morning bird walks and the Easter Ecstasy spring wildflower walks (and annual Eas-ter egg hunt). The April wildflower walks join the Tell a Tale Troupe Dinner Theatre, performing such classics as *The Red Badge of Courage*. Full Moon Cruises are available Apr through Oct.

Campers are charged $19 for water and electrical hookups and a dump station, with bathhouses containing hot showers also available. Or, if you believe this, you can Rent-A-Yurt for $55 per night. The park, which is off Highway 7, 6 miles north of I-30 at Caddo Valley (21 miles south of Hot Springs), also has an 18-hole golf course, a pro shop, and a marina and offers guided trail rides on horseback.

Scenic Highway 7 ends at Bismarck, but if you take US 67 south through the Caddo Valley beginning at Malvern, the picturesque 20-mile stretch will take you by a number of antiques shops (one in a town's restored train depot), a restored antebellum cabin, a petting zoo, and an old-time general store with woodcrafts and smoked meats. US 67 is the old route to Texas; if you want to get off I-30, this is the way.

Bismarck is the home of *Jo Ann Diffee Gallery.* Jo Ann is a self-taught artist who specializes in portraits but also does landscapes, wildlife, and still lifes. Her work reflects the colors of the mountains and desert and the feelings of the Southwest, where she grew up. Her gallery, in the former post office at 7214 Hwy. 7 in Bismarck, is a small, red, traditional building that actually looks as though it were built to be a gallery. She also carries raku pottery by Morgan McMurry. Jo Ann spends her time in the studio there and loves to talk to people who come by. The gallery is open Wed through Sat 10 a.m. to 4:30 p.m. or by appointment if you would like to commission a portrait. Call (501) 865-4990 for information or visit joanndiffee.com.

The Bar Fifty Ranch is a beautiful cattle and horse ranch situated on 200 acres near Bismarck, just 20 minutes from Hot Springs. At the **Bar Fifty Ranch Bed & Breakfast,** 18044 Hwy. 84, you will be invited to relax and enjoy the soothing sounds of the country. Stay at the ranch and enjoy the lovely patio and cabana with sauna and hot tub and the swimming pool, which is open May through Oct. You can enjoy fishing and paddleboating on one of three ponds or ride horseback in the surrounding hills. If you are in search of the perfect vacation hideaway, the ranch has cedar-log cabins situated on a bluff overlooking a valley filled with beautiful flowing creeks and lush green woods. The large cabins have two bedrooms, one a loft with a queen-size bed and the other downstairs. The loft bedroom has a very private view of the valley and hills beyond from the Jacuzzi tub for two. Cabins also have a fully equipped kitchen and wood-burning stove to complement the central heat and air-conditioning. They rent for $13 to $150 per night. Cowboy rooms are $45 for two, and the lodge is $70 for two. There is horseback riding by the hour. Daily horse rental is $70. Call toll-free

(888) 829-9570, or visit barfiftyranch.com. You can bring your own horse for a $15 stable fee or park your RV with full hookup (electrical, water, sewer) for $25 per night.

The area around here is a rock hound's dream. *Magnet Cove,* on US 270 East near Malvern, is said to have one of the country's most varied deposits of rocks and minerals. It is named for the magnetic iron deposits in the area.

The city of *Malvern* has such historical attractions as the *Boyle House Museum,* where you'll find artifacts and memorabilia relating to local history, Caddo Indian pottery and quilts, and antique furniture. Call (501) 337-4775 for hours and more information. From Malvern take Highway 171 west past *Lake Catherine State Park.* This park has 17 cabins. Some are rustic single units, where on chilly evenings you can enjoy a warm fire in the stone fireplace; others are modern duplexes. They are situated on a little peninsula on the lake, and most are on the lakeshore; the price is $84 to $179, double occupancy. You can also rent a yurt here for $55. But if you want to try your hand at roughing it, Rent-a-Camp provides tents, cots, a stove, and other camping equipment for $40 a night. The park has 10 miles of hiking trails and a nice swimming area. Call (800) 264-2422 for cabin reservations, (501) 844-4176 to make reservations for campsites, or check out arkansasstateparks.com.

The Ouachitas

Built along the bluffs of the Ouachita Valley, *Arkadelphia* was a river port during steamboat days. Now it calls itself the Wildflower Capital of Arkansas, and acres of them have been planted along the roadways and on public land. Take home a T-shirt saying GROW WILD IN ARKADELPHIA! The town has two universities literally across the street (and a ravine) from each other—Henderson State University and Ouachita Baptist University—and this arrangement has created one of the country's more interesting rivalries; their fierce athletic competition is legendary. Ouachita Baptist houses the personal library and memorabilia of Senator John McClellan, and Henderson State has a museum in a wonderful antebellum home featuring relics of the Caddo Indians. Both campuses are lovely, with huge oaks and interesting architecture.

The *Honeycomb Restaurant and Bakery,* at 7065 Main St., took quite a bit of damage in a 1997 tornado but survived. The restaurant is owned by Group Living, an organization to help adults with developmental disabilities. Because the group offers training and jobs to people, a big effort was made to get the restaurant going again—they served carryout foods until the building was fixed. Everything here is homemade. Breakfast omelettes, biscuits and gravy, and pancakes are served 8 to 10 a.m. Lunch, which begins at 11 a.m. and is served until 2 p.m. Mon through Fri, includes specials, such as chicken-fried steak, which come with a vegetable and salad, enough to feed a family of four. You can have one of their sandwiches—on homemade French bread—and dessert (with espresso!) until 4 p.m. Manager Barbara Eggar says absolutely nothing is ready-made, and the desserts are excellent. The restaurant is open for dinner 5 to 9 p.m. On the second, fourth, and fifth Tues of each month you can play bingo at the Honeycomb Restaurant. Games run 6:30 p.m. to about 9 p.m. The cost is $21 for 18 games. Call (870) 245-2333 for information or visit kdtsnr.wix .com/honeycomb.

The most recent renovation of *The Captain Henderson House,* at 349 North 10th St., has restored the mansion to its former majesty. This Queen Anne, exemplified by the round tower rooms and by the variously shaped

Peanut Brittle Capital

Arkadelphia is unofficially the peanut brittle capital of the state—there once were three shops all within 1 block of one another, and all good. But in March 1997 a tornado swept through this city, leveling most of downtown and killing 26 people. It was a most powerful and unusual tornado because it stayed on the ground for 26 minutes, according to news reports. This Class IV tornado was more devastating than Hurricane Andrew in the almost-mile-wide path it cut through the main part of the city. It left nothing but toothpick-size pieces of businesses and homes. (The only tornado worse is a Class V, which leaves nothing, not even toothpicks, in its wake.) One company, *Juanita's,* was blown away but has been rebuilt at 47 Stephenwood Dr. The new phone number is (870) 246-8542; or visit it online at juanitascandykitchen.com. In the wake of the tornado, then-President Clinton visited Arkadelphia and promised as much help as possible in its rebuilding.

roof and windows, also has Doric porch columns and other details of the neoclassical style, two architectural trends of the time. The home features elaborate wood paneling, ornate fireplace mantels, and fine pocket doors. You can call toll-free (866) HSU-INN1, locally (870) 230-5544, or fax (870) 230-5568 to contact innkeeper Vickie Jones. Rooms range from the Millsap Room, $90 per night, to the Regions Bank Suite (with sitting room) at $120 per night. View this magnificent mansion on the Web at hsu.edu. Click on the picture of the house.

US 67 rolls into *Gurdon*, where the *International Order of Hoo-Hoos Museum* will answer the questions of the curious about the history of the Supreme Nine, who handle the business affairs of the International Order of Hoo-Hoos. Ever wonder about the history of the Snark of the Universe, called the Supreme Hoo-Hoo, leader of eight other directors—the Senior Hoo-Hoo, the Junior Hoo-Hoo, the Scrivenoter, Bojum, Jabberwock, Custocatian, Arcanoper, and the Gurdon? Want to know more about the State Deputy Snark and the Viceregent Snark? You can get all the details here. "What's a Hoo-Hoo?" you ask. People in this timberland know that it's a fraternity of lumbermen. Its symbol is an arching Egyptian black cat with its tail curled into the number 9, and it was formed in 1892 to foster "elbow-rubbing" and the spirit of teamwork and is dedicated to health, happiness, and long life for its members. The museum is at 207 Main St. Hours are 9 a.m. to 4 p.m. Mon through Fri (it's closed at noon for lunch). Call (870) 353-4997 or (800) 979-9950 for information. The website is hoo-hoo.org.

Between Gurdon and Texarkana on US 67 (which parallels I-30) lies *"A Place Called Hope,"* birthplace of William Jefferson Blythe IV, who would become the 42nd president of the US. His grandmother's home, at 117 South Hervey St., is where he and his mother lived after his father's death. The

trivia

Ready for something spooky? Local folk legend surrounds the Gurdon Light, an unexplained phenomena of lights hovering in midair in a wooded area by railroad tracks. Locals explain the light appearances as a dead railwayman's lantern. Scientists have no explanation for the mystery. It was featured on the TV show *Unsolved Mysteries,* and the location is still used by the railroads.

home is now open for tours, which are free. In addition to the home there is a gift shop and replica of the Oval Office in an adjacent building. The tour runs about 30 minutes, but take time to enjoy the beautiful memorial garden planted in the backyard in honor of former president Clinton's mother, Virginia Kelly. The phone number here is (870) 777-4455. When Bill was four, his mother married Roger Clinton and moved to a home at 321 East 13th St. Bill Clinton attended Brookwood Elementary School.

If you want to see it all, go to the **Hope Tourist Center and Museum,** 100 East Division St., Hope, the renovated Iron Mountain/Missouri Pacific Railroad depot in the heart of the downtown area at the intersection of South Main and Division Streets, now dedicated to Bill Clinton and the town's history. Just as then-President Clinton said he "still believes in a place called Hope," others here have faith that the town will come alive now that more than 20,000 visitors a year from all over the world see it. In 1992 the presidential candidate visited the Hope depot to have campaign photos taken. When he was elected, the citizens of Hope decided to restore the depot to its original luster. The Union Pacific Railroad donated the station to the city in 1994, and the renovators used a federal grant and local funds to restore the building in 1995. Photographs chronicle Clinton's family, many on loan from local residents. One shows his father, William Jefferson Blythe III, who died in an auto accident before Clinton was born. Other artifacts include a bell from the kindergarten Clinton attended, one of his report cards, and a toy train he played with as a child. In a state-of-the-art audiovisual room, visitors can see two videos on the history of Hope and southwest Arkansas. Call (870) 722-2580 for information. Hours are Mon through Sat 8:30 a.m. to 5 p.m. and Sun 1 to 4 p.m.

Also in downtown Hope is **Cherry's Old Tyme Soda Fountain,** at 225 South Main (870-777-3424), where owner Cherry Stewart credits much of the revival to the efforts of the local businesspeople. Hope is a large watermelon-producing community, so in season have Cherry fix you a Watermelon Fizz. Hours are 11 a.m. to 2 p.m. ("When the bank closes, so do we," Cherry said.) Other downtown businesses include the **Little Herb Shoppe** at 203 South Main (870-777-2535). Hours are 9:30 a.m. to 4:30 p.m. Mon through Sat. **The Melon Patch** restaurant is at 104 South Elm, where you can stop in for lunch and have some very southern cooking (chicken and dumplings!). Call (870) 777-8802 for information. Hours are Mon through Fri 11 a.m. to 2 p.m.

Tailgater's Burger Company at 101 Main St. serves hot dogs and sandwiches in addition to signature burgers. The brick walls and decor make it a nice place for a casual meal. They are open for lunch and dinner, Mon through Sat 11 a.m. to 9 p.m. Call (870) 777-4444 for information.

Hope's old-fashioned sit-around-drink-coffee-and-talk-politics place is the *City Bakery and Dining Bar* at 200 East Second St., downtown. Owner Randal Ross says, "You'll love our buns," and you will also love the ham and biscuits for breakfast and the soups and sandwiches for lunch. Hours are Tues through Fri from, yes, 6 a.m. until 2 p.m. and on Sat 6 a.m. until 1 p.m. Please stop in, Randal says, "We knead the dough." Call him at (870) 777-6661.

Stick around for the annual *Hope Watermelon Festival* in Fair Park in August. Join in the melon-eating and seed-spitting contests, and of course, the melon judging. This town has two claims to fame: President Clinton and the world's largest watermelons.

If you plan to be at the southwest tip of the state to visit the *Conway Cemetery Historic State Park* near Walnut Hill, you might enjoy the ride across the river; then you can sing "Remember the Red River Valley" with more meaning. The park is dedicated to the memory of James S. Conway, the first governor of the state. The half-acre family cemetery where the governor is buried is on the 11.5-acre site, which also contains the governor's plantation home, Walnut Hill. Take Highway 29 to Bradley and then Highway 160 West for 2 miles to Walnut Hill. Turn left onto the county road and proceed 0.5 mile to the park entrance. No camping or visitor services are available. Visit arkansasstateparks.com.

If you take Highway 355 about 10 miles to the east of here, you'll come to the little town of *Stamps,* population 2,200. It was here that acclaimed poet Maya Angelou lived with her grandmother and other relatives off and on from about age 2 to 12. A neighbor woman became a mentor of sorts to Angelou, encouraging her to read and to express herself in writing. Angelou says her formative years in Stamps contributed to her award-winning novel *I Know Why the Caged Bird Sings*. City leaders are in the process of establishing a memorial to Angelou, including a regular poetry contest at the town's library.

Texarkana: The name of the town is derived from TEXas, ARKansas, and LouisiANA, three states that border nearby. Photographer's Island, at the front entrance steps of the post office, is a spot where you can photograph yourself standing in Texas and Arkansas at one time. Scott Joplin, the "King of Ragtime Composers," grew up here. A colorful outdoor mural depicting his life is a must-see stop. Before the coming of the settlers, the territory around Texarkana was the Great Southwest Trail, for hundreds of years the main line of travel between the Native American villages of the Mississippi Valley and those of the West and Southwest. The Grand Caddos tilled rich fields, fished, and hunted along the Red River, where they raised maize, beans, pumpkins, and melons.

trivia

Half the post office in Texarkana is in Arkansas, half is in Texas.

In the 1850s the builders of the Cairo and Fulton Railroad pushed through to meet the Texas and Pacific Railroad here. One of the first town lots sold in 1873 now houses the Hotel McCartney. Quite a few really interesting sites are on the Texas side of the line; there is a walking-tour map available that will lead you to many of them. So be sure and do the "trail of two cities" beginning on Stateline Avenue, where the only post office in the country that is in two states is situated, and then follow the 10-block walking tour to the other sites.

The 1920s have returned to Texarkana at the ***Texarkana Historical Museum of Regional History,*** at 219 State Line, actually in Texas, but a trip to the town wouldn't be complete without a visit to this museum. "This side of Paradise: the Jazz Age in Texarkana," at the museum, takes a close look at what the 1920s were all about in this part of the country and in a border town. Prohibition, automobiles, and a change in women's attitudes are all documented here. Hours at the museum are Tues through Sat 10 a.m. to 4 p.m. Call (903) 793-4831 for information. Admission is $5 for adults, $3.50 for children age 5 and up, and $4 for seniors and students. Visit texarkanamuseums.org.

Texarkana has a good place to call home for the evening. Sandra and Jeral Willard invite you to stay

trivia

One of Texarkana's attractions is the circa 1924 Perot Theater, a restored facility that features Broadway plays.

with them at **Oak Hill Bed and Breakfast,** 5522 Tennessee Rd. There are two bedrooms with private baths and a continental breakfast. Rates start at $100. Call (870) 645-2667.

Established in 1824, the town of **Washington** was, for more than 50 years, the jumping-off point for the unknown Indian Territory and Texas, a welcome sight for travelers on the Southwest Trail. The trail was an old Indian path and an important route for settlers, stretching diagonally across the territory from Missouri to Texas, forming part of the path that 3,000 Choctaw Indians traveled when they were forcibly evicted from Mississippi and sent to Oklahoma on the Trail of Tears.

The town of Washington is intertwined with **Old Washington Historic State Park,** a time warp back to those days. Like Williamsburg, Virginia, it's an authentic re-creation—as authentic as modern restoration and archaeology can make it—of a frontier boomtown of the 1850s. The entire town of Washington lies in a state park. Private homes are mixed with historic structures in the 1-square-mile area, along with the state's largest and most magnificent magnolia tree. The narrow dirt roads were laid out about 160 years ago when thousands of people were headed for Texas and stopped at the hotels in town to buy supplies. Davy Crockett, Sam Houston, and Stephen F. Austin passed through Washington headed west. During the Civil War Washington served as the Confederate state capital after Little Rock was captured by the Union army in 1863.

A blacksmith shop stands on the site of an earlier one, and inside the glowing metal is still fashioned by leather-aproned men who hammer out knives like the first bowie knife, designed here by smithy James Black for Jim Bowie. Today people travel from great distances to learn the ancient art of knife making at one of the world's few schools of bladesmithing, classes sponsored by Texarkana College and the American Bladesmith Society. The shop is open year-round.

Spring brings splashes of yellow jonquils, scattered over the hillsides, along roadsides, and in flower boxes all over the city to celebrate the annual Jonquil Festival in the middle of March. The quiet town of 148 is inundated with visitors, more than 40,000 at last count, who come to see the bright display of flowers, some of which are descendants of bulbs planted by the pioneers—as are the aging, gnarled catalpa trees that shade the gravel streets. During the festival craftspersons carve walking sticks of sumac, make brooms of straw with antique tools, and weave rugs on looms. Bowie knives are displayed in the park's gun shop, which also contains a 17th-century Chinese matchlock gun, muzzle-loading rifles (demonstrated by costumed traders in town), and a German machine gun from World War II.

Take a stroll around (and through) the impressive Royston Magnolia Tree, which was planted in 1839 by one of Washington's original residents, Grandison Royston. This tree is debatably both the oldest and largest magnolia in the state of Arkansas.

The Pioneer Cemetery is filled with pre–Civil War tombstones. Small markers dot the area where wagons bogged down in the bottoms of the Saline and Ouachita Rivers and where attacks by Rebel troops at Poison Springs, Marks' Mill, and Jenkins' Ferry killed 700 people. All these can be seen on the walking tours of the town. Tours take about 2 hours and begin at the 1874 Hempstead County Courthouse, which houses the park's visitor center. There are plenty of other sights visitors can explore on their own, too. A printing museum shows the evolution of printing during the 19th century; the B.W. Edwards Weapons Museum contains a collection of more than 600 weapons; and the Black History Museum, housed in a doctor's office built circa 1895, portrays the important role African-American Arkansans played in the history of Washington.

trivia

The Grand Caddos farmed this area and maintained six villages along the banks of the Red River. They were hospitable to the explorers and settlers. In 1840 a permanent settlement was established at Lost Prairie 15 miles east of Texarkana. Today all that remains are a number of mounds and other traces of the Indian civilization left behind as the native population moved westward.

Williams Tavern Restaurant, kitty-cornered to the courthouse and operated by the park, began as a "stand" on the road, an open house where, for pay, John W. Williams entertained travelers. It was one of the best-known spots between Memphis and the Red River. Today the menu is posted on the blackboard and features such homemade specialties as chicken and dumplings, potato cakes, and apple cider. Hours are 11 a.m. to 3 p.m. The Pioneer Grocery also serves sandwiches. And the nearby Tavern Inn re-creates the feeling of the pioneer era: The bar has an antique brass rail, and pre–Civil War bottles line the shelves, just as in frontier days. Phone (870) 983-2890 for more information.

There are several Greek revival homes, among them *the Royston house* and *the Sanders-Garland home.* At both places women in period dress check their hoopskirts in the petticoat mirror before greeting visitors. The Royston home towers behind huge magnolia trees, and flowers line the dirt drive leading up the hill to the front door, which has stained-glass windows depicting the four seasons. (Looking through one blue-paned glass makes things appear as though a blanket of snow were on the ground.) The house is filled with Empire furniture. The L-shaped, 1845 Sanders-Garland house has a large back porch where the family spent warm evenings. A portrait of daughter Sara hangs over the fireplace. A third house, the Dr. James Alexander Purdom home, circa 1850, features exhibits on early medicine.

The Confederate capitol of Arkansas (from 1863 until the end of the Civil War) is open to the public, as is the 1874 redbrick courthouse. For those interested in research, Washington is also the home of the *Southwest Arkansas Regional Archives (SARA),* dedicated to collecting and preserving source materials for the history of the area. SARA is in the Old Washington Courthouse and can be used by all serious researchers, including grade-school students. Although materials cannot leave the archives and must be used in the research room, copies can be made of most materials that are in good condition. The park is open year-round 8 a.m. to 5 p.m. daily. Admission is $7 for adults and $4 for children. Call (870) 983-2684 for information.

A block west of the courthouse is the oldest active Methodist church in the state. The congregation dates from 1818. *The Old Washington Jail* behind the church is the original 1872 Hempstead County Jail. Up until just recently, it was a privately owned bed-and-breakfast. At the time of this writing, the state park was in the process of buying the jail and reopening it for lodging. The previous owners were kind enough to let lodgers know that a resident ghost was included in the amenities. I imagine the specter will be included in the sale. For information on rates and availability, call the park at (870) 983-2684.

Another unique state park lies north of Washington on Highways 4 and 27. If diamonds are a girl's best friend, then women have a lot of pals around Murfreesboro—not in the quaint town square but in nearby *Crater of Diamonds State Park,* because there are not only diamonds forever but also

DeQueen for a Day

Originally, **DeQueen** was to be called *DeGoeijen,* after the turn-of-the-20th-century Dutchman who was to be the namesake of this town. The word proved too much of a tongue twister—it's pronounced *de-gwen*—and people soon decided that it would be a terrible handicap for a town to start life with such difficulties (plus the mail problems). Because his friends called him *DeQueen* anyway, that was the name that stuck when the town was incorporated in 1897. In the fall of that year, the first passenger train ran from Kansas City to Port Arthur. In a special car were Arthur E. Stilwell, Jan DeGoeijen, and his wife, Mena, after whom Mena, a town in northwest Arkansas, was named.

In 1828, when Sevier County took in several other counties, Paraclifta was selected as the county seat. The town took its name from a Choctaw chief at a nearby village who achieved a peaceful settlement when some pioneer men were accused of stealing horses. In the 1840s R. C. Gilliam built Paraclifta's most imposing house, with two ground-floor rooms leading from a large entry hall and two more rooms upstairs. (On the fireplace mantel you can see where Gilliam carved the initials of his wife, Frances.) Gilliam was a cotton planter and was killed during the Civil War's Battle of Marks' Mill. The town of Paraclifta is now almost totally gone except for the mansion. Tours of the **Gilliam-Norwood House** (also called Paraclifta House) may be arranged by contacting the Sevier County Historical Society Museum at 717 North Maple, DeQueen, in Dierks Park, or by calling (870) 642-6642.

Outside the **Sevier County Museum** stands the last red caboose from the Kansas City Southern Railroad, which linked the fertile Midwest plains to the deepwater port on the Texas Gulf Coast. Arthur E. Stilwell built that line with the help of Jan DeGoeijen, who was a young banker in Holland with the foresight to embark on this project when others had refused.

The museum also has a small village behind it. Antique Village has eight small buildings, including the Red Dog Saloon, the Sevier County Jail, and a church that is available for weddings and memorial services. Across the street is the 1940s House, a good example of the homes of that era; World War II memorabilia, a treadle sewing machine, and a satin wedding dress lying on the mahogany bed make you feel like you just came home. The details go right down to a piecrust ready to bake in the kitchen. If you are in town the second weekend in October, you will be treated to Hoo-Rah Days, a festival that celebrates the railroad's coming to town. Museum hours are Tues through Sat 10 a.m. to 5 p.m. For more information, call (870) 642-6642.

practically free. These are not phony "diamonoids." They are the real thing, and this is the only—repeat, only—diamond mine on the North American continent. There is a $8 charge for adults and a $5 charge for children age 6 to 12 (age 5 and under are free) to enter the digging area, but after that anything you find is yours to keep. Yes, diamonds are free here; all you have to do is pick them up. It's finders keepers, no matter how valuable they are, and almost 1,000 diamonds are found every year—the average is three a day. More than 60,000 diamonds have been found in the 80-acre crater. It's tricky; all that glitters is not diamonds. But here's a secret that makes this book worth the cover price: Dirt won't stick to diamonds like it does to other rocks, according to Michael Hall, park superintendent. And most diamonds are found in kimberlite breccia, which is a greenish rock. The gems are said to be from 95 million to more than three billion years old. Diamonds come in yellow, brown, pink, and black. And even if you don't find diamonds, you may find other semiprecious stones, such as jasper, opal, agate, quartz, amethyst, and garnet. There is even a geologist on the park staff to verify the gems, which are identified and weighed for you. The 40.23-carat Uncle Sam diamond is the record, but the 34.5-carat Star of Murfreesboro or the 15.31-carat Star of Arkansas wouldn't make a bad piece of jewelry, either. Speaking of jewelry, the Kahn Canary was found in the park in 1977. The uncut 4.25-carat stone is considered flawless, with a pleasing, natural triangular shape, and is mounted in a ring designed for former first lady Hillary Rodham Clinton for her husband's inauguration in 1993. They are among the biggest, and for most visitors, they whet the urge to dig.

The diamonds should be all gone by now, you say? Wrong. Geological forces push the diamonds upward slowly through the kimberlite soil, and the park plows the crater occasionally to increase the chance of bringing

trivia

DeQueen is the birthplace of country music singer Collin Raye, a three-time nominee for Male Vocalist of the Year by both the Country Music Association and the Academy of Country Music and a member of the Arkansas Entertainers Hall of Fame. Raye's number one country hits have included "Love Me," "Little Rock," and "One Boy, One Girl." Each June for the past decade, Raye has performed a benefit concert in DeQueen.

them to the surface of this 35-acre field, which is the eroded crust of an ancient volcanic pipe.

After a hot day of digging for diamonds with the kids, you can cool off at the park's *Diamond Springs Water Park.* It has over 4,000 square feet of water jets, slides, and waterfall hideouts as well as a covered deck area with lounge chairs. Water park admission is $6 for adults and $4 for kids. Hours are noon to 6 p.m. daily from Memorial Day weekend to mid-Aug and then on weekends only from mid-Aug until Labor Day weekend.

trivia

More than 70,000 diamonds have been found in Arkansas. The largest was found in 1924 and weighed 40.35 carats. A 16.37-carat diamond was found on the surface in 1975.

If you're hungry, you can grab breakfast and lunch at the *Kimberlite Cafe.* Hours are 8 a.m. to 4 p.m. daily from Memorial Day weekend to mid-Aug and then on weekends only from mid-Aug until Labor Day weekend. The park is on Highway 301 about 2 miles southeast of town and is open daily from 8 a.m. to 5 p.m. Between Memorial Day and Labor Day, hours are extended to 8 p.m. each day. Call (870) 285-3113 for information or visit craterofdiamondsstatepark.com.

Murfreesboro is a real gem (you should excuse the pun) of a town. It is just northwest of the park on Highway 301. Every Sat night during the summer, there is free entertainment at 8 p.m. in front of the *Conway Hotel,* which also has a flea market and an outlet for the art and crafts of local artisans. The hotel is on the National Register of Historic Places. The *Jif-E Corner Bakery and Deli* is on the courthouse square at 101 West Main. The sausage and biscuits are a fine way to start your day, but if you're here at lunchtime, there is a buffet lunch every day but Sat 11 a.m. to 1:30 p.m. The bread for the submarine sandwiches is baked fresh daily here, and there is fried chicken on the menu if a sandwich is not quite enough. The deli's long summer hours are 6 a.m. to 8 p.m. Mon through Sat and 11 a.m. to 8 p.m. Sun. Call (870) 285-3314 during other times of the year.

The *Queen of Diamonds Inn* is at 318 North Washington St., 1 block north of the square. Al and Jane Terrell bought the house and renovated it a few years ago, managing to combine Victorian charm and modern convenience. The office is in the 1902 home, which is filled with authentic furnishings. Motel rooms were built behind the home, and the 41 guest rooms there are new and modern. A complimentary continental breakfast is served in the cheery breakfast room in the house. Rooms are based on the number of people (over 14). For two people, they run $89 or $109 for four; call (870) 285-3105 for reservations.

The **Ka-Do-Ha Indian Village** is near Murfreesboro, about 1.5 miles off Highway 27 on Caddo Drive. It is the site of a prehistoric Indian settlement—home of the Caddo Mound Builders—and many artifacts are on display. The village is a combination archaeological dig and museum. You can tour the mounds and hunt for arrowheads on the surface, but state laws prohibit digging at the site. The mounds are in fields surrounded by woods; they are open, although some greenery has grown up around them, and you can see the remains and artifacts. An article about the mounds appeared in *Archaeology Today* magazine, but as yet the mounds are relatively undiscovered by tourists and there are no great crowds here. The gift shop and the Happy the Prospector gemstone mine are here, too, selling bags of rough minerals you can take to the water sluice and wash for your own gemstone. Hours at the village are 9 a.m. to 5 p.m. in winter and to 6 p.m. from Memorial Day to Labor Day. Admission is $4 for adults and $2 for children. Manager Sam Johnson offers a wealth of information about most places around town. Call (870) 285-3736.

Diamond hunting isn't the only outdoor activity that glitters near here. The Little Missouri River flows clear and cold and is the home of possibly the best fly fishing for rainbow trout in the state. It is also home to the scrappy smallmouth bass that provide some of the best action for sport anglers. The tailwaters below the dam are icy, and you can fish from a canoe or flat-bottom boat or just wade in and do it the old-fashioned way. If that experience has made you happy, continue north about 9 miles on Highway 27/US 70 to Glenwood, where you will find the **Caddo River**—a beautiful, spring-fed stream full of those same smallmouths. It is floatable year-round, and canoes and guides are available in Glenwood for pack-in trips in the wilderness. Crawfish is the bait of choice.

You can see why fishing enthusiasts favor this part of the state. **Daisy State Park,** in the foothills of the Ouachita Mountains near the northern end of crystal-clear Lake Greeson, is famous for its 30-pound lunker-class striped bass, northern pike, and walleye. Above the lake on the Little

Missouri lurk fighting rainbow trout, too. But this park has something more: It caters to motorcyclists with the 31-mile **Bear Creek Cycle Trail** on the west side of the lake. The trail goes to Laurel Creek and is open to motorcycles, all-terrain vehicles (ATVs), and nonmotorized bikes as well, although if you are pedaling, a mountain bike would be a good choice; this is a 31-mile one-way trip, and it's mountainous. ATVs are not allowed in the park except on the trail. There's a parking lot at the trailhead to off-load your ATVs, and motorcycles can be driven to the parking lot by roadway. The trail and park are open year-round 7 days a week. Call (870) 398-4487 for information.

In October the bike tour from Daisy to Crater of Diamonds Park, 23 miles away, is an annual event. There is an entry fee, but you get a free T-shirt for the tour. An interpretive program of guided hikes, games, crafts, and evening slide and movie shows in the park's outdoor amphitheater is free during summer. Campsites have electric and water hookups, but half of the 21 tent sites are for hike-in camping only. The clear waters of the Caddo River begin their path to the sea in the Ouachita Mountains near Mena, and the Caddo Valley is ideal for camping in primitive campsites on the abundant sand and gravel bars. From the town of Daisy on US 70, go 0.25 mile south. Call (870) 398-4487 for information or visit arkansasstateparks.com.

At **Pea Patch Ranch Cabin,** 179 Pea Patch Ranch, Caddo Gap, Chris Warren has 1.5 miles of riverfront on his 570-acre cattle ranch. He has built Pea Patch Cabin about 50 feet off the Caddo River. This cabin has a bath with shower and a fully equipped kitchen. The loft above the living area has a queen bed, and a futon in the living room will sleep two more. An 8 by 16-foot deck (with a chimenea for warmth) overlooks the river. It is a very private, secluded, and romantic spot and not too primitive. (There is air-conditioning and heat.) Rates are $125 per night (or $100 per night if you stay for 4 nights or more). The Buena Vista Cottage sits on a hill with pretty views of the ranch and the Ouachita Mountains. It has two bedrooms, one with a queen bed and one with a full, and two bathrooms. The cottage is $150 per night. You will have to stock your own supplies for cooking, though, since this is not a bed-and-breakfast arrangement, but that is what makes it different. Call (870) 356-2353 to talk to Chris or visit peapatchranch .com. To find the ranch, come into Caddo Gap from the south and take the only left turn in town; cross the Caddo River and it is the first drive on the right. There is a sign that says PEA PATCH RANCH.

Two beautiful sights in this region are the 4-mile Winding Stair portion of the *Little Missouri Trail* and the *Little Missouri Falls* near the Albert Pike Campgrounds north of Langley. To get there from US 70, west of Hot Springs, take AR 369 north. *Note:* AR 369 is 5 miles west of Daisy and 4 miles east of New Hope.

Follow AR 369 to the fork with FR 73 (about 6 miles). Continue north on FR 73 to FR 43 (about 3 miles). Turn left (northwest) and continue to FR 25 (about 4 miles). Turn left (west) and continue to FR 539 (about 0.5 mile). You have to hike in to see the falls, but they are almost accessible by road via a short (0.2 mile) hike from a picnic area with parking. The falls are a series of 10-foot stair-step falls in an area designated as "wild," meaning that all roads are barricaded and closed year-round. This walk is a bit of a test for older people because of about 25 yards of steps. But the trail winds along the river and through rocky, tree-shaded canyons, and the only sounds are the rocks kicking up riffles and the birds and squirrels chittering in the trees. If you are still feeling your oats, you can camp at Albert Pike and hike 6.3 miles along a trail of shortleaf pine, old-growth American beech trees, American holly shrubs, and plenty of white oak, hickory, and red cedars—a trail that parallels the Little Missouri River to the falls. The trailhead is at FR 106, a good dirt road, 2 miles from the Albert Pike Recreation Area. Watch for the Forest Service emblem marking the trailhead.

The falls are only 6 miles from the headwaters, and the river is not wide at this point. The trail fords the river at the southern end and crosses a creek near the northern trailhead, so some wading is required. The falls are between Round Mountain and Hurricane Knob. To drive to the picnic area from the Albert Pike Campgrounds, go north on CR 73 about 2 miles; then take a left turn on CR 43 and go about 5.5 miles, taking CR 25 to the left for 1 mile and CR 593 to the left about 0.25 mile. There are five picnic tables there, as well as parking. Be sure to bring your camera or sketch pad.

If you prefer a canoe or kayak, the river is peaceful and shallow and lazes along in summer, looping around wide gravel bars, forming deep swimming holes and rock towers. After spring rains, though, the Winding Stairs portion of the river is crooked and steep and capable of producing Class III rapids after a big storm—not easy to navigate for beginners.

East of Langley on Highway 84 and then Highway 4, you can meet "Beauty and the Beast" if you are in the mood for danger and adventure.

"Beauty and the Beast" is what they call the Cossatot River, and 11 miles of the most rugged and spectacular river corridors pass through *Cossatot River State Park* near Wickes, where Highway 4 meets US 71. The river begins in the Ouachita Mountains southeast of Mena and rushes south for about 26 miles into Gillham Lake. The waters are the home of two fish found only in the southern Ouachita: the leopard darter and the Ouachita Mountain shiner. The park covers more than 4,200 acres of wooded slopes and cascading, clear water. There are Class III, IV, and V rapids on this wild-running river, making it a favorite with rafters, kayakers, and canoeists. They say that Cossatot means "skull crusher," and the river can be dangerous. It flows over and around upended layers of bedrock, sometimes dropping 60 feet per mile, and contains narrow valleys and lengthy rapids and falls. Called "probably the most challenging" whitewater in the state, the river is not recommended for the inexperienced. Call (870) 385-2201 for information about the river or visit arkansasstatepark.com.

Mena is where US 71 runs into Scenic Highway 88. The city is in the shadow of Rich Mountain. The newly restored 1920 *Kansas City Southern Railroad Mena Depot Center,* at 514 Sherwood St., is a combination museum and visitor center. It houses the Mena Chamber of Commerce, a

trivia

The Ouachita Mountains run east and west, rather than north and south like most other American ranges. This makes the area difficult for pilots of small planes and backpackers, who often become disoriented in the unusual terrain.

tourist information center, and railroad displays and memorabilia. Quality crafts from a 60-mile area are for sale inside. The center is run by community volunteers, who know their way around the area quite well.

Raspberry Manor Bed & Breakfast, at 300 Raspberry Ln., is a secluded, romantic spot with 2.5 miles of quiet hiking trails. Fishing and rowboating are available on a private lake. Innkeepers Kathy and Don Rook treat people like family and "just turn them loose on the place." The huge 1,400-square-foot deck on the north, west, and south sides of the house overlook the mountains and lake, and there is the 65-foot-high "eagle's nest" for panoramic views. Inside, a 22-foot-high stone fireplace in the living/dining area is the perfect spot to get warm and watch the rotating chandelier in the living room. The manor also has one Victorian bedroom, one 1920s eclectic bedroom, a dance floor, a pool table, a game room, and an antique private bar. The Rooks serve a full breakfast ("with dessert of waffles or pancakes and syrup," Kathy says; now that's a full breakfast!). You can check out the website at raspberrymanor.com, or call (479) 394-7555; fax (479) 394-7618. Rates are $150 for the Fishin' Shack (this is not a cutesy new place—it really is rustic) or $115 to $150 for the bedrooms in the house.

Highway 88 shows off the 54 miles of twists and turns along **Talimena Drive** as it winds along the crests of forested mountains between Mena and the Oklahoma border, within the boundaries of the 1.6-million-acre **Ouachita National Forest,** covering almost all of Montgomery County. The drive spans the highest mountain range between the Appalachians and the Rockies. Getting off the road is full of pleasures, too. Hiking trails wind through the forests along ridges, lakes, and streams. It's a heaven for nature lovers. The area is one of America's oldest landmasses, and the rock there tells the geologic history of the area. At the crest of Rich Mountain a historic fire tower stands 2,681 feet above the valley.

Rising high above the clouds on Rich Mountain, **Queen Wilhelmina Lodge,** 3877 Hwy. 88 West in **Queen Wilhelmina State Park,** was destroyed by fire in 1973 and rebuilt in a style that reflects its past, with stone fireplaces, comfortable rooms, and a spectacular view. It is perched on the highest elevation in the park on steep and winding Highway 88. The first lodge was constructed in 1896 by the Kansas City, Pittsburgh and Gulf Railroad and was designed as a retreat for passengers on the line. The 3-story lodge became known as the "Castle in the Sky" and was named for Holland's young queen (there was largely Dutch financing for the lodge). A royal suite was set aside for her in hope that she would decide to make an official visit someday, but she never did. Dining in the lodge's restaurant gives you a view above the clouds. Rooms are $95 to $165 (for a room with sitting area and fireplace).

trivia

Queen Wilhelmina State Park has an extraordinary display of wildflowers from mid-Apr through early May. Wild iris, hyacinths, and violets carpet the hiking trails. Hike up to Lover's Leap Trail (1.3 miles) to see dogwood trees in bloom, Jacob's ladder, and a grand glimpse of the Ouachita National Forest.

Other attractions in the park include a small railroad, miniature golf, camping, and an animal park with creatures to pet. Queen

Wilhelmina State Park is 13 miles northwest of Mena on Highway 88, but in bad weather it is advisable to take US 270 to Highway 272 and then to go south for 2 miles. Continuing west takes you to the Pioneer Cemetery historical marker before crossing the state line into Oklahoma. Call (479) 394-2863 or you can find the lodge on the Web at queenwilhelmina.com. Talimena Drive crosses Highway 259 and begins to climb along the spine of the Winding Stair Mountains. There are several interesting spots along the drive: Billy Creek Recreation Area, Emerald Vista (which has not only camping but interpretive and equestrian trails), Lake Wister, Cedar Lake Recreation Area, Horsethief Springs, and Old Military Road historical sites all perch on the ridge of the mountains. You will have a sweeping view of the Poteau River Valley.

Highway 88 East from Mena leads to the only town in America named after a radio show—***Pine Ridge.*** If you are old enough to remember radio days and are at all nostalgic for them, first close your eyes and listen to your memories and then open your eyes and take a look at Dick Huddleston's ***Lum and Abner Museum*** (4562 Hwy. 88 West) or the "Jot 'Em Down Store." Is it the way you thought it would be? You will never see Fibber McGee's closet. You will never see the Shadow ("Who knows what evil lurks in the hearts of men?"), but this museum is on the National Register of Historic Places. You can walk right in and let your imagination take you back to those nights in front of the radio. Arkansas natives Chester Lauck and Norris Goff, better known as Lum and Abner, entertained listeners during the 1940s with a radio show filled with down-home humor, and today the store looks just as it did, or how we imagined it looked, back in the 1940s—an old potbellied stove near the post office window in the general store (with the museum situated in the next room). The museum is open Tues through Sat 9 a.m. to 5 p.m. and Sun noon to 5 p.m., Mar 1 through mid-Nov. You can call (870) 326-4442, and although neither Lum nor Abner will answer, postmistress Kathryn Stucker will. Visit lum-abner.com to see the movies that made Lum and Abner stars.

If you have followed Highway 88 East, you will be entering an area called the "Quartz Crystal Capital of the World," and there are several commercial mines around here. ***Wegner Quartz Crystal Mines,*** 3 miles south of Mount Ida on Highway 27, are one of the few mines where you can find your own crystals. They are open 8 a.m. to 4:30 p.m. Mon through Fri in winter and 7 days per week in spring and summer. You don't have to dig very deep to find crystals in one of the three mines. The digging fee ranges from $6 for deposits nearby to $20 a day to travel to the mines—groups of 10 or more only, and you can keep what you find. Tim, the manager, says that finding a crystal is almost guaranteed. One of the mines is a hike—0.25 mile up a mountain slope, a strenuous walk not recommended for older people—but you can be driven to the other location (in Tim's pickup truck), where you can dig in the red clay until you find all the crystals you want. Six-sided, single-point crystals are the most common and can be clear or cloudy quartz. The clusters are more difficult to find; they require more work and some luck, too. Crystals range in size from a quarter of a pound to 10 pounds. Richard Wegner, owner of the mines, also has showers and campsites available near the retail area, which is 5 miles south of Mount Ida on Highway 27. Call (870) 867-2309 for information, or visit their website at wegnercrystalmines.com.

Some nice side trips to resorts and picnic areas can be found along US 270. This beautiful part of the state offers scenic drives worth exploring for an afternoon or a weekend. Premier among them is the twisting drive to the summit of Hickory Nut Mountain that leads to a panoramic view of **Lake Ouachita** and its many islands. This region is remote and natural, with small towns sprinkled throughout the hills. It is a fine place to escape the hustle of city life and enjoy the beauty of the Natural State.

Surrounded by the Ouachita National Forest on Lake Ouachita, family-owned **Mountain Harbor Resort and Spa** has drawn visitors for nearly 50 years. Bill and Debbi Barnes and their friendly staff have made this gigantic complex feel warm and comfortable for five generations. It is one of the finest spa/resorts on the lake, because "off the beaten path" doesn't always mean roughing it in a primitive cabin. If you check in to the Harbor North Cottages, you will have a beautiful view of the lake and hot tubs on the deck. (Rates begin at $308 during the week and weekends begin at $469.) But wander over to the Turtle Cove Spa and enjoy the luxury of a massage, facial, pedicure, or any other holistic body treatment you want or need, on the outdoor spa cabanas overlooking the lake. Clean water, pure air, ahhh, it doesn't get any better than this. Of course, there is fishing and guy stuff, and things for the children, too, so it can be seen as a family vacation where mom actually gets to vacation as well. Go to mountainharborresort.com for a better idea of what's there or call (870) 867-2191 in Arkansas or (800) 832-2276 from out of state.

More Places to Stay in Southwest Arkansas

ARKADELPHIA

Best Western Continental Inn
136 Valley Rd., I-30/
Highway 67, exit 78
(870) 246-5592
Inexpensive

Quality Inn
150 Valley
(800) HOLIDAY or (870)
230-1506
Inexpensive

HOPE

Best Western
I-30/Highway 278,
exit 30; 1800 Holiday Dr.
(870) 777-9222 or
(800) 429-4494
(Bill Clinton slept here.)
Inexpensive

HOT SPRINGS

Best Western
2520 Central
(501) 624-2531
Inexpensive

More Places to Eat in Southwest Arkansas

ARKADELPHIA

Fishnet Family Restaurant
5000 Valley St.
(870) 246-7885
Inexpensive

HOT SPRINGS

Porterhouse Steak & Seafood
707 Central Ave.
(501) 321-8282
Expensive

CHAMBERS OF COMMERCE IN SOUTHWEST ARKANSAS

Arkadelphia Chamber of Commerce
2401 Pine St., Ste. B
Arkadelphia 71923
(870) 246-5542
arkadelphia.dina.org

Hope Chamber of Commerce
200 South Main, Hope 71802
(870) 777-3640
hopechamberofcommerce.com

Hot Springs Chamber of Commerce
Box 6000, Hot Springs 71902
(501) 321-2277
hotsprings.org

Southeast Arkansas

Several of the counties of southeastern Arkansas share the Ouachita River, but high bluffs, unspoiled forests, and the river bottoms give each area a distinct personality. If you enjoy gentle currents, a float on the Ouachita with your fishing gear is perfect.

In the early 1700s, French trappers encountered the Ouachita Indians living in small villages on the banks of the river. Ouachita is the French way of spelling the Indian word, which sounds like "Washita," but the meaning of the word has been lost—perhaps "good hunting" or "river of many fish," some say.

This is where the timberlands begin, past the Ouachita Mountains, on the way to the Mississippi Delta. The timberlands are where the Gulf Coastal Plain and the Arkansas River Delta meet, too. This lush area, covered with vast forests of southern pines and drained by sleepy bayous and sloughs, is a favorite with sports enthusiasts because of the exceptional fishing and hunting it provides.

The longest bayou in the world, Bayou Bartholomew, meanders through the timberlands. The history of the country is seen from a southern view in this part of the state, and

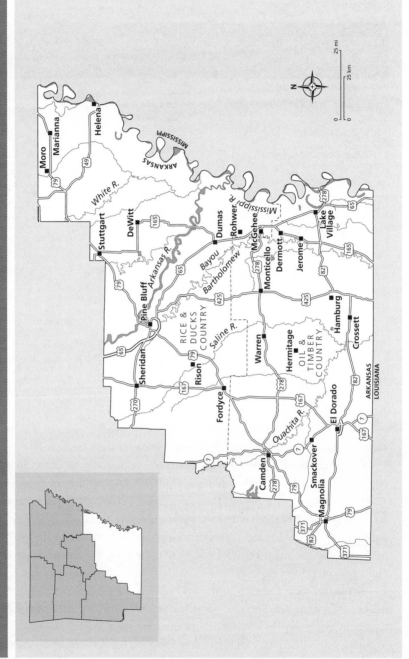

SOUTHEAST ARKANSAS

BEST ATTRACTIONS IN SOUTHEAST ARKANSAS

Big Boy Toys and Interior Story
Magnolia
(870) 234-8899

Dallas County Museum
Fordyce
(870) 352-7202

Delta Cultural Center
Helena
(870) 338-4350
deltaculturalcenter.com

La Bella Gourmet Gifts and Delicatessen
El Dorado
(870) 862-4335
labelladeli.com

Lakeport Plantation
Lake Village
(870) 265-6031 or (870) 972-2803
lakeport.astate.edu

Margland II
Pine Bluff
(870) 536-6000
margland.net

plantations and antebellum homes dot the Mississippi bottomland along the mighty river.

Oil & Timber Country

Camden stands on a bluff at a horseshoe curve of the Ouachita River. The Quapaw Indians, a branch of the Sioux, were friendly to early Spanish explorer Hernando de Soto when he made his trip up that river in 1541. The distance is 5 miles around the river's bend but less than a quarter mile across the neck of the curve. In fact, a man named Woodward once set more than 100 slaves to digging a bayou, which, had it been completed, would have become the main channel of the river, leaving the town sitting high and dry on the loop.

If you are near Camden at the end of September, you can join one of the largest annual arts and crafts festivals in the state. The *BPW Barn Sale* has been going on for over 50 years now and is a juried, one-day event featuring more than 180 exhibitors and vendors. Local entertainers perform throughout the day. There is an antique car show at the high school campus, and since so many visitors are in town, local organizations have a bake sale, pancake breakfast, spaghetti supper, whatever, that are different each year, so food is plentiful. Shuttles transport people from parking at several area churches to the barn, high school, etc. For more information call (870) 836-4560.

Camden is an old Deep South city where cotton bales once lined the streets leading to the wharf. A varied collection of restored antebellum homes, including the circa 1847 **McCollum-Chidester House,** at 926 Washington St. Northwest, attests to this heritage. The house, which is haunted (more about that in a moment), was used as headquarters by Sterling Price, a Confederate general, and Frederick Steele, a Union general, during the Battle of Poison Springs in April 1864.

The house is filled with the original furniture and even has some bullet holes in the plastered walls of an upstairs room where stagecoach drivers slept: Union soldiers shot at stagecoach driver Colonel John T. Chidester—who had allowed Confederate soldiers to read Union mail he was carrying on his stagecoach—as he was hiding in a secret room near the stairwell. A pair of crystal hurricane globes, a mahogany and walnut secretary, and a sewing machine date back to 1850, along with Mrs. Chidester's needlework and clothing. The original dining table is set with Mrs. Chidester's silverware and china (which were buried under a tree in the yard to keep them safe from Union soldiers). The east bedroom is haunted by an apparition of a man dressed in a long coat, carrying a cane or sword. It appeared reflected in a mirror in a photo taken by a member of the historical society in 1985; copies of the photo can be purchased here.

The historical society has built a carriage house in the backyard. Because this was a stagecoach stop, a replica of one of Chidester's Concord stagecoaches and a turn-of-the-20th-century surrey are parked there. The home is open 9 a.m. to 4 p.m. Wed through Sat. Tours are $5 for adults and $2 for school-age children. Call (870) 836-9243 for information.

trivia

During the Civil War near St. Charles on the White River, a cannonball was shot through a porthole of the federal ironclad *Mound City,* killing almost 100 soldiers when it hit a steam pipe. Historians call it the single most destructive shot of the war.

The winters have been fairly harsh in southeast Arkansas for the past few years, which makes the annual *Daffodil Festival* in Camden each March that much more welcome. During the second weekend in March, the town literally blossoms with billions of daffodil bulbs planted by the city and private residents. The festival includes a tour of five historic homes and their gardens, street dances, gardening demonstrations, and arts and crafts. Call (870) 833-2443 for more information.

The *Oakland Cemetery* at the junction of Adams Avenue and Maul Road, less than a mile from town, is the resting place of the more than 200 unknown young men killed in battle here. It has many other interesting stories of the lives and times of the early settlers. Beautiful examples of the almost-forgotten craft of wrought-iron work appear in fences around many plots. One unusual gravesite contains only four weathered posts and a heavy iron anchor chain connecting them. It is said to be the grave of a child who died on a steamboat trip. The boat stopped only long enough to bury the little girl, and the crew used what it had onboard to mark the spot.

From Camden take Highway 24 West to *White Oak Lake State Park,* which has 725 acres of timbered hillsides. Here in the hardwood forests, the Beech Ridge Trail offers a glimpse of the Gulf Coastal Plain. The gentle trail is 2 miles long and takes you from the thick underbrush of the edge of the woods into the shaded forest floor where life abounds. As the elevation drops, the pines of the uplands meet the lowland hardwoods, where the Caddo Indians lived some 200 to 300 years ago. Boardwalks cover the bottomland part of the trail to protect the unusual plants that live in this moist soil. Orchids grow here—in the early spring the twayblade orchid and later other orchids and arums (such as the jack-in-the-pulpit) are seen here. The park has 45 campsites with electricity and water.

A bridge takes you across the stream, where the soil is mostly white sand, the remnant of an ancient shoreline that was formed as the Gulf of Mexico receded from the area more than a million years ago. The fine white sandhills lead around a slight curve and ascend into the sand barren, an isolated spot where the soil is infertile and few plants can survive—but the ones that do are unique to these zones. Riddel's spikemoss, for instance, looks like little sand castles and, like moss, dries up and waits for rain to revive it and release its spores. But unlike moss and more like fern, it has roots and, like pine trees, has a conelike megaspore. It is unique to the

BEST ANNUAL EVENTS IN SOUTHEAST ARKANSAS

Winter Wings Festival
Lake Chicot State Park; first weekend in Feb
(870) 265-5480
Birding, lake cruises, and levee tours

Armadillo Festival
Hamburg; first weekend in May
(870) 853-8345
Armadillo derby and crawfish boil

Magnolia Blossom Festival
Magnolia; third week in May
(501) 833-2443
World championship steak cook-off

Crossett PRCA Rodeo
Crossett; second week in Aug
(870) 364-9277

Grand Prairie Festival of Arts
Stuttgart; Sept
(870) 673-1781
Juried show and sale, top exhibitors, miniature art show

BPW Barn Sale
Camden; Sept
(870) 574-4560

Arkansas Blues & Heritage Festival
Helena; second weekend of Oct
(870) 572-5223

World's Championship Duck Calling Contest & Wings over the Prairie Festival
Stuttgart; Thanksgiving weekend
(870) 673-1602, (800) 810-2241
Gumbo cook-off and the Great 10K Duck Race

sandhills and sort of a missing link between lower and higher plant levels. Call (870) 685-2748 or (870) 685-2132 for information or go to arkansasstate parks.com.

The park is adjacent to **Poison Spring State Forest** on the shores of White Oak Lake. There are regular sightings of great blue heron, egret, osprey, and green heron. In winter bald eagles live on the shoreline. Of course there are always great-horned owls and pileated woodpeckers along the many hiking trails.

Logging trucks rumble down the highways, and trucks stacked high with chicken crates cruise in a confetti of feathers: Forestry and chicken ranching are the main businesses as you head south. But along US 79 between Camden and Magnolia, you'll see what is perhaps not the most beautiful of yard ornaments (but better than a birdbath)—oil wells—gracing lawns.

Six miles north of Magnolia on CR 47, just off US 79 near the McNeil Highway junction, is *Logoly State Park.* This is not pronounced to rhyme with "by golly" but rather sounds more like *Low-ga-lie.* The name has nothing to do with the loblolly pine, either. It is actually an acronym of the names of three families who gave the land to the state—the Longinos, the Goodes, and the Lyles. The park has medicinal waters bubbling up in 11 natural springs in the forest; people once traveled from far away to drink and bathe in the mineral waters. Logoly was also the state's first environmental education park, and observation stands and photo blinds dot the trails for nature observers and birders. The mineral springs and unique plant life make it worth exploring.

The visitor center houses exhibits of the park's history and natural environment. Hours are 8 a.m. to 5 p.m. daily. Call (870) 695-3561 for information or visit arkansasstateparks.com.

The *White House Cafe,* at 323 Adams, is a nice choice for lunch or dinner. This place has been open since the early 1900s, when it was built for railroad workers who were putting lines through for the lumber business, and has the oldest beer license in the state. It offers more than 50 kinds of beer, both domestic and imported, and is famous for cheeseburgers and steaks. One of its specialties is Mexican food. Owner Teresa Lampkin, who doubled the size of the restaurant seating when she bought it, also brought in her family's personal collection of antique beer cans. Customers spend hours searching the walls for their favorite brand. Hours are 11 a.m. to 10 p.m. Mon through Sat. Call (870) 836-2255 for information.

If you'd like to see how Camden does fine dining, visit the *Postmasters Grill.* At 133 Washington St. inside the 1896 Camden Post Office building, the menu features American cuisine created with fresh ingredients. Lunch is 11 a.m. to 2 p.m. and dinner is 5 to 9 p.m. Tues through Sat. Call (870) 836-5579 for reservations or for more information, or visit postmastersgrill.com.

South of Camden on US 79 lies the city of *Magnolia.* As the name tells you, flowering trees grace this city's landscape. The courthouse is surrounded by them, and fragrant blossoms burst into bloom just in time for the *Magnolia Blossom Festival,* which includes a parade, treasure hunt, art and craft shows, antique cars, motorcycles, fishing tournament, dog show, and steak cook-off the third week in May. The steak cook-off has become one of the biggest events around here. They cook 4,000 rib eyes, sold for

$20 with a drink, baked potato, salad, and roll. This is the *official,* nationally sanctioned steak-cooking championship, attracting steak cookers from all over the country with a prize purse of over $10,000. **Big Boy Toys and Interior Story,** at 24 Hwy. 79, is another must-see place. It is a combination art gallery, collectibles shop, and sort-of museum. Owner George Black says that some items are not for sale, like the 1915 Model A car hanging on a wall. There are model trains, fountains, and a chandelier made of deer antlers (which is for sale). A good collection of emerging-images art is on display, too. In these paintings, nothing is quite as it seems at first glance. Something might appear to be clouds, but when you get closer you realize it is a herd of buffalo running across a prairie. By the front door stands a Christmas tree decorated in a western theme. George recently added 4,000 square feet to the store, mostly to accommodate his hunting and fishing village, a separate room in the center of the store. In addition to antique hunting and fishing items, you'll find mounted animals, such as elk, deer, and bobcats. Some of them were shot by George himself right here in southeast Arkansas. George is an artist. He designs barbecue grills that look like a horse, a pig, or a rocket ship. One of George's grills is 70 feet long! The front of the shop is a boutique with gifts and home decor run by his daughter Heather to lure the ladies into the shop, too. You have to climb the stairs to get to the big boy toy department. The shop is open 8 a.m. to 5 p.m. Mon through Fri. Call (870) 234-8899 for information.

If you are looking for a place to eat, search out the **Backyard Bar B Que,** at 1407 East Main. It is well known around here for its baby back ribs and homemade pies. Glenda Jones is the "pie lady," and she has been here since the beginning. People line up outside for her special pies. You never know what kind of pie will be offered—it depends on her mood—but some of the favorites are chocolate chip cherry cheesecake, lemon icebox pie, any kind of cheese pie you can imagine (chocolate and raisin are two favorites), and pecan cream cheese pie. Hours are Tues through Sat 11 a.m. to 9 p.m. Owners David and Susan Greer know that a lot of people are weight conscious, so they also have a low-fat menu. What, you might ask, could a barbecue and pie place have on a low-fat menu? Picture this: a rolled, steamed 10-inch tortilla with greens, chicken breast, steamed asparagus, carrots, fat-free cheese, and tomato slices. Call (870) 234-7890.

Walk around the town square and feel the magnolia pride in this lovely town. Each shop represents the city's flowering trees in some small way, it seems. A gift shop sells marble eggs, music boxes, and items covered in magnolias. A framing gallery features prints with magnolias, and even the pharmacy has magnolia mementos. You can browse the antiques mall and give your feet a rest in the Let's Do Lunch loft while your eyes continue to shop, or be wild and find the *Magnolia Bake Shop,* which produces such mouthwatering treats as pecan sticky buns, rum cakes, and crullers. At 103 North Jefferson St., the bakeshop has been turning out fresh cinnamon rolls since 1928. Original owner Joe Stroope Sr. has passed the business on to his sons Joe Jr., Stephen, and Willie, who continue to make luscious baked goods daily. They have expanded beyond doughnuts and cookies, though, and now offer almost anything your sweet tooth can desire. Along with great bread, cakes (German chocolate), pies (apple, peach, and pecan), and Danish pastries, the men make fresh biscuits and sausage rolls for the breakfast crowd. (How does a German smoked sausage tucked inside a fresh roll sound? Or breakfast sausage inside a hot biscuit?) Everything is baked fresh daily, and the bakery opens at 6 a.m. and stays open all day until 5:30 p.m. Tues through Fri and until 4 p.m. Sat, so you can go from early Danish to late-afternoon sausage roll. Call (870) 234-1304 for information.

trivia

If you hear bells while walking around the town of Magnolia, don't think you've gone nuts. The campus of Southern Arkansas University is home to a 180-foot-tall bell tower that chimes every 15 minutes, 365 days a year. The sound carries for miles. During the Christmas holiday season, the tower is decorated and lit to look like a huge candle, and the music played reflects the season.

Shopping for exclusive designer clothes, something in the $200 to $1,200 price range? Then stop by *Lois Gean's,* at 109 South Jackson St. The shop is listed right there with the high-dollar department stores in *Vogue* magazine as the place to buy designer clothes. The ad says, "Lois Gean's, Magnolia," with no state mentioned—because people "in the know" know where Lois Gean's is. People who want Donna Karan, Escada, and Anne Klein clothing and who like Valentino bags shop here and have come from miles around to do so since 1948. Lois Gean's started as a small gift shop and has bulged sideways to take in 4,400 square feet of the neighboring buildings. The rustic entrance, with its cast-iron stove and old brass mailboxes, belies the polish inside, and dynamic owner Lois Gean Kelly travels to New York on buying trips. The shop is open Mon through Sat 10 a.m. to 5 p.m. Call (870) 234-1250 or for information. Check the website at loisgeans.com.

Open for tours is **Albemarle's Artificial Marsh,** 7 miles south of town on US 79. The National Aeronautics and Space Administration–inspired marsh is an environmentally safe wetland that serves as a natural water-purification system. There are more than 80,000 aquatic plants and feeding stations to encourage the habitat of beavers, otters, and raccoons as well as ducks, hawks, egrets, and other waterfowl. A teaching station explains the development of the marsh, and a freshwater aquarium is filled with Japanese koi, minnows, frogs, catfish, goldfish, and turtles. To schedule a tour call (870) 235-6000.

Southern Arkansas University's (SAU) Working Farm, at the north edge of Magnolia, also takes an environmentally conscious approach. The 670 acres of livestock, poultry, and plants are cared for by 75 students in the country's largest agricultural work-study program. The farm focuses on ways to reuse waste products, studies the benefits of tillage versus nontillage crop growth, and does applied research into breeding techniques and equipment. SAU is also home to the state's only official National Collegiate Athletic Association rodeo team, whose horse and practice stock are housed on the farm. The farm, which draws people from all over the country, can be toured by appointment by calling (870) 235-4340.

The **Weyerhaeuser Company Reforestation Center,** just outside Magnolia on Calhoun Road, is where 50 million seedlings a year are born from some 600 parent trees. The people at Weyerhaeuser know the ancestry of each tree ("It's sort of a stud farm for trees," says Lester Hutchins of the Magnolia Chamber of Commerce) and have chosen the area because the environment is perfect for reproducing pines. The birth and upkeep of these native trees are a full-time job in this timberland. In spring, seeding operations can be seen; in summer the seedlings grow, covering the acreage with a soft green fuzz; in fall, cone harvesting and processing go on; and in winter the seedlings are harvested to sell to forest products companies and individuals in a five-state area. Although southern pine predominates, other trees—different kinds of oak and some cypress—are grown in the forest. Respect and care for the environment are demonstrated in this area, despite the logging that sometimes strips hillsides bare before they are replanted. This is an environmental education stop worth a visit. Two videos are available: The first shows the birth and growth of the trees cultivated here; the second relates the life cycle of the forests. To find the forest, go south on US 79 to the first intersection (less than 1 mile), turn east onto Calhoun Road, and proceed about 6 miles to the center. Hours are 7:30 a.m. to 4 p.m. Mon through Fri. Call ahead at (870) 234-3537; group tours can also be arranged.

After all this exploring, if you're looking for an unique place to get a relaxed meal, stop by *The Flying Burger* at 101 Hwy. 79 North, in Magnolia (there is now a second location in El Dorado at 704 S. Timberlane Dr.). Along with great burgers (they don't actually fly) you'll also find southern seafood dishes like crab legs, shrimp, po' boys, catfish, salads, and fish tacos. They are open for lunch and dinner, Mon through Sat 11 a.m. to 9 p.m. Takeout is also available if you're in a hurry. Call (870) 234-3701 for more information.

Driving east on US 82 brings you to the city of *El Dorado.* In 1921 the town prospered when black gold began gushing and the sweet smell of crude oil pumping onto the land and into the once-pristine waters of the Ouachita River drew the get-rich-quick crowd of promoters, drillers, roughnecks, and thieves. The town filled with itinerant oil workers, and the population jumped to 30,000 persons who needed to be fed. A 3-block area called Hamburger Row sprang up. Now, more than 70 years later, more sophisticated restaurants line the street, and the city is not to be missed if good eating is high on your list of things to do while traveling.

Most of the buildings downtown were constructed in the boom days, when oil flowed freely from the wells around here. Now one of two "Main Street" cities in the county, El Dorado has been restored, and brightly colored awnings, pear trees, and park benches have been added to the old lampposts that line the streets. The place boasts handsome old homes and the *South Arkansas Arts Center.* The old *Union County Courthouse* on the town square, the heart of the community, is a massive, neoclassical building with more columns than any other structure in the state. *The Rialto Theater,* built in 1929 at 117 East Cedar St. on the square, has also been restored and is the state's only working art deco theater, with gilded, vaulted ceilings and waterfall curtains. To take a tour or to find out what's showing, call (870) 881-8771.

La Bella Gourmet Gifts and Delicatessen, at 101 East Main St., features delicious sandwiches, soups, meats, cheeses, and salads, as well as gift baskets. It is also well known for its cinnamon rolls, powdermilk biscuits, and "almost world-famous" turnip green soup. The building was an old department store built during the oil boom. It has a ballroom upstairs for parties and every day serves crawfish étouffée with red beans and rice that is so good people from Louisiana take some home with them. The 100-seat deli sells such wonderful things as cream and butter fudge. The more adventurous fudge lovers clamor for the smoked chipotle and jalapeño flavors. La Bella uses Italian meats shipped in from "Yankee Land" (Massachusetts) and was twice given honorable mention as one of the best delis in the state. At Thanksgiving and Christmas you can order a Cajun fried turkey and dressing made with jalapeño corn bread and have it shipped to you. Jim Robinson is the owner of this place (you can't miss him, he's the big, smiling man with the beard). It's open Mon through Sat starting at 8 a.m.; Mon through Wed it closes at 6 p.m., Thurs through Sat at 8 p.m. Call (870) 862-4335 for information or visit labelladeli.com.

While you are downtown on the square, find *JJ's Barbeque & Catfish* at 1000 East Main. You will not believe the size of the menu here. They have just about everything. Not just barbecued ribs and catfish, but anything else a card-carrying carnivore could crave. Every night is certified Angus steak night or, you can indulge in the All-You-Can-Eat Catfish Feast (or chicken, ribs, or other meats) with side dishes and hush puppies. Ed's Country Fries are more like potato chips and an indulgence worth the calories. Now let's talk about dessert. Leave room for homemade sweet potato pie, blueberry pie, or the special Italian cream cake. Owners Joe and Joyce Gallea know how to keep customers coming in. Hours are Mon through Thurs 11 a.m. until 8 p.m. and Fri until 9 p.m. Call (870) 862-1777.

The **South Arkansas Arboretum** is a 17-acre arboretum adjacent to the high school and city park. It has walking trails, pavilions, and picnic areas that are used for educational purposes and also for weddings. The arboretum is open 8 a.m. to 4 p.m. Mon through Sat and 9 a.m. to 5 p.m. Sun. Call (870) 864-7160.

If you are going to spend a few days in El Dorado, there are a multitude of fascinating places like *Creative Means,* at 114 West Main, where Colleen and Mike Means do quilt stretching and have work by local artists, as well as custom framing of prints and posters. Hours are 10 a.m. to 4 p.m. Tues through Sat (870-862-9881).

The *Old Towne Store,* at 113 North Jefferson St., is a bakery and bulk-food shop offering foods prepared only with natural ingredients—home-made soups and sandwiches (with whole-grain breads) and freshly baked pies and pastries. The aroma of baking bread and cookies fills the shop. Hours are 8 a.m. to 6 p.m. Mon through Fri and 9 a.m. to 5 p.m. Sat. Call (870) 862-1060 for information.

Even though it's tempting to spend the day on the square, the rest of the city has some surprises, too. There are plenty of antiques shops and restaurants tucked around town.

El Dorado

El Dorado stands among the proudest of the small towns. While others have lost retail business to outlying areas, El Dorado enjoys a 95 to 100 percent retail occupancy. It has the last grand movie palace in the state, the Rialto, still showing movies each night. When my husband and I went to El Dorado, I had just finished two terms on the city council and one term as mayor of our town. Our city had taken the same Downtown Redevelopment money used in El Dorado, but we accomplished very little compared with this site. I was so amazed at El Dorado that I just couldn't leave without visiting every business on the square and talking to the owners. We stayed for dinner and saw the downtown blossom into a night center, too.

The courthouse is magnificent, and many of the retail businesses are upscale specialty stores, located in a historic district that has been restored to reflect a 1920s ambience. Because of the four restaurants and the theater, however, there is a slight parking problem, something every small town in the country wishes it had.

In the 20-block downtown area, 750 trees were planted, and the courthouse was relandscaped with more than 300 plants, including London plane trees, the street tree so common in Europe. There are old English phone booths, information kiosks, and street clocks dotting the square. Turn-of-the-20th-century light poles and sidewalk planters make the square a fine place to stroll.

Smackover, north of El Dorado on Highway 7, is worth a side trip because it is the other "Main Street" city in this county. The name comes from nearby Smackover Creek, which got its unusual name from the French explorers who found the banks of the creek to be covered with sumac and so named it Sumac Couvert. (Sumac Couvert soon became pronounced "smackover.") Boomtown murals are painted on the facades of the stores alongside Kennedy Park on Broadway Street; 1923 was a time when oil and money flowed freely and the town was prosperous.

The *Arkansas Museum of Natural Resources,* 3853 Smackover Hwy. 1 mile south of the oil-rich town on Highway 7 Bypass, is surrounded by 20 acres of woodlands. Six operational exhibits are on-site, including a working oil well, pumping rig, and seven derricks. And, surprise! Inside the 25,500-square-foot exhibition and research center, there's an art gallery, too, where local talent exhibits in the spacious auditorium. Each artist donates a piece of his or her work to the ever-growing collection in the 14 galleries now being designed. This is the largest museum in south Arkansas and has a full-time staff to direct visitors through the permanent and changing exhibits made up of the archives and artifacts covering subjects that include geology, refining oil and brine, use of petroleum and bromine, and paleontology, as well as social subjects such as women's role in the boom era. Stop first at the information desk in the lobby for pamphlets describing the indoor and outdoor exhibit areas. Temporary and traveling exhibits are displayed in the exhibition center, with two video presentations depicting the discovery of oil and brine in the state. No admission fee is charged to see the machinery and equipment that made this area explode in the 1920s, when the Busey Number 1 oil well blew in. Notice the colorful murals by Phillip Grantham that depict the history of the oil boom. Videos, tapes, and transcripts of oral histories of the roustabouts and roughnecks who lived and worked in the boom era are available to the public. A gift shop in the museum offers a variety of unique gifts related to the petroleum industry and the 1920s, as well as locally produced treats of jellies, hams, and syrups. Visit arkansas stateparks.com.

The *Smackover Oil Field* was the largest in the country for a 5-month period in 1925. Oil Field Park, the outdoor portion of the exhibit, has a 1920s standard rig and a 112-foot wooden derrick, the tallest known wooden derrick structure in the country. There's a spot to picnic, but if you want to see the real thing, you can get a tour through the 40-acre Smack-over Field, just north of the museum, with acres of salt flats where the oil pioneers disposed of salt water that came from the ground along with the oil (residue of the oceans that once covered the southern part of the state). The museum, at 3853 Smackover Hwy., is open Sun 1 to 5 p.m. and Mon through Sat 8 a.m. to 5 p.m. There is no charge for entering this facility, but donations are accepted. Call (870) 725-2877 for information.

Returning from Smackover, driving east from El Dorado north on High-way 15 is one of the more scenic routes in the southern part of the state. The 14-mile drive from **Moro Bay** to **Hermitage** is a tranquil journey on a good county road. Houses along Highway 15 are a mixture of Victorian and modern styles. There used to be a free ferry to whip you across the Ouachita River by **Moro Bay State Park.** It is now dry-docked, and you can walk through it. This is where Moro Bay and Raymond Lake join the Ouachita River.

Christmas is quite a sight in the town of **Warren,** off Highway 15. A multimillionaire from Little Rock had a huge display of Christmas lights that annoyed his neighbors, who took him to court to douse the array and won. The lights were donated to the town of Warren, and now Christmas on the Courthouse Square is lovely. If you are lucky enough to be here during the holiday season, be sure to go by **Massey Florist,** at 205 West Cedar, because Jimmy Massey turns his place into a Christmas paradise for a couple of months. He has a huge gift shop, and you can finish off your list here. Hours are Mon through Fri 8:30 a.m. until 5:30 p.m. and Sat until 5 p.m. Call (870) 226-3822.

As long as you're shopping, a couple of other places in town are worth looking for. **The Spinning Wheel,** 210 South Main St., has upscale clothes, gifts, and all manner of things. Hours are 10 a.m. to 5 p.m. Mon through Fri and until 4 p.m. Sat. Call Jean Claycomb at (870) 226-6127. **The Sandwich Shop,** at 106 East Cedar, is owned by Jennifer and Johnny Bradford. They serve ice cream, sandwiches, beef stew, potato soup, and other good things at tables, the soda bar, or booths. Lunch and dinner are offered 7 days a week. There's even a pool hall in the back. Hours are Mon through Thurs 11 a.m. to 3 p.m. and Fri and Sat until 8 p.m. Call (870) 226-3920 for information.

If you decide to go southeast from El Dorado on US 82 toward Crossett, you will be passing through the **Falsenthal National Wildlife Refuge,** which has a visitor center off US 82 at Grand Marais. Lifelike dioramas show the 65,000-acre Ouachita River bottoms with wildlife, native plants, hardwood trees, uplands, and permanent water. In the Native Inhabitants diorama, an archaeologist (an animated mannequin) unearths ancient artifacts and tells the story of Native Americans from the Felsenthal Basin. Pay attention during the tour. You can take a computerized test at the end to see how much you learned. The Saline River flows from the Ouachita foothills to the Ouachita River at the wildlife refuge, and here you'll find the world's largest green-tree reservoir—home to such rare species as the red-cockaded woodpecker, an endangered species that brings birders from far away (the loblolly pine is the only tree in which these birds will nest), bald eagles, and alligators—as well as good bass fishing. Call (870) 364-3167 for information.

The town of **Monticello** (pronounced Mon-te-cell-o) is a 150-year-old timber town, and probably the oldest home there is the **Trotter House,** at 404 North Main St. Innkeeper Margaret Reddick will welcome you to this incredible 3-story Victorian home. It takes up a full city block and was built in 1896 by Virgil Trotter, who raised a family here. The kids used the third-floor attic for roller-skating, and the dining room table at which they ate is still in use in the main dining room today. The home has the original stained-glass windows from 107 years ago. A magnificent wraparound porch stretches three-quarters of the way around the house, and there's another on the second story.

This home is just a block from the town square but has a very large tree-filled backyard that's home to birds and squirrels, with walks on the grounds and benches under old magnolia trees that date from before the house was built. There are six bedrooms, all upstairs. A sitting room, a library/office, and a large main dining room, with another smaller dining room adjacent to it, are on the main floor. Antique furniture fills the home, some of it the original furnishings, and the house has been restored according to original blueprints. Margaret serves a full breakfast of omelettes, muffins, pancakes, or whatever sounds good to her that day. She also honors special needs of her guests. Rates are $75 to $95, and there are special packages for honeymoons (with champagne, special sweets, and a Jacuzzi in the Magnolia Room), girls' night out, and Mother's Day. One room has huge claw-foot tub that is bigger than the Jacuzzi. This was the first home in Monticello with indoor plumbing. Now there are computer and fax outlets in each guest room, as well as central heat and cooling.

Margaret will tell you where to shop and visit in town. Since it's a college town, there are plenty of restaurants and fast-food spots and an eight-screen cinema with matinees. There is also a public golf course. Call Margaret at (870) 367-0200 for information and reservations.

The Allen House at 705 N. Main St. is interesting to both history buffs and ghost hunters. The home, originally built in 1906 for Joe Lee Allen and his family, has been investigated for paranormal activity several times, and the current owners, Mark and Rebecca Spencer, have had several personal interactions with ghosts inside the house, which is their private residence. Mark has written a book about the house and the Allen family, centered around historical information and the love letters that he found wedged under a floorboard in the home's attic.

The house is an interesting combination of architectural styles: neo-classical, Gothic, and Queen Anne. It also has a large carriage house that served as living quarters for servants. The Allen House is open for tours by appointment for groups of six or more. If you're visiting at Halloween, the house is open to the public every Oct 30 and 31 6 to 11 p.m. for tours. The guided tour offers historical information punctuated by Allen family artifacts that are still in the home. During the Halloween tours, you also get to hear five of the voice phenomenon that were recorded during one of the para-normal investigations. Cost is $10 per adult and $5 for children ages 3 to 9. Call (870) 224-2271 to make reservations, or visit allenhousetours.com for more information.

If you liked the shop in Warren, then you will like ***The Spinning Wheel*** at 310 North Main St. here in Monticello, as well. It has the same hours, 10 a.m. to 5 p.m. Mon through Fri and until 4 p.m. Sat. It also carries toys, gifts, and clothing. Call (870) 367-3216.

Crossett, on US 82 east of Lake Jack Lee, is a former sawmill town started by a lumber company in 1903. It has a multifaceted gem of a city park, with a 3-mile paved hiking trail circling Lucas Pond—a quiet little lake stocked with bass and crappie for fishing—cutting through thick woods filled with honeysuckle and grapevines, and ending near the zoo, which has alligators, wolves, and peacocks. East of the pond in a wooded setting is ***Wiggins Cabin.*** The original cabin, circa 1830, was the oldest building in Ashley County until it burnt down in 2002. The cabin was rebuilt by the Crossett Cultural and Historic Society. Members worked closely with the Arkansas Historical Society to make sure the cabin replica is authentic. It is constructed from hand-hewn logs pulled from the bayou, hand-writhed shingles, and individually fired bricks. The cabin, a square-hewn cypress log dogtrot (with two living areas under one roof and a breezeway between), shows the labor of a man skilled with a whipsaw, broadax, and adze. The cabin represents the settlement's earliest days in the "Great Wilderness" of towering cypress, canebrakes, and rattan vines of the Bayou Bartholomew. Today it looks as though someone lives there, right down to the strips of fabric trailing from a rocker onto the floor, as if Mother had just stopped her rug-braiding to fix dinner.

Next door is the *Old Company House,* built before 1910 by the Crossett Lumber Company for its employees. It, like all the other company houses, was painted "Crossett Gray," one of the cheapest paints sold at the time. It, too, looks lived in. A "four-eye" wood-burning stove with a pancake griddle and teakettle stands in the kitchen. Nearby is a washtub used for everything from scrubbing clothes and bathing to cleaning hogs. A bare bulb hangs in each of the three rooms. Tours may be arranged by calling the Crossett Chamber of Commerce at (870) 364-6591.

Visit the *Crossland Zoo,* one of only two licensed zoos in the state. It is set along a 2.8-mile concrete walking, biking, and skating trail within the Crossett city park that also connects to the Wiggins Cabin and Old Company House. The zoo features a petting zoo and 50 different mammal, reptile, and avian species. There is also a picnic area so that you can bring lunch. At 1141 Parkway Dr., the zoo is open daily and admission is free. Hours are 9 a.m. to 5 p.m. Mon through Sat and 1 to 5 p.m. Sun. Call (870) 364-7732 for more information.

The Georgia Pacific Corporation has gained national recognition for its tree-farming methods. The *Levi Wilcoxon Demonstration Forest* at *Hamburg,* north of Crossett on US 82, has three distinct types of forest, interconnected by a nature trail winding around Lake Georgia Pacific. The forest contains 250-year-old virgin growth, as well as pine seedlings and pine sawlogs more than 70 years old. Near the forest stands the giant Morris Pine—a loblolly pine tree 130 feet tall that measures more than 197 inches in circumference at its base. It is estimated to be more than 275 years old.

Hamburg is also the site of the Armadillo Festival held the first weekend in May, made world-famous by the Armadillo Derby. Say no more—you just have to be there and see it for yourself.

Lake Village sits on the west bank of **Lake Chicot**, the state's largest natural lake, an enormous oxbow of the great river forming the eastern border of the state. Lake Shore Drive follows 18 miles of waterfront through the city; it passes a marker designating the spot from which Charles Lindbergh made aviation history with his first nighttime flight. US 65 is only 6 miles north of the Louisiana border, and the rich alluvial soil reaches a depth of more than 1,000 feet (the world average is 7 inches); this is prime cotton-growing country, and with the Mississippi River just a few miles from town, offers beautiful scenery.

You can't go to Lake Village without visiting **Rhoda's Famous Hot Tamales.** The worn-out sign above the door has a subtitle of "also hamburgers, pies, and hot lunches," but you're really there for the tamales. And probably the pie, if you don't stuff yourself on the tamales, that is. Rhoda's tamales really are famous—she and her husband James have been written about by *Southern Living, Gourmet,* and many a food writer. You might think that would disqualify her as an "off the beaten path" type of place, but once you enter Lake Village and find the unassuming corrugated metal building that is home to Rhoda's, you'll see why she's still in. In addition to her now world-famous tamales, Rhoda has a gift for making pies. She even makes pies that are half sweet potato and half pecan for folks who can't decide what kind to try. Call (870) 265-3108 to find out how many tamales Rhoda has saved for you. You'll find her little restaurant at 714 St Marys St.

In 2007 **Lakeport Plantation** was opened. It is the last remaining antebellum home on the Mississippi River in Arkansas that has not been destroyed or altered significantly. It is considered one of Arkansas's foremost historic house sites. Tours of the Lakeport Plantation are available at 10 a.m. and 2 p.m. Mon through Fri. Admission is a $5 donation; $3 for senior citizens, school-age children, and groups of eight or more. Please call in advance for group tours: (870) 265-6031. For more information about visiting the plantation, call (870) 972-2803 or visit lakeport.astate.edu. The Lakeport Plantation is off Highway 82 near the bridge to Greenville, Mississippi. Turn south from Highway 82 onto Highway 142 and go 2 miles to the Lakeport

Plantation on the left. The gravel drive entrance is between cotton fields at a bend in the highway. A sign at the entrance says, epstein land company. On your way north out of Lake Village on Highway 65, stop off in **Dermott** to visit **The Amish Country Store.** Here you'll find over 200 handcrafted Amish and Mennonite products including fresh bread; canned goods like jams and jellies, pickles, and salsa; cheeses and meat; cider, soap, and furniture. You can also stock up on snacks and candy before you continue on your travels. Hours are Mon through Sat 9 a.m. to 5:30 p.m. The store is at 3040 Hwy. 65 North. Call (870) 538-9990 for more information or visit amishandcountrystore.com.

Rice & Ducks Country

The city of **McGehee** is one of the old railroad towns in the southeastern part of the state. A proposed Rails-to-Trails Corridor, 74 miles of railroad tracks that are being converted to hiking trails, threads through the area.

For lunch, **Kelley's Drug Store,** at 104 Holly St., has a genuine soda fountain and really great sandwiches. Hours are 8 a.m. to 5:30 p.m. Mon through Fri. Call (870) 222-5071.

If you're a fan of barbecue, be sure to check out **Hoots BBQ and Bakery,** 2008 Hwy. 65 North. Don't let the fact that the restaurant is inside a converted gas station fool you—Hoots is well known among locals as the best barbecue in the land. There are many other options on the menu as well. Try the Hoot's Burger, topped with a fried egg, caramelized onions, bacon, and cheese, with a side of homemade fries. For dessert, you can select from the cakes, pies, and cookies in the bakery. Hours are Mon through Thurs 11 a.m. to 10 p.m., Fri 11 a.m. to 11 p.m., and Sat 5 to 11 p.m. Call (870) 222-1234 for more information.

The **World War II Japanese American Internment Center Museum** at 100 South Railroad St. in the south building of the McGehee Railroad Depot opened in 2013 and houses data, memorabilia, and artifacts that exhibit the plight of the 17,000 Japanese Americans who were interned in relocation camps located in the nearby towns of **Rohwer** and **Jerome** after the bombing of Pearl Harbor. (See "Lest We Forget.") The exhibit, called *Against their Will,* highlights the history of the two camps and the people who lived there. There is also a gift shop with books and souvenirs. Hours

Lest We Forget

A *Japanese-American Relocation Center* site was established September 18, 1942, by the federal government at Rohwer in the aftermath of the bombing of Pearl Harbor.

Today all that is left at the 500-acre site is the cemetery, the monuments, and a large brick smokestack. The monuments, exceptional works of sculpture built in 1944, show the fine artistic skills of the internees who were detained here during World War II. One monument is dedicated to the Japanese Americans from the camp who died while fighting for the US Army in Europe; this monument is shaped like a tank, with a star-topped column rising in the center. Another is dedicated to those internees who died while in the camp; it features a column covered with elaborate Japanese script and topped by a globe with an eagle perched on it. The simple concrete grave markers were also made by the people living in the camp.

The center is on the National Register of Historic Places and currently undergoing refurbishment. New signage is being installed and the monuments and cemetery are being repaired. A replica small-scale guard tower serves as an informational kiosk. Take the self-guided walking tour along the southern boundary of the original camp, where you will find interpretive kiosks and an audio narration by former child internee, actor George Takei (best known for his role of Sulu on *Star Trek*), who discusses the history of the site and personal anecdotes from his time there. The camp is about 12 miles north of McGehee on Highway 1 toward Rohwer. A sign on the road will direct you toward a gravel road leading to the site, which open during "daylight hours."

are Tues through Sat 10 a.m. to 5 p.m. Admission is free. Call (870) 222-9168 for more information or visit rohwer.astate.edu.

On Highway 65 north of McGehee, you'll find the town of *Dumas.* Plan a visit to *Taylor's Steakhouse* for a unique dining experience. As the name would imply, Taylor's is known for their steak, which they serve dry-aged. You'll also find some other Cajun menu items here, including shrimp and grits, crawfish enchiladas, blackened duck breast, and swamp pasta. At 14201 Hwy. 54, Taylor's is only open for dinner at the end of the week: Thurs 5:30 to 9 p.m. and Fri and Sat 5:30 to 10 p.m. Call (870) 382-5349 to make reservations (walk-ins are also welcome).

In 1673 two Frenchmen, Catholic missionary Father Jacques Marquette and explorer Louis Jolliet, set out to explore the Mississippi Valley, traveling down the river from a French outpost on the north end of Lake Michigan to where Helena stands today. In 1682 they were followed by French explorer René-Robert Cavelier, sieur de La Salle, who wanted to establish forts along the river. One of his officers, Henri de Tonti, stayed and established a trading post where the Arkansas and Mississippi Rivers converge. It marks the first permanent settlement in the lower Mississippi Valley and was known as the Arkansas Post.

Homesteading began and, because the rich soil was perfect for cotton, was soon followed by slaveholding planters. Cotton became king. The **Refeld-Hinman House,** built about 1877 near Hinman Bayou, is an old log house that now serves as headquarters for the **Arkansas Post Museum** at 5530 Hwy. 165 South. The main building is pioneer homestead–style, with an open fireplace in the kitchen, complete with cooking pots, offering a glimpse of how cooking and household chores were done. The 1930s Child's Playhouse contains built-to-scale furniture and a wood-burning fireplace. The Peterson Building's lifestyle exhibits include one of pioneer wash day, as well as a country store, a farm workshop, and a vintage 1910 Stoddard-Dayton automobile. The gift shop is at the entrance to the Arkansas Post National Memorial. The museum is open year-round Tues through Sat 8 a.m. to 5 p.m.; Sun and national holiday Mon 1 to 5 p.m. Admission is free. Call (870) 548-2634 for information.

The **Arkansas Delta** is land built by rivers and has its own special vocabulary for the lowlands—words like levees, bottoms, backswamps, point bars, and oxbows. When dueling was outlawed, the islands of the Mississippi were used as dueling grounds because they were out of the jurisdiction of lawmakers. Hunters flock to this area, just as the ducks do. A large number of hunting clubs and lodges lie along the Mississippi Flyway, and when the season is right, they fill up fast.

Rising above a bustling Mississippi port, **Helena** is an old river town on the slopes of Crowley's Ridge. It is steeped in history, with antebellum, Edwardian, and Victorian homes and buildings scattered among rolling hills. Because of its position on the river, Helena was of strategic importance during the Civil War, when control of the river meant cutting the Confederacy in half. The Battle of Helena was one of the bloodiest in the state. The Confederate Cemetery on Holly Street contains a monument to the war dead and a panoramic view of the Mississippi.

The *Moore-Hornor House,* at 323 Beech St., is a Greek revival/ Italianate–style home. It was built in 1859 and placed on the National Register of Historic Places in 1987. Situated in a central position during the Battle of Helena in July 1863, the backyard of the home was a battleground with intense hand-to-hand combat in the struggle for Graveyard Hill. Restoration of the Moore-Hornor home incorporates archaeology, living history, and special programming in its interpretation. Go to deltaculturalcenter.com for more information.

Across Beech Street from the Moore-Hornor House is New Fort Curtis. This fort is a replica of the original Fort Curtis, which was built by the Union army when they occupied Helena in 1862. On July 4, 1863, 4,129 Union officers and men were positioned in and around the fort to fight against 7,646 Confederate troops. These outnumbered Union troops successfully defended Helena from the Confederate attack. Today, you can explore the earthen fort firsthand. You'll find interpretive panels and exhibits that tell the story of the fort, including how freedom-seeking former slaves helped with construction. Huge 24-pounder guns on display give you a sense of the type of heavy weaponry used to defend Fort Curtis. Admission is free. For more information, call the Helena Advertising and Promotions Commission at (870) 714-2844 or visit visithelenaar.com/content/fort-curtis.

Helena, founded in 1833, is Arkansas's major *Mississippi River* port and one of the oldest and most beautiful communities in the state. Here wharf boats once tied up indefinitely to the landings on the river, with every kind of store and concession onboard. Dozens of offices on Water and Ohio Streets made it a busy area. The street nearest the river began to drop off bit by bit as the river ate at its shores, and many buildings were moved from

Catfish—Anyway You Like It

You may have figured out by now that more catfish is eaten in Arkansas than in any other state of the Union. The fish is almost always dipped in egg and corn-meal and fried to a crispy finish on the outside with a soft, flaky, moist interior. Of course, you may also have noticed that everything else in Arkansas is fried, too— unless it's barbecued. This is not California. Even former president Bill Clinton takes a lot of ribbing (pun intended) about his love of barbecue and fried foods.

Water Street to save them. Most of the caving in of the riverbank occurred just after the Civil War. Soon Cherry became the main street.

Helena has built a park embracing the river that gave the town its life. There's a boardwalk, fishing spots, picnic areas, campsites, and docks big enough to accommodate the *Mississippi Queen* and *Delta Queen* steamboats. Watch all the activities on the riverfront by taking a 1.3-mile walk along the paved path atop the levee.

The ***Delta Cultural Center,*** at 95 Missouri St., in Helena's downtown area, portrays the city's blues heritage and pioneer life, an outgrowth of the rich cover of topsoil left by the winds and rivers of the area partly in the Helena Train Depot, built in 1913. The building's arched windows and orange tile roof reflect the sunlight and sounds of the adjacent river. The museum contains exhibits of the changes in landscape and lifestyle of the Delta, with themes covering early inhabitants, the Civil War, and music of the region, using artifacts, film, and music. The gift shop offers handmade crafts, railroad memorabilia, and posters. A reconstructed houseboat porch lets you live the story of the "river rats" who inhabited the Black and White Rivers. A caboose, with its railroad sounds and elevated navigation seats, gives kids a hands-on sense of the railroad era. The most popular portion of the center is the darkened corner room, where music flows from hidden speakers. The rough wooden floor and counter stools evoke the hard life and gritty work of the early inhabitants of the Delta. Photos and artifacts from the clubs of the city recall the blues legacy of such musicians as B.B. King and Sonny Boy Williamson and of the roadhouse bands of rockabilly favorites Conway Twitty and Charlie Rich. The center has opened an educational complex with computers for children and free Internet access. Their website is deltaculturalcenter.com.

The city has built a dock where riverboats from Memphis deliver passengers to the riverwalk. The cultural center is at the corner of Natchez and Missouri Streets at the harbor, at the end of the city's business district. Hours are 9 a.m. to 5 p.m. Tues through Sat and Mon that are national holidays. The center is frequently open late on Fri to accommodate special programs open to the public. Admission is free. Call (870) 338-4350 for information.

The area around the center is filled with shops and restaurants. One such place is ***Cotton & Kudzu.*** At 413 Cherry St., this combo antiques/gift shop carries home and garden decor, antiques, jewelry, handbags, children's clothes and accessories, and more. Hours are Tues through Sat 10 a.m. to 5 p.m. Call (870) 338-8339 for more information.

Cherry Street along the levee was once filled with many whites-only saloons. The black bars were on Elm Street, the neighborhoods segregated. Helena, like other Delta towns that relied on sharecropping and shipping cotton by river, had its rough side and its hard times. The great blues musicians like Roosevelt Sykes and Robert Lockwood let it all show in their music. In fact, this is the home of the Sonny Boy Williamson Blues Society.

While you're on Cherry Street, stop in at *Granny Dee's* for fantastic soul food. At Granny's they cook dishes including greens, fried chicken, mashed sweet potatoes, and peach cobbler with recipes that have been passed down through the generations. If you can't decide what to order from the menu, you can always choose the buffet! The buffet, along with breakfast and plate lunches are served Tues through Sat 8 a.m. to 3 p.m. Call (870) 338-8862 for more information.

Freedom Park, at 700 South Biscoe, was once the location of a Contraband camp (Contraband was a term used for escaped slaves who were seeking freedom during the Civil War). Now, the park interprets the lives of the African Americans who lived in this area during the war. Five exhibits include a plantation house and a refugee dwelling, as well as life-size figures that help tell the story. Freedom Park is the first location in Arkansas designated as a National Underground Railroad Network to Freedom site. The park is open 8 a.m. to 5 p.m. Sun through Thurs and 8 a.m. to 8 p.m. Fri and Sat. For more information, call the Helena Advertising and Promotions Commission at (870) 714-2844 or visit visithelenaar.com/content/freedom-park.

Slowly, more of Helena's fine old buildings and private homes are being restored to their former elegance.

The circa-1896 *Pillow-Thompson House,* at 718 Perry St., is the grande dame of the Victorian homes. Turrets and gables of many shapes grace the roofline. Curved porches bedecked with gingerbread surround it, and a row of porthole windows gives it a unique look. It is every little girl's idea of a dollhouse and was built for fancy-dress balls. Five generations of Pillows lived in the house until it was donated to Phillips Community College by Josephine Pillow Shinault Thompson and her son, George de Man. Members of the Pillow family were among those serving on fund-raising and restoration planning committees. Much of the original furniture was given with the house. This wedding cake–style home is on the National Register of Historic Places.

On the first Thursday of each month, the Pillow-Thompson House hosts a luncheon. A rotating group of local caterers provide the prix-fixe meal 11 a.m. to 1 p.m. Reservations are required. Cost is $12 per plate. It's a unique way to enjoy the ambience of the home while also enjoying a wonderful locally made meal. You can also register for etiquette lunches and business etiquette classes if you'd like a lesson on formal dining in a fitting atmosphere. The home is open for public tours Wed through Sat 10 a.m. to 4 p.m. It may also be rented for parties because of its commercial kitchen. Call (870) 338-8535 for more information, or visit pccua.edu/pillowthompson.

There are three historic districts in Helena, each with its own interesting sites and a fine collection of antebellum and Victorian homes and festivals celebrating the town's Deep South heritage. Tours of the homes and a downtown walking tour of the city are available from the chamber of commerce.

In *Life on the Mississippi,* Mark Twain said, "Helena occupies one of the prettiest situations on the river," and so it does. Hernando de Soto crossed the river here, followed in 1673 by Father Jacques Marquette and explorer Louis Jolliet. The city is filled with large modern homes as well as dozens of sturdy Victorians. Rolling hills, trees, and deep Bermuda lawns line the wide streets. This is obviously a town of old money.

The blues have influenced all the styles of America's musical heritage, including jazz, rhythm and blues, and rock and roll. Such greats as Sonny Boy Williamson, Robert Junior Lockwood, and Robert Nighthawk have been broadcast on the *King Biscuit Time* radio show on KFFA in Helena since 1941, and the **King Biscuit Blues Festival,** also known as the **Arkansas Blues & Heritage Festival** is celebrated in October to commemorate it. Helena is also the hometown of lyric soprano Frances Greer and country singer Harold Jenkins, better known as Conway Twitty. It offers 4 stages with 78 bands and performers over the 3-day festival. There is food and arts and crafts for sale. This is a must-see show. Call (870) 572-5223 or visit king biscuitfestival.com.

For almost 75 years now, the annual **World's Championship Duck Calling Contest & Wings over the Prairie Festival** has been held in

November. The 2-day festival has the usual arts and crafts, carnival rides, and live music, but it also features—what else?—the World Championship Duck Gumbo Cook-off. Call (870) 673-1602 or visit stuttgartarkansas.com.

The deep yellow *Edwardian Inn Bed and Breakfast,* at 317 South Biscoe St., was built in 1904. It was the home of William Short, a cotton broker and speculator who spent more than $100,000 in 1904 to build his family's dream house. The home contains eight original fireplace mantels, detailed woodwork, wainscoting, and paneling. It has unusual wooden floors of "wood carpeting" parqueted in Germany from strips of 1-inch-wide wood mounted on canvas and shipped to town in rolls. The huge wraparound porch is a fine place to rock on a warm afternoon. The building is one of the most interesting structures in this historically significant town and is on the National Register of Historic Places. Owners Dana and Lynn Chadwick watch over 12 comfortable rooms: The home has nine rooms and three suites, each with private bath, phone, and television. A full breakfast is served in the cheerful, latticed sunroom. The cost is $95 to $100 per night. Call (870) 338-9155 or (800) 598-4749 for reservations. The website is edwardianinn.com.

trivia

Birders! The ivory-billed woodpecker, thought to be extinct for more than 60 years, has been spotted in the Cache River and White River National Wildlife Refuges in the Arkansas Delta Byways region. It was, and now is again, the largest woodpecker in North America. During the 1880s and 1940s, millions of acres of virgin forest throughout the South were destroyed and this majestic bird was long thought to have been destroyed along with it, until 2005, when firm evidence in videos led to further searches in the state. For more information on the ivory-billed woodpecker in Arkansas, go to agfc.com.

The city of *Marianna* lies in the heart of the fertile Delta and on the edge of the St. Francis National Forest, which has abundant wildlife, hunting, and fishing. The *Marianna-Lee County Museum,* at 67 West Main St., has a small collection of Civil War artifacts found in the area, as well as artifacts from the Quapaw Indians, who once called this region home. Other displays focus on agriculture of the area. The museum is open by appointment. Call (870) 295-0145.

The county museum, at 67 West Main St., has a small collection of Civil War artifacts found in the area, as well as artifacts from the Quapaw Indians, who once called this region home. Other displays focus on agriculture of the area. The museum is open by appointment. Call (870) 295-0145.

The sign on US 79 says welcome to stuttgart. Take the *t*'s out of the name and you have the word *sugar,* so it's called "Sugartown." Would you have figured that out? **Stuttgart** began in 1878 when a Lutheran minister born in Stuttgart, Germany, brought his congregation to the Grand Prairie region of Arkansas; 9 years later the city was incorporated and named after the founder's birthplace.

Sugartown calls itself the "Rice and Duck Capital of the World." Farmers need oceans of water to produce rice, and this land is perfectly suited to this crop. The waterproof layer of clay, known as "hardpan," stops the water from seeping past the topsoil. Farmers use the "flush-and-flood" method: Fields are covered with water just after planting to germinate the new seeds; it stands for a day or two. When the shrubby plants are about 6 inches tall, the fields are flooded and left underwater for the duration of the summer. Although rice does not need standing water to grow, the water serves as a weed-control device. That's why ducks have always been plentiful hereabouts; 1.3 million acres of rice are just too tempting to the migrating flocks. Ever since the Quapaw Indians tied decoys to their heads and submerged themselves up to the nose in the water among the cattails and weeds to wait for the ducks when they landed nearby (the Native Americans grabbed the birds by the legs, clipped their wings, and took them home to a pen), hunting has been as important as agriculture here. As agriculture increased, the duck changed from "an acquired taste" to a tasty delight because the birds started out eating wheat in the Dakotas,

trivia

The **Smoke Hole Natural Area,** north of Stuttgart, is a 455-acre tract of land that is a good example of a forested wetland. The name "smoke hole" refers to a small, chimney-like opening in the tupelo brake within the area, which makes a perfect environment for the river otters and wood ducks that live there. Part of the area is flooded from 60 to 90 days each year, and most is flooded permanently. Marshes, swamps, and bogs covered in shallow water are home to plants and animals found in wetlands.

then dined on corn in Illinois, and finished up on Grand Prairie rice as they migrated south.

Life wasn't easy for farmers on the prairie. But when the chores were done and they put the hoe down, they knew how to have fun, too. The *Museum of the Arkansas Grand Prairie,* at 921 East 4th St. (at Park Avenue), depicts the history of the pioneers who farmed the Grand Prairie of eastern Arkansas from the 1880s until 1921. You can see how they worked and how they played. The first families came to the area under the 1862 Homestead Act. An 1880 home is beautifully furnished from the era. A rustic prairie home and scaled-down reproductions of actual buildings once here on the prairie—a mercantile, a doctor's office, a photography shop, a millinery, a grocery store, a post office, and, of course, a jail— are all part of the intriguing outdoor displays. A beautiful new mural has been painted in the equipment room depicting the history of the prairie. The area was settled by German Lutherans, and the museum has a lovely little church, a two-thirds-scale replica of the one that existed in the settlers' day. Displays give visitors insight into how farm families lived, with everything from old Victrolas and early kitchen equipment to a corner filled with the attire of a 1923 wedding. The place is huge. In the Wings of Grand Prairie, a minitheater, you can feel the modern-day thrill of a "crop duster turn" riding in the cockpit of a crop duster's plane. A display of antique musical instruments and fine needleware fills much of a recent 20,000-square-foot addition.

Because ducks are the other half of the economy hereabouts, it is no surprise that one of the more popular exhibits is the Waterfowl Wing, which houses a re-creation of a morning duck hunt, complete with circling birds, duck blind, cypress boat, and backgrounds painted by artist Don Edwards. All the world-champion duck callers from the Wings over the Prairie Festival held each Thanksgiving weekend are represented here, and visitors can listen to the 37 varieties of ducks that come through the Mississippi Flyway each year. Spotlights highlight each bird.

Famed wildlife artist William D. Gaither created realistic scenes for wildlife in its natural habitat, and the museum offers taped information on the flora and fauna of the Grand Prairie. Arkansas has one of the largest fish farming industries in the country, and the exhibit of live catfish is one children enjoy. The museum is open Tues through Fri 8 a.m. to 4 p.m. and

Sat from 10 a.m. There is no admission fee, but donations are accepted. Call (870) 673-7001 for information.

The *Arts Center of the Grand Prairie,* at 108 West 12th St., Stuttgart, features rotating exhibits of local and state artists' paintings, sculptures, and other artwork. Art-related activities are going on here all the time. Performing arts are presented, too. The Art Center Thespians, a community theater group, has several productions a year. A musical production runs in conjunction with the Grand Prairie Art Council's annual Grand Prairie Festival of the Arts. Call (870) 673-1781 for information.

You can take your fine arts experience even further in Stuttgart by paying a visit to **Grand Prairie Center** at Phillips Community College. The 60,000 square foot facility plays host to a full season of shows from Aug through May. Performances such as Cirque ZumaZuma, Seven Brides for Seven Brothers, the Arkansas Symphony Orchestra, and children's theater productions can all be taken in here. Grand Prairie Center is located at 2807 Hwy. 165 South, on the southern edge of town. Call (870) 673-4201 for show times and ticket prices, or visit pccua.edu/GPC.

It's a Grand Old Flag!

The people of Arkansas trace their state flag to Miss Willie Hocker, a member of the Pine Bluff chapter of the Daughters of the American Revolution. It was this group, in 1913, that became concerned when the **USS Arkansas** was about to be christened that the state had no flag. A statewide contest ensued with 65 entries, some designed by schoolchildren with crayons, others by accomplished seamstresses.

The 25 stars on the flag's blue diamond border signify that Arkansas is the 25th state in the Union, which is represented by the color selection of red, white, and blue. The diamond shape is because Arkansas is the only diamond producer in the Union. The single star above the name Arkansas represents the state's role in the Confederacy, and the three stars below represent the three countries that have owned the region: France, Spain, and the US.

Miss Hocker's design was officially adopted by the state legislature on February 26, 1913, and the Pine Bluff DAR chapter commissioned her to make the first flag for the USS *Arkansas* battleship.

Nancy Garot is the owner of *Gallery G Antiques in DeWitt.* This shop, in a historic 2-story bank building at 200 Court Sq., offers fine antiques, furniture, silver, and estate jewelry in an elegant location. Shop hours are Thurs through Sat 10 a.m. to 5 p.m. Phone (870) 946-2593 or visit gallery-g.com.

South of Stuttgart on US 79, *Pine Bluff,* the second-oldest city in the state, was founded in 1819 by Joseph Bonne, a French-Quapaw Indian, who built a log cabin on a pine-covered bluff overlooking a bend in the Arkansas River. Pine Bluff is now a trade center of the southeastern part of the state. It's a pretty town, with big old houses and wide streets. The University of Arkansas at Pine Bluff is here, and those interested in history will enjoy the "Persistence of the Spirit" exhibit in the campus Fine Arts Center, which chronicles the lives of Black Arkansans from pioneer days to the present. Call (870) 547-8236 for information.

The *Delta Rivers Nature Center* in Pine Bluff is the first of four such centers operated by the Arkansas Game and Fish Commission. The theme of Arkansas wetlands is presented with live animals, plants, and habitats, along with short films and exhibits. If you have never been to a swamp, this is your chance to see the wetlands up close. It is a diverse homeland to alligators, deer, owls, and other creatures. The center is built on what was once the main channel of the Arkansas River, at 1400 Black Dog Rd., off US 65B in the city's Regional Park. The main structure is reminiscent of the tin-roofed houses built on stilts in wetland areas. You walk up a sloped wooden walkway passing a swampy pond. Lily pads, young cypress trees, and bamboo are home to ducks and other birds. A mosaic map of the *Arkansas Delta* is the centerpiece, tracing the rivers and bayous. Behind glass are snakes, lizards, tarantulas, and the shallow-water salamander without back legs—called a siren—that buries itself in the mud.

trivia

American Legion games are played on a fine baseball field in Pine Bluff. Taylor Field was originally built for professional baseball with a grandstand, a press box, and regulation 90-foot base paths. The field now hosts national and regional tournaments.

Here is where the fun begins for the children. Below the lobby is a mock-up of a yellow biwinged crop duster. You can take a seat on the lower wing and watch a flyover of the Delta fields and lakes. Then on to the River Rat Boat Theater, a mock-up of a river barge, where a short film traces the history of the Delta's people, from Native Americans to the taming of the Arkansas River. Exhibits showing the richness of the swamp habitat explain how it filters pollutants and absorbs floods. You can even step on a scale and compare your weight with a record fish caught in the Delta (a 215-pound gar). Feeding time in the alligator pen is popular.

Outside, a paved loop trail leads to Black Dog Bayou, and a bird blind overlooks Black Dog Lake. There is a longer primitive loop trail for those who want to explore further.

Admission is free. Open year-round Tues through Sat 8:30 a.m. to 4:30 p.m., Sun 1 to 5 p.m. Call (870) 534-0011 for more information, or preview the center on the Web at deltarivers.com.

The **Arkansas Railroad Museum,** 1700 Port Rd., at the Cotton Belt Railway Shops in Pine Bluff, re-creates railroading in the 1940s. The 60-year-old engine is the last 4-8-4 steam locomotive ever built and was donated to the city by the railroad. This major restoration project, called "The Pride of Pine Bluff," utilized all-volunteer labor. Several cabooses and passenger cars have been added. Call (870) 535-8819 for more information. The museum's hours are 9 a.m. to 2 p.m. Mon through Sat. Admission is free, donations are accepted.

The **childhood home of Martha Mitchell,** wife of former attorney general John Mitchell and media darling of the Nixon years, is a stately blue Victorian house in Pine Bluff built in 1887. Martha's old homeplace, at 902 West 4th St., is open for tours. It has been restored and has several pieces of the original furniture dating from 1900 to 1930. Wallpaper was duplicated from scraps of original wallpaper for the renovation. The upstairs porch is decked in white gingerbread.

Photographs of Martha and clippings about her time in the capital—including a framed *Life* cover—adorn the walls of one bedroom. Bob Abbott bought the house from Martha before she died in 1979 at age 57 after battling cancer.

Tours are free but by appointment. Call Bob at (870) 535-4973 or the Pine Bluff Visitors Bureau at (800) 536-7660, ext. 2145, or go to atol.com/martha.

There is a cluster of lovely bed-and-breakfasts on 2nd Avenue in Pine Bluff, and all of them can be rented by the week or month at better rates. ***Margland II,*** at 703 West 2nd Ave., is one of four homes owned by innkeepers Wanda Bateman and Ed Thompson. All have been restored and decorated in an elegant fashion and serve as bed-and-breakfasts. This one, a 1903 colonial revival house, is a Bermuda cottage of "shingle style" architecture and done in pastels—blue, mauve, and pink. The detailed beauty is filled with Victorian antiques and touches of the nearest holiday—Christmas offers particularly outstanding decorations. Three of the bedrooms have lofts. A large, modern kitchen at the back of the house overlooks the brick-paved yard, which has a gazebo and small wrought-iron tables scattered about. The first floor and yard are used for private parties and wedding receptions. It's a popular wedding and honeymoon spot.

Margland III is next door at 705 West 2nd Ave. and is done in a bold wine color scheme inside. Even the bathrooms are decked out in lovely detail. This structure was built as a duplex in 1894. Guests have use of the kitchen if they desire.

Margland IV, at 709 West 2nd Ave., is a 1907 home with chambered projecting bays, round corners, and a porch with round corner turns. An exercise room, a whirlpool bath in each suite, and three loft bedrooms at the top of spiral staircases are part of the six suites, which all have private baths. Each is decorated with its own theme—country, art nouveau, Pennsylvania Dutch. A full breakfast is included, and other meals may be had by reservation.

The newest, ***Margland V,*** at 704 West Barraque, is, of course, as beautiful as the others. Call there for weekly and monthly rates.

And where is Margland I, you might ask? It's in the town of Earle and was called Margland Farm. It's where Wanda Bateman's husband grew up. Call Wanda at (870) 536-6000 for reservations at any of the homes or visit their website at margland.net. Prices range from $65 to $110.

Sissy's Log Cabin, 2319 Camden Rd., has long been a Pine Bluff tradition for gift shopping. For more than 33 years, it has been an international gathering spot for people who love fine jewelry and good service. Sissy Jones is justifiably proud of her custom-designed jewelry. Her trademark "slide bracelets" were born of her antiques business in the log cabin off US 65 on US 79. She used antique Victorian clasps and mounted them on two 14-karat-gold rope chains, and because they seemed to be an instant hit, she found herself in the jewelry business. Now the store designs its own clasps. But there are many other original pieces to admire, too. Former first lady Hillary Rodham Clinton owns several pieces of Sissy's jewelry. Sissy's is open 10 a.m. to 5:30 p.m. Mon through Sat. During May and Dec it's open Sun, too. Call (870) 879-3040 for information or visit sissyslogcabin.com.

Other places to check out in Pine Bluff include the ***Arkansas Entertainers Hall of Fame*** at the Pine Bluff Convention Center, 1 Convention

Digging Southeast Arkansas

Modern archaeology buffs will make the drive to Sheridan, on US 270 west of Pine Bluff, because literally digging up the past is what Elwin Goolsby, the county historian and the founder of the **Grant County Museum,** is famous for. The museum, at 521 Shackleford Rd., looks like an old mercantile store but is packed with things that preserve the history of the area. The retired history teacher has gathered thousands of historical items using a metal detector and a shovel. He and his team of amateur archaeologists—his students—have uncovered gas pumps made of solid iron dating from 1919; a rusted-out moonshine still, whiskey barrel hoops, and a lantern apparently smashed by ax-swinging feds in the 1930s; abandoned farming equipment; and 200 roadside signs. There are also musket balls, pistols, and scabbards from the Civil War. But probably the favorite items are the remains of a B-17 bomber that crashed in a swampy area north of town while on a training mission. The plane was left to sink into the bog, but when a road grader turned up a rusty pistol, Goolsby and his gang grabbed shovels and uncovered a machine gun, canteens, oxygen masks, and the dog tags of some of the nine crew members who died there.

The museum area contains not only photographs and microfilm genealogical records but also log cabins, barns, corncribs, and a Depression-era church on the grounds. Each is filled with small items that tell a story—a tiny shoe from a little girl named Leola, who died in a house fire; a slave's tombstone—reflecting the history of Grant County. An acre of ground about 1 mile from the site, now called Heritage Square, is being used to save historic buildings scheduled for demolition, including a Victorian folk house, circa 1904, and a small 1927 cafe, complete with kitchen utensils and dishes of food. The museum is open 9 a.m. to 4 p.m. Tues through Sat. Call (870) 942-4496 for information or visit grant countymuseumar.com.

Center Plaza, where you can see an "animatronic" Johnny Cash sing five songs when you punch his buttons. The museum chronicles the many entertainment stars who have called Arkansas home: Glen Campbell, Allan Ladd, Tracy Lawrence, Al Green, Charlie Rich, Mary Steenburgen, Conway Twitty, Billy Bob Thornton, Dick Powell, Floyd Cramer, and Harry Thomason (producer of *Designing Women* and *Evening Shade,* as well as many other well-known television shows). Recent inductees include Jerry Van Dyke, K. T. Oslin, Bronco Billy Anderson, and William Warfield. Call (870) 536-7600 for more information. The hall is open Mon through Fri 9 a.m. until 5 p.m. It's open on weekends seasonally.

The **Jefferson County Historical Museum,** at 201 East 4th St., has displays of items from 1830 to the present. There are tools, dolls, cotton-farming implements, Victorian and Civil War clothing, and an interesting assortment of waterfowl, as well as a multitude of other things to see, including a large collection of WWI and WWII items. The building itself is on the National Register of Historic Places, since it served as a Union train depot during the Civil War. Call (870) 541-5402 for more information, or go online to pbjcmuseum.org. Hours are 10 a.m. to 4 p.m. Wed through Fri.

Jerry Horne is his name (it really is), and he loves old band instruments. So much, in fact, that he used his vintage band instruments collection, which was taking up too much space in his music store (Wallick Music Company, nearby), to open **The Band Museum** in a circa 1890 building at 423–425 Main St., Pine Bluff. Jerry, who looks a lot like Mitch Miller, says his collection was a "semiretirement project," and he enjoys showing visitors the sousaphones, piccolos, trumpets, double-bell euphonium (Remember it from "76 Trombones" in *The Music Man?*), and a double-bell trumpet, an odd instrument that has a bell at either end and no mouthpiece. Many of the 700 instruments date from the 1700s, and all are from bands—marching bands, swing bands, symphonic bands, and jazz bands. Jerry, a former band director, not only is an accomplished trombone player, but he also can play the slide trumpet or something as simple as a carved whistle.

The museum features exhibits on circus bands and a history of the Smiles Girls Band, a group of girls from Fort Smith who traveled around the country in the 1930s playing signal horns made in Germany for the Hitler Youth movement. The Arkansas Heritage Hall of Fame in the museum pays tribute to jazz musicians like the late Art Porter and Louie Jordan. Unusual instruments, such as a trumpet made of plastic because of the World War II brass shortage, are displayed in the History of Trumpets section. Visitors will also see such instruments as those made by the Holton Company, which have highly engraved gold-plated bells, and a folding brass drum made in 1917.

This is more than just a museum, though. There is a 1950s-style soda fountain where you can sit and sip a cherry phosphate and listen to the rockin' jukebox, which is filled with songs from the 1950s and '60s. Jerry says he can fix just about anything you could buy at a soda fountain in the 1950s. In fact, he used to be a soda jerk, so the festive black-and-white checkered floor and the antique-oak bar make him, and a lot of other people, feel right at home.

Vintage orchestra posters, old photographs, and sheet music decorate the walls. A colorful Chinese drum, antique percussion instruments, flutes, and saxophones will keep your interest, as will Jerry, who is a virtual one-man band. Admission is free, and hours are 10 a.m. to 4 p.m. Mon through Fri and by appointment on Sat and Sun. Call (870) 534-HORN (4676) for more information or visit bandmuseum.tripod.com. A gift shop features items related to music, and exhibits change periodically.

trivia

Why is a county that lies in the heart of cotton country named Grant? Why is the county seat named Sheridan? They are named for two US Army generals, Ulysses S. Grant (commander in chief of the Union Army) and Philip Sheridan (infamous Union cavalry leader), because the county was formed during Reconstruction. Local folks blame the Yankee carpetbaggers.

After you have browsed the museum and had a phosphate, you can explore the history of the town, beginning in the early 1700s, through a series of impressive outdoor murals. Start on Main Street at Barraque Street.

The town has a colorful history. Legend has it that a Quapaw hero named Saracen, born about 1735, rescued two pioneer children from marauding Chickasaws. When the Quapaws were sent into Indian Territory in Oklahoma, Saracen was allowed to stay on land along the river at today's Port of Pine Bluff. His remains lie in the Catholic cemetery.

World-famous archer and bow hunter Ben Pearson once lived in the home at 714 West 4th Ave. The 1860 home served as Union army headquarters during the Civil War. The first shots in the war may actually have been fired at Pine Bluff in April 1861, before Confederate gunners opened fire on Fort Sumter, South Carolina. The Jefferson Guards fired warning shots and halted federal boats headed upriver with garrison supplies, which the guards seized for the Confederate army. A real battle happened here later when, in 1863, Confederate General John S. Marmaduke was unsuccessful in taking the city from Union General Powell Clayton.

The mural at 2nd Avenue and Main Street portrays the story of the oldest public institution in the state with an African-American heritage, today's University of Arkansas at Pine Bluff, which was formed as Branch Normal College. Among the dignitaries on the mural is Joseph C. Corbin, first principal of that school. Another mural at 3rd Avenue and Main Street shows the 1892 fire station and other handsome structures from the turn of the 20th century.

Lybrand's Bakery & Deli, at 2900 Hazel St., was voted best bakery in southeast Arkansas, and it has been cooking since 1946. It offers delicious sandwiches, soups, salads, quiche, and lasagna. Open 6 a.m. to 5:30 p.m. Mon through Fri and 6 a.m. to 1:30 p.m. Sat. Call (870) 534-4607 for information and daily lunch specials, or check out lybrandsbakery.com.

trivia

Sheridan Timberfest is held in Oct to celebrate this town's ties to the timber industry.

Pine Bluff is full of surprises. Who would expect a town of 58,000 people to raise $4.35 million for an arts and science center? The 22,000-square-foot facility, *The Arts & Science Center for Southeast Arkansas* can be found at 701 Main St. The three spacious art galleries display exhibitions and selections from the center's 1,400-piece permanent collection as well as traveling exhibits. A fourth gallery is Adventure Space, a hands-on science center. The theater is filled for performances of Broadway musicals. Hours are 10 a.m. to 5 p.m. Mon through Fri and 1 to 4 p.m. Sat. Call (870) 536-3375 for information, or visit artssciencecenter.org or pinebluffonline.com.

About 9 miles southwest of *Sheridan* on Highway 46 is the *Jenkins' Ferry Battlefield,* one of three sites in the state commemorating the Union army's Red River Campaign. The point where the Union army escaped the pursuing Confederates by crossing the rain-swollen Saline River on April 30, 1864, is now a National Historic Landmark. For more information call (501) 844-4176 or go to arkansasstateparks.com/jenkinsferry.

Drive south of Sheridan on US 167 to Fordyce, which each spring celebrates its railroad industry with the popular, weeklong **Fordyce on the Cotton Belt Festival.** Ole Number 819, one of the few remaining steam locomotives in operation, rolls into town from Pine Bluff for rides. The childhood home of Paul "Bear" Bryant is a short drive from downtown on Highway 8; the Alabama football coaching legend grew up here and played football for the Fordyce Redbugs.

The **Dallas County Museum** is in a 1907 building at 221 South Main St. The children's museum on the second floor has more than 3,500 square feet of hands-on historical activities for kids. Also on the second floor is a communications exhibit. The building that houses the museum was once the Fordyce Telephone Company, so much of the exhibit was already in place. Hours are Tues through Fri 10 a.m. to 4 p.m. and Sat 10 a.m. to 2 p.m. There's an antiques mall next door full of real bargains. Call (870) 352-7202.

Southeast of Fordyce at the junction of Highways 97 and 8 is **Marks' Mills State Park.** This park is the site of a 1864 Civil War skirmish in which Confederate troops captured a Union supply train. This battle resulted in the Union army retreating toward Little Rock. In addition to picnic sites, you'll also find interpretive exhibits, and the Marks' Mills Cemetery here. For more information, call (888) AT-PARKS or visit arkansasstateparks.com/marksmills.

More Places to Stay in Southeast Arkansas

CAMDEN
Holiday Inn
1450 US 278 Southwest
(870) 836-8100
Inexpensive

CROSSETT
America's Best Value Inn
1400 South Florida St.
(870) 364-4101
(800) 870-1182
Inexpensive

DUMAS
Days Inn
501 US 65 South
(870) 382-4449
Inexpensive

EL DORADO
Holiday Inn Express
1819 Junction City Rd.
(800) HOLIDAY
(870) 881-8900
Inexpensive

LAKE VILLAGE
Days Inn
912 US 65/82 South
(870) 265-4545
Inexpensive

CHAMBERS OF COMMERCE IN SOUTHEAST ARKANSAS

Camden Chamber of Commerce
Box 99
Camden 71701
(870) 836-6426

Crossett Chamber of Commerce
101 West 1st Ave.
Crossett 71635
(870) 364-6591

El Dorado Chamber of Commerce
201 North Jackson
El Dorado 71730
(870) 863-6113
boomtown.org

Helena Chamber of Commerce
111 Hickory Hills Dr.
Helena 72843
(870) 338-8327

Magnolia Chamber of Commerce
Box 866, Magnolia 71753
(870) 234-4352

Pine Bluff Chamber of Commerce
510 South Main
Pine Bluff 71601
(870) 535-0110
pinebluff.com

Stuttgart Chamber of Commerce
507 South Main
Stuttgart 72160
(870) 673-1602, (800) 810-2241
stuttgartarkansas.com

MAGNOLIA

Hampton Inn
128 US 79
(870) 234-1800
Inexpensive

PINE BLUFF

Holiday Inn
3620 Camden Rd.
(870) 879-3800
Inexpensive

STUTTGART

Stuttgart Best Western
Duck Inn
704 West Michigan
(870) 673-2575
Inexpensive

WEST HELENA

Best Western
1053 West Hwy. 49
(870) 572-2592
Inexpensive

More Places to Eat in Southeast Arkansas

CROSSETT

Chen & Chen Chinese Restaurant
107 Unity Rd.
(870) 304-2410
Inexpensive

MAGNOLIA

Miller's Cafeteria
2402 North Vine
(870) 234-2181
Inexpensive

MARIANNA

Lucky Star
378 W. Chestnut St.
(870) 295-5601
Inexpensive

SHERIDAN

The Yellow Jacket Drive-In
101 North Rock St.
(870) 942-2486
Inexpensive

Central Arkansas

The hub of the state is its central region. Here the capital, Little Rock, and its sister city across the river, North Little Rock, are the core of the state's government, cultural, and financial life. Cosmopolitan and urban, the city and its surrounding suburbs offer sophisticated shopping, fine dining, and big-city nightlife.

Several state parks are nearby, too. Toltec Mounds, an archaeological site to the east; Pinnacle Mountain, an environmental education park—and trailhead to the challenging Ouachita Trail—to the west; and Woolly Hollow State Park, north of Conway, can be part of your travel plans when you are based in the capital city.

Towns with such names as Pickles Gap, Toad Suck, and Romance dot the heart of the state, and there are surprises everywhere. There's a 33-room mansion on a plantation that is still growing cotton and even an elephant breeding farm hidden away near this metropolitan center.

The Heart of Arkansas

Start in *Little Rock,* called the City of Roses because of the abundance of the lovely flowers planted all over the city.

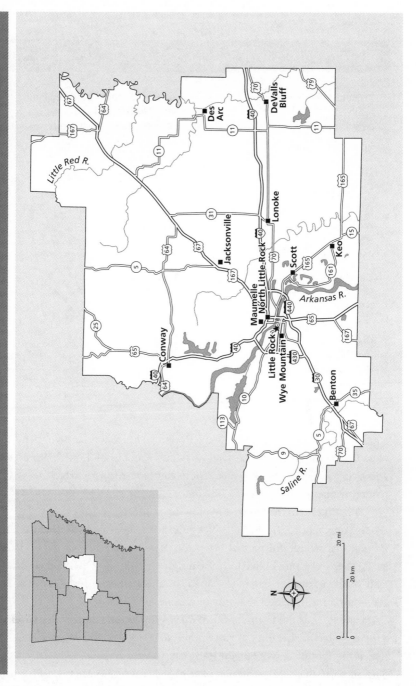

CENTRAL ARKANSAS

BEST ATTRACTIONS IN CENTRAL ARKANSAS

Argenta Arts District
North Little Rock
argentaartsdistrict.org

Marlsgate Plantation
16 miles southeast of Little Rock on
old US 165
(501) 961-1307

Mount Holly Cemetery
Little Rock
(501) 376-1843
mounthollycemetery.com

Ouachita Trail
at Pinnacle Mountain State Park
near Maumelle
(501) 868-9150

Purple Cow
Little Rock
(501) 221-3555

**Riddle's Elephant Breeding Farm
and Wildlife Sanctuary**
between Guy and Quitman
(501) 589-3291
elephantsanctuary.org

Silvek's European Bakery
Little Rock
(501) 661-9699

Soho Modern
Little Rock
(501) 372-4884

Toltec Mounds
southeast of Little Rock
off US 165
(501) 961-9442

Little Rock sits on a rocky bluff overlooking the Arkansas River. The best view of the river is from the walkways and terraces of 17-acre *Riverwalk Park* at the foot of Rock Street. There the little rock for which the city is named is marked by a bronze plaque.

The *River Market* area downtown is a fun place to spend a day. It is an amazing renovation in Little Rock, and it is booming. You can wander around this wonderful part of town for days and not see or get a taste of it all. There is a fine collection of eating places in the Ottenheimer Market Hall—Middle Eastern, Japanese, Spanish, and barbecue restaurants, a bakery—and a meat market as well.

Little Rock is the home of the *William Jefferson Clinton Presidential Library*—having beaten out Hot Springs and Hope. Concrete and steel now rise at the foot of newly named President Clinton Avenue. Located within a 30-acre park, the library extends over mile 118.2 of the Arkansas River on a brief stretch of Markham Street (which was renamed for the president after his supporters failed to get the entire street named for him). It has a futuristic "glass curtain," which extends from the shore on stilts in a way intended to memorialize the "bridge to the 21st century" that former president Bill Clinton mentioned in his acceptance speech at his renomination in Chicago in 1996, according to museum designer Ralph Applebaum, whose credits include the US Holocaust Memorial in Washington, D.C.

The library is just up the street from the Old State House in the now-booming River Market Zone, where nightlife is expected to blossom—a district dotted with hotels, restaurants, bars, and shops. The library has a $160 million price tag and is a triumph over lawsuits, the slings and arrows of Clinton critics, and even onetime union friends. It is a home for Clinton-related exhibits, complete with a full-scale replica of the Oval Office to be outfitted as it was for the president. A timeline frieze of words and images is at the center of the 20,000-square-foot space. Within the 110-foot-long, 2-story centerpiece exhibit are official schedules for each of Mr. Clinton's 2,923 days in the White House, including the only House impeachment and Senate acquittal of a US president in history. It includes elements of joyous celebration, as well as the tension of being in the world of politics. It may be a misnomer to refer to the Clinton facility as a library, because it is more of an information warehouse. History's wordiest president has left an abundance of paper and e-mails unmatched at other presidential repositories (76.8 million pages, plus 40 million e-mails), according to the National Archives and Records Administration (NARA). More than 79,000 gifts and "artifacts," including 4,500 official gifts from abroad, and 1.85 million photographs will also be part of the collection.

Since former president Bill Clinton was the first president of the Internet age, this site functions as the first truly virtual presidential library. Visitors can search for information, communicate through chat rooms, create a dialogue, and participate in moderated sessions. Have a bite at **Cafe 42** (named after the 42nd president). Hours are Mon through Sat 9 a.m. to 5 p.m., Sun 1 to 5 p.m. Admission is $7; $5 for seniors, students, and military; $3 for children over 6 years old.

There is even a tomb fit for a president. Clinton's epitaph may, literally, be here in "Contemplation Grove," a quiet and secluded stand of trees at the south end of the grounds, designed to hold a small chapel and a burial facility.

The University of Arkansas Clinton School of Public Service is also located within the park. For more information visit clintonlibrary.com or call (501) 376-4282.

Nearby is the historic *Cathedral of St. Andrew,* at 617 Louisiana St. It is on the National Register of Historic Places. This English Gothic–style granite building with its European stained-glass windows, 3,000-pipe organ, and tower bell has been dominating the Little Rock skyline since 1881. Visitors always comment on the oversize Stations of the Cross. They were actually made for a very large cathedral under construction in Chicago and were mistakenly sent to the much smaller St. Andrew building site, where they were installed. Tours can be arranged for groups by calling (501) 374-2794. Sat evening Mass is at 4:30 p.m., Sun mornings at 8:30 a.m. and 12:05 p.m. Visit cathedralsaintandrew.org for a virtual tour of the cathedral.

Little Rock is an interesting city for history buffs, for it houses three state capitols, making Arkansas unique in this respect. The first is the *Historic Arkansas Museum,* formerly known as the Arkansas Territorial Restoration. On these grounds, at 200 East 3rd St. (park at the intersection of 3rd and Cumberland Streets), are some of the oldest buildings in the state on their original sites. Among them are the 1830s Hinderliter Grog Shop, the 1840s McVicar and Brownlee Houses, and the 1820s *Arkansas Gazette* Print Shop. Huge old magnolia trees shade the area, and there is a feeling of leaving the modern world and returning to a different time. The houses are held together by white oak pegs and graced by original hand-carved mantels and doors. Costumed interpreters heighten the sense of originality in the tours offered on the hour Mon

trivia

The *Little Rock Zoo* (off I-630 exit 4 at 1 Jonesboro Dr.) has more than 600 native and exotic animals. There is a tropical rain forest, a penguin exhibit, and a cheetah conservation center. The zoo is also home to the Arkansas Carousel. This over-the-jumps-style carousel dates from the 1920s and is the only fully operational carousel of its kind in the world. The zoo is open daily 9 a.m. to 5 p.m.

through Sat 9 a.m. to 4 p.m. and Sun 1 to 4 p.m. Tour tickets are $2.50, $1.50 for seniors, and $1 for children under the age of 18.

An important component of the museum is Arkansas Made, an area devoted to the best of Arkansas's decorative, mechanical, and fine arts. A permanent collection includes the state's premier paintings, silver, pottery, textiles, and furniture produced by Arkansas artists over the past 200 years.

Admission to the museum is free. Call (501) 324-9351 to learn about traveling exhibits and special programs for children and families. You can also visit historicarkansas.org.

The second capitol, the circa 1836 **Old State House,** at 300 West Markham St., is a perfect example of Greek revival architecture. It is one of the most beautiful buildings in the South and the oldest standing state capitol building west of the Mississippi. The museum inside covers the political and social history of Arkansas, but many come to see the beautiful display of 31 gubernatorial inaugural gowns worn by Arkansas first ladies. Hours are 9 a.m. to 5 p.m. Mon through Sat and 1 to 5 p.m. Sun. There's no admission charge. Call (501) 324-9685, or visit their website at oldstatehouse.com.

The new capitol, circa 1900—a downscaled model of the nation's capitol that is made of Batesville marble quarried in the state—finishes the list. This, of course, is where former president Clinton was Governor Clinton, and more and more tourists want to see the building—constructed, by the way, by convict labor where the old walled penitentiary stood. A 2-ton brass chandelier hangs in the rotunda. Six massive brass doors from Tiffany's reflect the morning light on the eastern facade—doors so sensitive to fingerprints that they are roped off except on Inauguration Day. Sunlight pours into the chambers of the House and Senate through stained-glass domes and into the central halls through barrel-vaulted ceilings. Here the "Dash" bus sprints from the capitol to downtown for 25 cents, making lunch and shopping easy for both tourists and politicians. For information on tours of the building, call (501) 682-5080.

Follow 7th Street from the capitol to the **Quapaw Quarter,** with its renovated Victorian homes and buildings. It extends from the capitol to I-30 and from the Arkansas River to Roosevelt Road and is an interesting place to spend the whole day. Every spring, gardeners open their homes to the public during the Quapaw Quarter's annual tour. Homes and gardens in the event change each year. The walking tour includes the governor's mansion and the Old Methodist parsonage in addition to private homes. For information about the tour, call (501) 371-0075 or go to quapaw.com.

The Quapaw Quarter contains some magnificent houses, such as the fabulous Gothic Queen Anne mansion at 2120 Louisiana St., which is now *The Empress of Little Rock Bed & Breakfast Inn.* It is a tour house, too. Owners Sharon Welch-Blair and her husband, Bob, share the history and beauty of their home with everyone. Dressed in period costumes to lead the tours, Sharon acknowledges that Bob is the resident, and very accurate, historian. The beautiful structure was finished in 1888 by a Mr. Hornibrook, who owned a bar. Because of his occupation, he was blackballed from the then-prestigious Scott Street. He got his revenge by building the most magnificent mansion in Little Rock. The home is made of native materials. Beyond the curved front doors—with a stained-glass transom—rises a dramatic double staircase. There are five fireplaces, four with their original Eastlake mantels, on the first floor. The woodwork alone is worth seeing. There are three different styles of parquet wood floors. The tower is octagonal, as are many of the rooms. Legend has it that Mr. Hornibrook held illegal poker games in the tower. In fact, during renovation, one of the workers encountered a ghost in the attic. Bob insists he has seen a gentleman in a homburg hat descending the staircase. Ask him to tell the story.

There are five rooms and four spa suites, each with a private bath and telephone. Rates are $139 to $329. The owners would rather not have guests under 10 years old. If you just want to see this stunning home, tours are at

Haunted Little Rock

Many of the Little Rock points of interest covered in this chapter are considered to be haunted. In addition to the apparition at The Empress of Little Rock, you also might have the chance to experience paranormal activity at Mount Holly Cemetery, MacArthur Museum of Arkansas Military History, Curran Hall (home to the Little Rock Visitor Information Center and the Quapaw Quarter Association), and the Old State House.

11:30 a.m. and 3 p.m. Mon through Thurs for $7.50 a person. Call (501) 374-7966 for reservations and information, or visit theempress.com.

The Rosemont *Inn and Cottages,* also in the Quarter at 515 West 15th St., has rooms ranging from $99 to $145, or you can rent a cottage for $160 to $400 per night. Call (501) 374-7456 or rosemontoflittlerock.com.

MacArthur Park, also part of the Quapaw Quarter, was the site of the Little Rock Arsenal, built in 1836. General Douglas MacArthur was born in the arsenal in 1880. His father, Captain Arthur MacArthur, with Mrs. MacArthur, came to the arsenal as commandant during the Reconstruction after the Civil War. There are a couple of interesting places in the park. One is the *Arkansas Arts Center,* at 9th and Commerce Streets, where you can be an active participant in the arts. You can develop your talents in many creative areas, such as photography, pottery, woodworking, painting, and drawing. The spacious halls are filled with contemporary crafts by Arkansas artists and works by Picasso, Cézanne, and Degas. Handcrafted jewelry and toys are also available. Call them at (501) 372-4000, or check out arkarts.com.

Best Impressions restaurant is a project of the Fine Arts Club, the center's volunteer organization. There's a nice range of American fusion-style dishes available from the a la carte menu. The arts center is open 10 a.m. to 5 p.m. Tues through Sat and 11 a.m. to 5 p.m. Sun. Lunch is served 11 a.m. to 2 p.m. Tues through Fri and 10 a.m. to 2 p.m. Sat and

BEST ANNUAL EVENTS IN CENTRAL ARKANSAS

Lanterns Outdoor Winter Festival
Little Rock (Wildwood Park for the Arts)
mid-Feb
(501) 821-7275
wildwoodpark.org

Toad Suck Daze
Conway; first weekend in May
(501) 327-7788
toadsuck.org

Riverfest
Little Rock; Memorial Day weekend
(501) 255-3378

Annual Summer Bluegrass Show
Adona (Cypress Creek Park)
first week in June
(501) 662-4918
cypresscreekpark.com

Sun. Call (501) 372-4000, ext. 417, for information, or visit bestimpressions restaurant.com.

At the north end of the park, you'll find the **MacArthur Museum of Arkansas Military History.** This museum inhabits the last remaining building from the original Little Rock Arsenal, where General MacArthur was born. Its exhibits feature artifacts, photographs, weapons, documents, uniforms, and other military items that chronicle Arkansas's military history from its territorial period to the present. The museum address is 503 E. 9th St. Hours are 9 a.m. to 4 p.m. Mon through Sat and 1 to 4 p.m. Sun. Call (501) 376-4602 for more information.

The Arkansas Arts Center's **Decorative Arts Museum,** housed in the Pike-Fletcher-Terry Mansion at 7th and Rock Streets in the Quarter, is a 3-story beauty full of mirrors, silver services, and carved wooden decorative items used in homes over the years. The museum has both permanent collections and changing exhibits. The Crystal Room is a mirrored area filled with crystal and glass displays, almost resulting in a fun-house effect. Each room has its own fireplace. In 1839 the original house—a seven-room brick home—was built on grounds large enough to make it self-sufficient, including slave quarters, a smokehouse, and a detached kitchen. It was occupied by federal troops during the Civil War. In 1916 it was remodeled into its current colonial revival style, complete with a leaded-glass skylight opened by a pulley in the attic. The museum is open Mon through Thurs and Sat 10 a.m. to 5 p.m., Fri until 8:30 p.m., and Sun 2 to 5 p.m. Admission is free. Call (501) 372-4000 for more information.

Across Highway 630 at 1423 Main St. you'll find **The Green Corner Store** nestled inside the circa 1905 Lincoln Building. This unique shop proclaims itself to be the "first and only eco-lifestyle retail store in Arkansas." Inside you'll find products ranging from daily necessities to toys and games, and even items for your pets. The Lincoln Building was home to the C. H. Dawson drugstore and soda fountain for 60 years. The store owners have gone back to the building's roots by adding an authentic soda fountain in 2012. Be sure to pull up a stool and enjoy handcrafted ice cream from the local Loblolly Creamery and novelties from bygone days including phosphates, egg creams, and malts. The Green Corner Store is open 10 a.m. to 6 p.m. Mon through Fri, 10 a.m. to 5 p.m. Sat, and 10 a.m. to 3 p.m. Sun. Call (501) 374-1111 for information, or visit thegreencornerstore.com.

If it's a nice day, you can take your ice cream and wander down Main Street to where it intersects with Daisy Bates Drive. There you'll find ***Bernice Garden.*** This privately owned garden is open for public use. It also serves as an event venue and hosts the neighborhood farmers' market every Sun from mid-Apr to mid Nov. Originally the site of a fast-food restaurant, the garden now boasts rotating sculpture exhibits and a lighted canopy whose roof collects rainwater to sustain the garden's beautifully landscaped areas. It's definitely worth a stroll. Call (501) 410-3938 for information, or visit thebernicegarden.org.

Mount Holly Cemetery is 4 blocks west of Bernice Garden. This unlikely location will excite both history and art buffs alike. Known as "The Westminster Abbey of Arkansas," the cemetery is the burial ground for 11

The Search for the Perfect Burger

Former president Clinton is known for his love of burgers. The search for the perfect burger in Arkansas continues in his honor—even though he now lives in New York. (Unless otherwise noted, all the following are located in Little Rock.)

Arkansas Burger Company
7410 Cantrell Rd., 72207
(501) 663-0600
Sit-down burgers, both meat and veggie. Bonus: great Greek salad.

The Burger Box
1023 West 7th 72201
(501) 372-8735
Politically incorrect flyers on the wall and great greasy burgers. Bonus: beer.

Gadwall's Grill
7311 North Hills Blvd.
Sherwood 72116
(501) 834-1840
Burgers, white chili, and more. Bonus: beer and wine.

Salem Dairy Bar
6406 Congo Rd.
Benton 72019
(501) 794-3929
A local institution. Bonus: Real milk shakes made to order.

Shorty Small's
11100 North Rodney Parham Rd., 72212
(501) 224-3344
Noisy burger and sandwich joint. Bonus: a full bar.

Sports Page
414 South Louisiana St., 72201
(501) 372-1642
Fat burgers and grilled sausage, turkey, or ham sandwiches. Bonus: great crispy fries.

governors, seven senators, generals (all Confederate), black artists, two Pulitzer prize winners, 22 mayors, veterans from every war in US history, and even a Cherokee princess. The land deed dates back to 1843, although there are grave markers with dates that are even earlier than that. Mount Holly was one of the first cemeteries placed on the National Register of Historic Places. From an artistic perspective, grave marker styles include classical, Victorian, art deco, and modern. The grounds feature beautiful landscaping, including vintage roses and huge shade trees. Structures from the 19th century include a bell house, a receiving house, and a cast-iron fountain.

Tours of Mount Holly Cemetery are $5 per person. Themes include Arkansas and Little Rock History, the Cherokee Removal and Indian Territory, Confederate Arkansas, Victorian Funerary Art and Symbolism, the Trees and other Flora of Mount Holly, African Americans in Mount Holly, and Famous Women of Mount Holly. Call Sexton Steve Adams at (501) 376-1843 to schedule one.

The cemetery is at 1200 South Broadway. If you want explore on your own, gates are open 8 a.m. to 5 p.m. in the summer and 8 a.m. to 4 p.m. in the winter. For more information, visit mounthollycemetery.com.

If you're looking for Thai food in Little Rock, head for **kBird** at 611 Beechwood in the Hillcrest neighborhood. But you're not looking for a restaurant. kBird is a food truck, owned and operated by Richard Glasgow and his wife, Aimee. Richard has always been passionate about cooking. In 2001 when the couple got married, they traveled the world for about a year and a half. Richard fell in love with the cuisine and culture in Southeast Asia. While working in Little Rock as a corporate lawyer, Richard recognized the lack of good Thai food in the city and decided to take matters into his own hands. Now, Thai staples like curry, pad thai, and fried rice are served alongside seasonal specials like mango with coconut sticky rice. You'll also want to try Aimee's ginger cookies. Richard sources his produce and meat locally, and the Glasgows travel to Thailand about every 2 years to gather new ideas and learn more about authentic regional flavors. kBird is open Mon through Fri 5 to 8 p.m. You can call ahead to place an order at (501) 352-3549. Menus are posted on Facebook and Twitter each afternoon. Entrees average about $10 each.

You can see more of what the food truck scene in Little Rock has to offer at Westover Church at 6400 Kavanaugh Blvd. on the second Wed of each month. Many of the city's food trucks gather here for a **Food Truck Meetup** 5 to 8 p.m. Hundreds of people turn up for these monthly events, so be prepared to wait in line for your dinner choice. Don't worry though, there's usually live music and plenty of people watching opportunities to keep you occupied.

The **Soho Modern** shop, at 2200 Cantrell, is filled with early- and mid-20th century designs and furniture. Remember Danish modern, lava lamps, and things our parents thought were too cool? They were handed off to us for our first apartment, and we hated them. (Of course, this depends on your age. Maybe you were sent off with the blond limed-oak furniture of the 1950s.) What goes around comes around, according to Becca Hayley, and what is ultramodern to one generation becomes hideously old-fashioned to another. But then along comes a new crop of young adults, and suddenly it's hot. Deco, retro, and things kitschy or made of chrome or vinyl —you name it, she has it. Becca studied design in Los Angeles and once performed in a techno-funk band. Now she is an interior decorator who can work with any style. The smooth lines of these home-decorating pieces appeal to her. Their unadorned curves and angles blend into any plan. Hours are 11 a.m. to 6 p.m. Thurs through Sat. Call (501) 372-4884 for information.

From Cantrell Road, turn north on Rebsamen Park Road or Riverfront Drive and follow it until it dead-ends into a parking lot at the foot of a strange-looking bridge. You've officially arrived at The Big Dam Bridge, the nation's longest specially built bicycle and pedestrian bridge. The Big Dam Bridge spans the Arkansas River and connects over 15 miles of the scenic **Riverside Trail,** which loops from downtown Little Rock to the bridge, through Burns Park, and back to the Argenta Arts District in North Little Rock. The bridge's name

trivia

The *Arkansas Democrat-Gazette,* published in Little Rock, is the oldest newspaper in continual publication west of the Mississippi River. It was first issued at Arkansas Post in 1819.

is not only fun to say, but points out the fact that it was built directly atop Murray Lock and Dam. Time your walk across just right, and you might get to watch a boat pass through. The bridge is lit at night with a rainbow of colors that can easily be seen while driving across the I-430 bridge to the west.

If you'd prefer to try out the bridge and the Riverside Trail that it connects on wheels rather than on foot, visit **Bobby's Bike Hike** in downtown Little Rock. They have bikes of all types and sizes, and if you don't want to do your own navigating, you can sign up for one of their guided tours. Rentals are by the hour, half day, or full day and range from $14 for 2 hours on a comfort hybrid to $55 for a full day on a high performance road bike. Kids bikes, toddler seats, and pull trailers are available as well. Seasonal hours are summer 8:30 a.m. to 8 p.m., spring/fall 8:30 a.m. to 7 p.m., and winter 9 a.m. to 6 p.m. Call (501) 613-7001 for information or visit bobbysbikehike .com/littlerock.

Once you have reached the Kroger store at 1816 Polk, Little Rock, look inside for **Silvek's European Bakery,** which specializes in Eastern European baked goods. A sign says that Silvek's will bake poppy stollen the last Fri of each month, for special orders only. If you plan to be in Little Rock awhile, it is worth the *weight*. Hours are 6 a.m. to 8 p.m. Mon through Sat and 6 a.m. to 7 p.m. Sun. Call (501) 661-9699 to order a stollen.

Cantrell Gallery, at 8206 Cantrell Rd., has more than 3,500 square feet of gallery area, featuring an eclectic group of artists from around the state. It is the largest commercial gallery in Arkansas. The gallery is open 10 a.m. to 5 p.m. Mon through Sat. Call (501) 224-1335 for information, or check out cantrellgallery.com.

After walking the gallery you might want some food, and the never-ending search for the perfect burger continues, of course. Well, you are in luck, because nearby, at 8026 Cantrell Rd., is the **Purple Cow,** where you can get a juicy cheeseburger for $5.85 and polish off a thick, hand-dipped butterscotch or strawberry milk shake to rejuvenate yourself. They also serve "adult shakes" with a shot of liquor. You will recognize the place right away by the purple doors. *Southern Living* magazine described it as "charmingly odd," but the corrugated metal siding isn't the reason—it's the Alka-Seltzer on the menu, which may, indeed, be necessary after wolfing down a cheeseburger with hot pepper cheese and jalapeños. Hours are 11 a.m. to 9 p.m. Sun through Thurs and 11 a.m. to 10 p.m. Fri and Sat (they serve brunch on Sat and Sun 9 a.m. to 2 p.m.). Call (501) 221-3555 for more information.

Families with young children will enjoy the climate-controlled respite of *The Wonder Place*. At the back of Breckenridge Village shopping center at 10301 N. Rodney Parham, The Wonder Place offers of 5,000 square feet of space for children to flex their imagination and creativity. Activity centers include a tree house, water table, stages for both people and puppets, an art studio, a kid-size cafe, veterinarian's office (the patients are all stuffed), and much more. Admission is $7.75 per person age 1 and older, and the second adult with a family is free. You can easily make a day of it—just get your hand stamped if you want to go and get some lunch, and then come back in the afternoon. Hours are 9 a.m. to 5 p.m. Mon through Sat. Call (501) 225-4050 for information, or visit thewonderplace.com.

Keep exploring and find *Pyramid Hearne Fine Arts* at 1001 Wright Ave. for a collection of African-American art. Call (501) 372-6822. Hours are Mon through Fri 9 a.m. to 6 p.m. and Sat 11 a.m. to 6 p.m.

Tucked away in an office park in West Little Rock is possibly the most well-hidden eatery in the city. *Milford Track* describes itself as "a gourmet deli-grill restaurant with menu offerings that can satisfy even the most discerning palate." Their breakfast and lunch fare truly is outstanding, but you have to find it to enjoy it. First, drive yourself to 10809 Executive Center Dr., Plaza 2, and park next to the Searcy office building that overlooks the lake. Head around the back of the building via the sidewalk and up onto the patio. Inside the doors at your right, you'll find Milford Track, waiting to fill your tummy with a selection of salads, sandwiches, and desserts all made fresh and very reasonably priced. Take your meal back out to the patio where you can sit and watch the swans cruise the lake while you eat. Milford Track is open 8 a.m. to 5 p.m. Mon through Fri and 11 a.m. to 2 p.m. Sat. Call ahead orders or for help finding the place at (501) 223-2257, or visit milford-track.com.

trivia

Outdoor sculptures are hidden all over Arkansas. There is an Easter Island near DeQueen, a tribute to woodsmen in Gurdon, and a Statue of Liberty at Paragould. *Stone & Steel: A Sculptural Tour of Arkansas* shows you where to find nearly 400 outdoor sculptures. Call (501) 324-9880 for the brochure and map.

Farther west, you'll find the hidden gem of **Wildwood Park for the Arts.** Take Chenal Parkway west and turn off at Kanis Road after you pass Kroger. As your surroundings turn more rural, turn right on Denny Road and watch for the signs pointing you toward the park. One part nature park, one part art institute, and one part festival venue, Wildwood offers something for everyone. The park is open on a daily basis with free admission unless there is a festival going on. Stop by to hike the trails around the lake and through central Arkansas's largest botanical gardens, where the native flora is marked with descriptive panels and several of the trees are marked with the names of the people who have "adopted" them. The park also boasts a performing arts theater as well as studios, classrooms, and production spaces. There is often art on display inside the theater building. If your timing is right, take advantage and attend one of the seasonal festivals that the park hosts. Hours are 9 a.m. to 5 p.m. Mon through Fri, 10 a.m. to 5 p.m. Sat, and noon to 5 p.m. Sun. Call (501) 821-7275 for information or visit wildwoodpark.org.

Here is a special note for serious hikers: The **Ouachita Trail** begins at **Pinnacle Mountain State Park,** north of Cantrell Road on the western edge of Little Rock's Chenal Valley. The mountain rises more than a thousand feet into the sky above the Arkansas River Valley, a wedge of rock jutting abruptly from the flat valley. Surrounded by heavily wooded hillsides, bright waterways, and rich lowlands, the summit offers a panoramic view of the eastern slopes of the Ouachita range. There are hiking trails for everyone in this day-use park, from the gentle 0.5-mile loop for the physically limited to the day trip for birders and wildflower hunters to the infamous Ouachita Trail that extends more than 250 miles into eastern Oklahoma for really serious hikers. The starting point of this awesome trail is just west of the visitor center and marked with blue blazes. If you are headed for Oklahoma, and not in a hurry, call (501) 868-9150 for trail information.

If it happens that you are driving through this area in the spring when the daffodils bloom, slip through the tiny community on **Wye Mountain** and see and smell 7 rolling acres of daffodils. You won't be alone; thousands of others will be doing the same thing. More than 30 different types of daffodils—ranging from light to dark yellow or orange—nod in the sunshine. Flowers usually bloom mid-March. The local Homemakers' Club offers barbecue and homemade cobbler at its annual arts and crafts fair held then. To reach Wye Mountain from Little Rock, take exit 9 from I-430, drive west on Highway 10 past Lake Maumelle, turn right on Highway 113, and drive 7 miles north until you see a small Methodist church surrounded by thousands of bright flowers.

If you're in the Wye Mountain area in May, June, or July, there will be another treat waiting for you. Make a visit to *Wye Mountain Flowers and Berries* to pick your own raspberries, blueberries, and blackberries. The farm is open Mon through Sat starting at 7 a.m. during the picking season. Buckets with liners are provided, and berries are sold by the container. There are over 3 acres of flower gardens, including sunflowers, lilies, and zinnias, so you can pick your own bouquet too. Please call (501) 330-1906 for harvest information. The farm is at 20309 Hwy. 113 in Bigelow. Bring sunscreen, a hat, water, and bug spray. Closed-toe shoes are also recommended. You can visit the website at wyemountain.net.

With Little Rock as the hub, explore some surrounding towns. Northeast in *Jacksonville* is the *Jacksonville Museum of Military History,* newly opened by a group of veterans and history buffs to chronicle everything from the Civil War battle of Reeds Bridge, which took place here, to the two World Wars. Jacksonville is the home of Little Rock Air Force

There's Peace in the Valley

Here's a secret for those of you headed for **Pinnacle Mountain State Park.** The vast majority of the 500,000 annual visitors crowd into the smaller west summit area. If you like crowds, shrieking children on playgrounds, and a hiking trail that sounds like a shopping mall and gives you an aerial view of the new Wal-Mart, well, then, sure, go ahead. But if you head west on Cantrell Road out of Little Rock, turn right onto Chenal Parkway (which merges with Highway 300), and do not turn at the first road into the state park, you will run into Pinnacle Valley Road. Turn right, and you are in the park. There you will find a visitor center, wildflower garden, an Environmental Education Pond full of wildlife, and a parking lot. The start of the East Summit Trail is here, and another 1.25-mile trail goes around the base of the mountain back to the west side (to join the crowd). For a serious walkabout, there is also an entrance to the Ouachita Trail near the visitor center where you can hike the 222-mile trail west all the way to Oklahoma. Visit partners forpinnacle.org.

Base and the former Arkansas Ordnance Plant, where artillery shells were made. There is a Christmas card signed by Adolf Hitler, machine guns, and Viet Cong booby traps. Admission is $3 for adults, $2 for military families and seniors, and $1 for students. Hours are 9 a.m. to 5 p.m. Mon through Fri and 10 a.m. to 5 p.m. Sat. Phone (501) 241-1943 or visit jaxmilitary museum.org.

The *Lower White River Museum State Park* is in the town of *Des Arc.* The museum shows 100 years of hard river life from 1831 to 1931. The diverse history of this life, when men fished with nets and dived for freshwater mussels, is in these three small rooms. Fish were brought up in seines, tammel nets, and hoop nets, one of which is in the museum. Stringers with metal hooks called crow's feet were dragged across the river bottom, and the mussels with shells open to feed closed on the hooks and were hauled aboard. A drag, a device that dredged the bottom and pushed mussels into a net, was also used. Catfish and buffalofish were caught and carried by rail from the White River to the rest of the country. Houseboats were owned by river workers. Meat of mussels was popular, and shells were used for buttons. Native Americans (Quapaw to the south, Osage to the north) used them for tools and jewelry, and newcomers built button factories at Claredon and DeValls Bluff. The museum has an early button-making machine.

Divers groped in the murky waters for the shells of creatures called bankclimber, hill splitter, hogshell, washboard, Wabash pigtoe, monkeyface, and purple pimpleback mussels. They often improvised, making diving helmets from things like the gas tank of a Model T Ford.

The river was the lifeline of the area and the highway for products grown in the region. Everything from canoes to steam-powered boats cruised the waters. Then the Civil War brought thousands of riverboats along the Mississippi and its tributaries.

Artist George Caleb Bingham's paintings, showing river life from 1811 to 1879, are on display. Admission is free. The museum is open 8 a.m. to 5 p.m. Tues through Sat and 1 to 5 p.m. on Sun. Call (870) 256-3711 for information.

Heading back to Little Rock on US 70, which parallels I-40, will take you through the little town of *DeValls Bluff* and a chance to try a couple of interesting eating places.

Since US 70 runs right smack through the middle of DeValls Bluff, **Craig's Bar-B-Q,** at the west end of town on US 70, will be easy to find if you're not in the mood for catfish. The sauce here makes the ribs or pork sandwich something to remember. But be careful. The mild is like the pre-launch rocket fire at NASA, the medium is launch-incendiary, and the hot: We have ignition! You can take home some sauce if you want the fire next time, too. Hours are 10 a.m. to 8 p.m. Sun through Thurs and 10 a.m. to 9 p.m. Fri and Sat. Call (870) 998-2616 for information.

Across the street, the words **Family Pie Shop** are hand-scrawled on an unpretentious white concrete block shop. But a cooling dessert waits inside. Mary Thomas's handmade creations are simply great. Try the Karo-nut pie—it's Mary's rendition of the classic southern pecan pie. If she doesn't have the kind of pie you like, just tell her and she'll bake one special for you. Hours are 9 a.m. to 5 p.m. Wed through Sat. The shop is closed on Sun, but you can buy her pies at Craig's then. Call (870) 998-2279 for information.

The largest and one of the oldest state-owned fish hatcheries is in Lonoke, a town named for the "lone oak" that originally stood on the site. Fishers should stop by and give the staff at **Joe Hogan Fish Hatchery and Lee Brady Visitor Center** a high five of thanks, as the hatchery produces over four million fish each year, the majority of which are used to stock various bodies of water across the state. Warm-water fish including catfish, largemouth bass, bream, crappie, striped bass, and hybrid striped bass are born and raised here. Inside the visitor center you'll find five aquariums with fish, alligators, and turtles on display. The visitor center and hatchery are open to the public Mon through Fri 8 a.m. to 4:30 p.m. Admission is free. Families and individuals can take a self-guided tour of the grounds, or you can call ahead to schedule guided group tours. Joe Hogan Fish Hatchery is at 23 Joe Hogan Ln. Call (501) 676-3188 or toll-free (877) 676-6963 for more information.

An impressive archaeological site, even though misnamed, **Toltec Mounds** lies southeast of Little Rock off US 165. An early owner thought these were the mounds of the Toltec Indians of Mexico, but the people who built the mounds and lived in the central part of the state had a cul-ture different from that of other contemporary groups in the Mississippi Valley. They were not nomads but lived in permanent villages where they

Romance in Arkansas

Arkansas has a place where "Romance" is never missing, but it is someone's job to cancel it every day: the postmaster of this little town called by that name ever since pre–Civil War settlers from Kentucky came in covered wagons and did a lot of courting by the creek there. *Romance* got its 15 minutes of fame when the US Postal Service selected the office to host the inaugural introduction of the 25-cent "Love" stamp in 1990. One of the best collections of Love stamps and stationery is housed here to accommodate the high volume of business around St. Valentine's Day. If you are seeking romance in Searcy on Highway 5, go west on Pleasure Street about 10 miles until you reach Joy, Arkansas; Joy will lead to Romance. Any letter can be sent to the post office with a request to cancel the letter there and forward it to someone.

built sturdy houses and farmed the rich soil. This is one of the largest and most complex Native American mound sites of its era in the lower Mississippi River Valley, and Arkansas's tallest mounds. For more than 15 years now, the Arkansas Archaeological Survey and volunteers from the Arkansas Archaeological Society have been digging for answers about the lives of a culture named Plum Bayou who lived here about AD 600 to 1050. Self-guided tours take visitors through areas of the central plaza and five of the original 18 mounds.

The early residents used the nearby Arkansas River for transportation and fishing and clay for pottery; the soil was fertile, and the surrounding uplands supported an abundance of animals for hunting. A dugout canoe measuring 24 feet was found in the Saline River, miraculously preserved, perhaps because of being quickly buried in mud. This and other artifacts are on display at the park. One of the mounds is thought to have been a religious site; another was a burial mound. Others were platforms for leaders' homes. Building the mounds took tremendous effort (250,000 basketloads of dirt were required for the largest one). In June you can watch digs under way by the Arkansas Archaeological Survey. The mounds are arranged to mark solstices and equinoxes as the sun's rays change with the seasons to time crop planting and hunting. They are covered with grass and trees now, but when they were used by the Plum Bayou, they were bare.

There are storytelling sessions featuring myths and legends, and during workshops visitors can learn "flintknapping"—chipping arrowheads from stones. The mounds are on Highway 386, 9 miles northwest of the town of England, off US 165. The visitor center is open Tues through Sat 8 a.m. to 5 p.m. and Sun 1 to 5 p.m. The self-guided tour is free. Guided tours are $4 for adults, $3 for children age 6 to 12, or $10 per family. Call (501) 961-9442 for information.

The city of Scott is at the junction of Highway 161 and US 165, and in an old store and post office built in 1912 is the *Plantation Agriculture Museum*, 4815 Hwy. 161, which focuses on the massive cotton plantations of the 1800s and the turn of the 20th century—and the small farms that surrounded them. These plantations ranged from 1,000 to 7,000 acres, and most had huge homes. Many of the plantations were like small towns, with housing for workers, a church, school, blacksmith shop, and cotton gin.

This is a constantly changing exhibit with live demonstrations often on the agenda: demonstrations on Wash Day (everything from washboards to a gas-engine Maytag operating); Homespun Day with spinning, weaving, and dyeing; or Hay Harvest Day. The most popular is Antique Power Days, featuring steam engines and draft animals. The self-guided tour is free. Guided tours are $4 for adults, $3 for children age 6 to 12, or $12 per family. Hours are Tues through Sat 8 a.m. to 5 p.m. and Sun 1 to 5 p.m. The museum is closed

trivia

Toad Suck got its name from steamboat captains traveling the Arkansas River who tied up there when the water levels were not right at the lock and dam. After they visited a nearby tavern, local residents said, "They *suck* on the bottle 'til they swell up like *toads!*" But research suggests it is a corrupted French phrase *taudis sucre,* meaning "sweet water" (referring, of course, to the rum being served at the saloon). The most likely answer is found on an Arkansas map dated 1853 that was used by riverboat captains: Toad Suck was listed along with Cow Suck and Bear Suck—a suck is an eddy, which is a good place to park a large boat in moving water.

P.S. Never use the "f" word (frog) in Conway during Toad Suck Daze. Frog is a dirty word and will get you in trouble—guaranteed. The Sat morning toad races and the "Chosen Toad" are serious business here.

Mon (unless it is a state holiday). Call (501) 961-1409 for information on the demonstrations.

You might want to grab a "Hubcap" Hamburger (that got your attention, didn't it?): three-quarters of a pound of beef on a 6-inch bun, with lettuce, tomato, pickle, and onion at *Cotham's Country Store and Restaurant.* The country store has been in business since 1919, and the restaurant started operating in 1984. Owners Larry and Linda Griffin have added lots of antiques to the store's merchandise. To find the hamburger the fast-food places can't match, leave US 165 and go to Highway 161. Turn right and drive 0.25 mile past the museum and post office. Hours are 11 a.m. to 2 p.m. Mon through Thurs for lunch, and food is served 11 a.m. to 8 p.m. Fri and Sat. Ask for a table in the back with a view of the Horseshoe Bayou. But be prepared to wait. Call (501) 961-9284 for information.

Sixteen miles southeast of Little Rock on old US 165, which parallels I-40, is *Marlsgate Plantation,* a working plantation with 2,000 acres of cotton and a beautiful 33-room mansion on Bearskin Lake, an oxbow lake, in the center of it. This wooded setting is where David Garner lives. The plantation, a lovingly maintained beauty, is a picture of Victorian elegance, and the ties between Arkansas and the Deep South are plain to see. This mansion, with its four Ionic capital square brick columns, was built in 1904 and is shaded by pecan trees. The interior features a stairway landing with stained-glass windows, 14-foot ceilings of pressed tin, each in a different design, oak woodwork, and a fireplace in every room. David serves lunches to groups of 16 or more and has an antiques, flower, and gift shop in the carriage house. The mansion is 5 miles off the road and not visible from the highway, but tours of this private home can be arranged on an individual basis by appointment. Call (501) 961-1307.

Keo is 15 minutes southeast of Little Rock. Dean Morris has turned the Morris farm into an antiques wonderland. *Morris Antiques* fills five buildings, and you will need all day to see everything. Buildings 3 and 4 contain mantelpieces, old pipe organs, Victorian sofas and chairs, Tiffany-style lamps, beautiful old clocks, and French furniture. There are glass bowls and jars of all kinds. Dean has warehouses in Chester, England, where an Englishman buys antiques as a hobby at garage sale–type events. He has another warehouse in Paris (not Paris, Arkansas, but the other place across the pond). To find Keo take US 165 southeast. It is 13 miles from exit 7 off I-440. Turn right onto Highway 232. Morris Antiques is on the right, behind the Methodist church. Hours are 9 a.m. to 5 p.m. Tues through Sat and noon to 5 p.m. on Sun. Call (501) 842-3531 for information or check out the website at morrisantiques.com.

If you get tired and need a lunch break, look for ***Charlotte's Eats & Sweets,*** in a lovely old drugstore at 290 Main St., where Charlotte Bowls will fix you a sandwich or dessert at the soda fountain (the pies here are beautiful). Ask about the Keo Classic, which is Charlotte's favorite. She also likes the coconut cream pie. Hours are 11 a.m. to 2 p.m. Tues through Fri and 11 a.m. to 3 p.m. Sat. Sorry, but it is closed on Sun and Mon. Call (501) 842-2123 for information.

Benton is southwest of Little Rock on I-30. The small ***Gann Museum,*** at 218 South Market St., is the former office of Dr. Dewell Gann Sr., built in 1883 by patients who could not afford to pay for their medical care. These amateurs sawed out porous blocks of bauxite by hand, allowed them to dry, then cemented them together. It is the only known building anywhere made of bauxite. The museum has a collection of the unique multicolored swirl-patterned Niloak pottery (*Niloak* is "kaolin" spelled backward, the high-quality clay found nearby and used in making Eagle Pottery in the early 19th century). Next door is Dr. Gann's Victorian home, which had the first telephone and indoor bathroom in town. The home has been restored to its original elegance but is not open to the public. The museum is open 10 a.m. until 4 p.m. Tues through Thurs. Call the executive director, Bernard Barber, for appointments for other times at (501) 778-5513.

trivia

Pickles Gap got its name when a German immigrant crossing the creek overturned his wagonload of pickles. Now you can stop at ***Pickles Gap Village*** at 5-A Gapview Rd. and eat (casseroles and homemade desserts at Pickle Barrel Fudge Factory & Cafe), drink, shop (the fudge factory has over 30 flavors, from apple to pumpkin), and send postcards. Stop by on Sat, and old-time music will be playing from the Pickin' Porch Music Store. It's a local jam session. Lunch is served Tues through Fri 11 a.m. to 2 p.m. and Sat 11 a.m. until 3 p.m. The shops are open Mon through Sat 9:30 a.m. to 5 p.m. Some shops are also open Sun noon to 5 p.m. in the summer. Call (501) 327-8049 or visit picklesgapvillage.com.

Driving north on I-40 from Little Rock, you'll find the city of Conway between the towns of Pickles Gap and Toad Suck. Lake Conway is a nearby 6,700-acre fishing lake, and Lake Beaverfork offers not only fishing but also swimming and waterskiing. Toad Suck Park is at a historic ferry site on the Arkansas River, and the Cherokee Trail of Tears Memorial can be found at **Cadron Settlement Park.**

The Cadron Settlement blockhouse, a 2-story log structure, is in the final stages of its third life. There is probably more history here—the geographical center of the state—than anywhere else. This settlement dates back 2 centuries. Spanish explorer Hernando de Soto's expedition passed by looking for riches, and the French explorers Marquette and Jolliet made their way here. After the French and Indian War, the British stripped France of its North American possessions. No one knows whether it was the French or the Spanish who made the first settlement here, but all recognized that the juncture of a broad creek made an excellent landing site for a trading post to trade in the beaver pelts found here. There was fresh water in a free-flowing spring, lots of timber and game, and the site was on a rocky bluff that would be safe from the floodwaters and easy to defend should the Quapaw become hostile. It was set to be the capital of the new territory, but somehow Little Rock won the prize. Cadron was a stopping point on the Trail of Tears—the Cherokee were forced to land here due to low water. Many died, and the dead are identified on a marker. The Civil War saw brutal and bloody guerrilla warfare here. More information can be found at conwayparks.com/Cadron.html.

Stop in at **The Mean Bean Cafe,** at 2501 Dave Ward Dr. (Highway 286 West), for an afternoon latte or cappuccino or for a spinach burrito. There is a daily lunch special, as well as the sandwiches and soup that Trisha Cooper and Susie Schwarznau turn out. Hours are Mon through Thurs 10:30 a.m. to 3 p.m. and Fri 10 a.m. to 8 p.m. Call (501) 336-9957 for more information.

If you're in the mood for a lively lunch or dinner while in Conway, head over to **Legends Restaurant at Back Achers Ranch** on 50 acres at 3725 College Ave. Legends will provide you with the unique opportunity to enjoy a western-style meal made from fresh, local ingredients while watching barrel racing, rodeos, or other events going on in the arena through large glass windows. Hours are 11 a.m. to 9 p.m. Mon through Thurs and 11 a.m. to

10 p.m. Fri and Sat. They are closed on Sun unless there's an event going on. Call (501) 327-8200 for information or visit legendsatbackachers.com. The **Baum Gallery of Fine Art** is in McCastlain Hall on the campus of the University of Central Arkansas. It is one of the largest academic galleries in the state and serves as a learning laboratory for visual arts. There are four gallery spaces that host a wide variety of international and national traveling shows and student exhibitions. Admission is free. Hours are Mon through Fri 10 a.m. to 5 p.m. On Thurs it is open until 7 p.m. Sun hours are 1 to 5 p.m. Call (501) 450-5793 for more information, or visit the website at UCA. edu/art/baum to see the exhibit schedule.

Mike Smith began making furniture in 1974 while working in his dad's shop. Now he has his own shop, **Smith Chair Shop**, in his home in a rustic setting near Conway, at 283 Round Mountain Rd. Mike's post-and-rung chairs and stools are custom pieces in oak, cherry, or walnut, and each is signed and dated. He begins with fresh cut lumber from sawmills in Arkansas. He then air-dries the boards and begins the process of sculpting. Rocker posts and rungs are made with an old-fashioned wood lathe and handheld chisels and gouges. Rocker runners are cut with a band saw, and the parts are carefully assembled. The combination of air-dried post wood and kiln-dried rungs allows the post wood to shrink around the dry rungs, creating a tight joint. The furniture is stained and finished to bring out the natural grain and color of the wood. Mike weaves the seats with a durable twisted-paper cord called fiber rush. The seats are sealed with a clear finish to preserve them. Rocking chairs are available in many sizes, from a child's chair to an impressive 44-inch man-size rocker. Child rockers start at $200, adult rockers start at $500. Mike also restores and repairs old rockers and chairs using the same processes. Call ahead for an appointment and directions: (501) 327-0385. "We're off in the country on a dirt road," Mike says.

Riddle: What does someone do with a baby elephant when it reaches 6,000 pounds? The answer is a Riddle, too—Scott Riddle, to be exact. **Riddle's Elephant Breeding Farm and Wildlife Sanctuary** is where Scott and his wife Heidi care for elephants from all over the world that are no longer wanted by the places that were once their homes. Elephants too old, too cranky, or injured in some way are routinely destroyed every year. Because they are almost extinct in many of their former ranges, because there are so few places left to support elephants in their natural environment, and because the Riddles wanted to do something for this endangered animal, the couple bought 330 acres off Pumpkin Center Circle between Guy and Quitman (on Highway 25) and took them in. The farm contains a spring-fed creek, a waterfall, a pasture, and forestland. The Riddles completed a 2,000-yard swimming hole for their 13 jumbo guests.

One such guest is Solomon, a 12-year-old African elephant that was to be killed in a culling, or herd-thinning operation, in his native land. A wealthy man who bought two as calves and then watched them grow to 6,000 pounds soon tired of caring for them (a full-grown male can weigh 6 tons and stand 12 feet tall). African elephant Willie (from the Nashville Zoo) joined Toby, a 19-year-old male, and Tonga, a 21-year-old female from a small Indiana zoo. Asian elephant Betty Boop came from a circus, where she was injured by an overwrought male (weighing only half as much as males and shorter by 4 feet, females are no match in a domestic dispute).

Riddle's most famous elephant was Mary, a 24-year-old Asian elephant with an artistic bent. Her paintings hang in galleries around the country,

Safari

The day began in Fairfield Bay at the home of friends. My mom and dad had driven to Arkansas with us to do some exploring. Actually, my dad and my husband had golf in mind, and my mom and her friend Terry had shopping in mind. I was thinking about elephants.

I had heard about a man who took in neglected pachyderms—somewhere between Guy and Quitman on the map—and who was open to seeing visitors. The men vetoed the elephant safari and headed for the golf course. Mom and Terry, always good sports in these matters, jumped into the car, and we headed out.

We arrived at **Riddle's Elephant Farm** in a cloud of gravel dust. Scott Riddle met us at the gate and took us on tour. I learned more about my mom than about elephants that day. She is fearless. She walked up to huge elephants and rubbed their trunks. She fed them handfuls of hay and even asked about riding one. She was fascinated with the sounds the elephants made—the high sounds and deep rumbles—when they communicated with each other.

I now have a great photo on my desk of my mom—smiling sweetly—with her arm around an elephant's trunk. It is one of my favorite pictures of her.

where they brought in as much as $350. (Asian elephants, a separate species, are smaller—if you can call it that—than their African cousins and often lack tusks.) Riddle, who is also an artist, calls Mary's style "impressionist." One gallery owner sees it as "abstract." But whether in the style of Monet or Picasso, Mary liked primary colors, "with red her favorite," Riddle says. Mary's talents didn't stop there. She also played the drum, the bell, the tambourine, and, believe it or not, the harmonica. Mary was the primary

trivia

Did you know that the bottom of an elephant's foot is not hard like a hoof, but rather a shock-absorbing pad that is able to contract, expand, and adapt to the terrain, allowing elephants to move quietly and with agility? Elephants walk on tiptoe. The bones of the toe point toward the ground but are protected by a thick fatty pad inside the sole of the foot.

fund-raiser. In the wild elephants eat 500 to 600 pounds of food a day—that's a lot of groceries—and even with high-nutrition elephant chow, 100 pounds a day is average. The nonprofit operation is constantly searching for ways to bring in funds.

Long-range plans include massive, pachyderm-size barns; medical facilities; and the corralling of a large pasture to allow all the elephants to roam unchained, as Boop does now. Scott also wants to open an elephant museum with his collection of more than 1,500 elephant items—ancient temple rubbings, figurines, and prints—and a large assortment of books on the subject.

The farm is home to a collection of geese, goats, dogs, cats, and chickens right now, but the designation "wildlife sanctuary" entitles the Riddles to take in any zoo or circus animal that might otherwise be destroyed. Most funding comes from individual memberships ($25) and corporate sponsorship of the farm. "This is not a job; it's a life," Riddle says. Call (501) 589-3291 for directions to the farm and a chance to hear the incredible vocabulary of sounds these gentle creatures use to communicate—25 different ones, ranging from high-frequency whistles to deep rumbles, two octaves below human range—and an unbeatable photo opportunity. Tours are conducted on the first Sat of every month between 11 a.m. and 3 p.m. or by appointment.

Riddle puts out a newsletter called *The Elephant's Trunk Nose News*. Volunteers are always needed to help with these wonderful creatures. Call

Gordon McIntyre, the volunteer coordinator, at (501) 589-3291 if you want to offer a helping hand. See more at elephantsanctuary.org.

Just across the Arkansas River from Little Rock is the city of **North Little Rock,** which actually started out as the town of Argenta, until the city of Little Rock annexed it in the early 1900s. The historic area near the river in North Little Rock is known as the Argenta Arts District and has a had a resurgence in the past decade.

Here you will find a unique collection of eateries and shops, including **Galaxy Furniture,** which sells authentic and reproduction retro furniture, new and used home and office furniture, and even art, collectibles, jewelry, and vintage clothing. You never know exactly what you will find at Galaxy, but there's bound to be something groovy. Galaxy, at 304 Main St, is open 9 a.m. to 5 p.m. Mon through Sat. Call (501)-375-DESK (3375) for more information, and check out galaxyfurniture.net.

Spend the night in Argenta so you can soak it all in. The **Baker House Bed and Breakfast,** at 109 W 5th St, is a beautiful circa 1898 Victorian home that offers modern amenities. There are five suites ranging in price from $89 to $115 per night. An added bonus to staying at the Baker House Bed and Breakfast is that it is right on the River Rail Trolley Line (see below). Call (501) 372-9930 for information or visit bakerhousenlr.com to make reservations online.

The **River Rail Trolley Line** is a great way to access both downtown Little Rock and North Little Rock without having to fight traffic. Three vintage replica streetcars run a 3.5-mile loop via an overhead power supply. Stops include easy access to many of the sights and activities mentioned in this book, running throughout the downtown/riverfront districts of both cities. You can pay per boarding, but a day pass is the true bargain at $2, as it allows you to get on and off at any of the 15 stops on the route throughout the day. The Blue line runs the entire route between North Little Rock and Little Rock while the Green line runs an abbreviated route, sticking to the Little Rock side of the river. Trolleys run Mon through Sat 8:20 a.m. to 10 p.m. with extended hours until midnight Thurs through Sat. Sun the routes run 10:40 a.m. to 5:45 p.m. Visit cat.org/river-rail for more details on routes and rates, or call (501) 375-6717.

North Little Rock's **Riverwalk Park** includes a pleasant, paved mile-long walking path along the banks of the Arkansas River. (This 1 mile of path is also part of the Riverside Trail system mentioned earlier in this chapter.) Near the east end of Riverwalk Park you'll find the **Arkansas Inland Maritime Museum** (AIMM) floating in the Arkansas River on a dock. One of the vessels they have anchored there can really sneak up on you. The **USS Razorback Submarine** was commissioned in 1944 and served on many missions in World War II, during Cold War operations, and in the Vietnam conflict. After being decommissioned in 1970, the USS *Razorback* became the USS *Muratreis* and served the Turkish army until 2001 when she was once again decommissioned. In 2004 she found her forever home, moored to the docks at AIMM. You can take a tour of the inside of the sub as well as a small museum exhibit of artifacts from the *Razorback*'s history. Or, if you really want an immersive experience, gather a group of 10 to 35 friends and stay on the sub overnight. Tour admission is $7.50, $5 for children under 12, seniors, and military. If you're feeling a little claustrophobic, you can do the museum only tour for $2. The submarine tour is not recommended for children under the age of 5. Call (501) 371-8320 for information or visit aimmuseum.org.

There is a familiar sight in **T.R. Pugh Memorial Park** in North Little Rock if you have seen *Gone with the Wind* as many times as some people. It is what appears to be an abandoned gristmill tucked away in a grove of pine and oak trees. **The Old Mill's** shingled roof overlooks a lazy stream gurgling around a rusted waterwheel. Bent persimmon trees form a natural bridge across the water. It looks authentic, but on closer inspection you will see that the "wooden" bridge, rain barrels, benches, and everything right down to the downspouts are made of concrete. Sculptor Dionicio Rodriguez created all of it in the tradition of *el trabajo rustico,* a Mexican folk art. Rodriguez sculpted painted concrete over copper forms, using lampblack and chemicals to give it the texture of weathered wood. It took 4 years to create and had its 15 minutes of fame as the background for the opening credits of *Gone with the Wind.* Time took its toll on the mill; it became dilapidated and was deeded over to the city in 1979. A major restoration project has returned the mill to its original appearance, and walking trails and picnic areas have been added. The Old Mill is in the T.R. Pugh Memorial Park at the corner of Fairway Avenue and Lakeshore Drive off Highway 107. Call (501) 758-1424 or (800) 643-4690 outside Arkansas.

You can find much of the history of North Little Rock in **Burns Park** at exit 150 off I-40. This is one of the largest city parks in the country and includes a log cabin dating from the 1850s, a covered bridge, fishing access for the disabled, multiple playgrounds, a child-size carnival ride park, miles of trails, and a 36-hole golf course.

More Places to Stay in Central Arkansas

LITTLE ROCK

Best Western
1501 Merrill Dr.
(501) 224-8051
Inexpensive

Holiday Inn, Airport (East)
3201 Bankhead Dr.
(501) 490-1000
Inexpensive

Little Rock Marriott
3 Statehouse Plaza
(501) 906-4000
Inexpensive

More Places to Eat in Central Arkansas

CONWAY

China Town
201 Skyline Dr.
(501) 450-9090
Inexpensive

Marketplace Grill
600 Skyline Dr.
(501) 336-0011
Inexpensive

LITTLE ROCK

The Dixie Cafe
1301 Rebsamen Park Rd.
(501) 663-9336
Inexpensive

Graffiti's
7811 Cantrell
(501) 224-9079
Inexpensive

CHAMBERS OF COMMERCE IN CENTRAL ARKANSAS

Conway Chamber of Commerce
900 Oak St., Conway 72032
(501) 327-7788
conwaychamber.org

Little Rock Chamber of Commerce
1 Chamber Plaza
Little Rock 72201
(501) 374-2001
littlerockchamber.com

Little Rock Convention & Visitors Bureau
Box 3232, Little Rock 72203
(501) 376-4781
littlerock.com

North Little Rock Visitors Bureau
Box 5511, North Little Rock 72119
(501) 758-1424, (800) 643-4690
northlittlerock.org

Index